Eric Williams and the
Anticolonial Tradition

Eric Williams and the Anticolonial Tradition

The Making of a Diasporan Intellectual

Maurice St. Pierre

University of Virginia Press
Charlottesville and London

University of Virginia Press

Printed in the United States of America on acid-free paper

First published 2015

9 8 7 6 5 4 3 2 1

Library of Congress Cataloging-in-Publication Data
St. Pierre, Maurice.
Eric Williams and the anti-colonial tradition : the making of a diasporan intellectual / Maurice St. Pierre.
pages cm.—(New world studies)
Includes bibliographical references and index.
ISBN 978-0-8139-3674-1 (cloth : acid-free paper)—ISBN 978-0-8139-3673-4 (pbk : acid-free paper)—ISBN 978-0-8139-3685-7 (e-book)
1. Williams, Eric Eustace, 1911–1981. 2. Williams, Eric Eustace, 1911–1981—Political and social views. 3. Prime ministers—Trinidad and Tobago—Biography. 4. Intellectuals—Trinidad and Tobago—Biography. 5. Historians—Trinidad and Tobago—Biography. 6. Anti-imperialist movements—Trinidad and Tobago—History—20th century. 7. Trinidad and Tobago—Politics and government—20th century. 8. Trinidad and Tobago—Intellectual life—20th century. I. Title.
F2122.W5S7 2015
972.98304092—dc23
[B]

2014015286

Cover photo courtesy of the Trinidad and Tobago Government Information Services

To my son, Mark St. Pierre, for teaching me the value of theory, and to the thousands of unsung heroes (male and female) who contributed to making Eric Williams the intellectual that he was

Contents

Acknowledgments

I WOULD like to express my gratitude to Bridget Brereton, who read and provided valuable comments on an earlier version of the manuscript, and Annette Palmer, who read a chapter and provided access to various data. I would also like to thank the two anonymous readers of the manuscript for their very helpful comments and suggestions. Thanks are also due to Jerome Teelucksingh and Carole Agard-Lamming, as well as Kathleen Helense-Paul, Sylvie Pollard, and Dr. Glenroy Taitt of the Eric Williams Memorial Collection, for their assistance during various visits to the Eric Williams Memorial Collection at the University of the West Indies at St. Augustine. Carmelite Coombs and Jeff Henry provided helpful information regarding life in Trinbago. I thank Aubrey Bonnett, Patrice Jones, Eusi Kwayana, Rupert Lewis, Perry Mars, Brian Meeks, Kimani Nehusi, Oryne Stewart, Tayla Stewart, Paul Sutton, Rosalyn Terborg-Penn, Godfrey Vincent, and especially Dolan Hubbard and James Patterson for their support. I also thank Rudolph and Bridget Morris and Drew and Lynette Patterson for their hospitality while I was away from home. I am grateful to Erica Williams-Connell, for her unflagging interest and for providing me with various documents, and to my wife, Charlotte St. Pierre, who also helped in the collection of data. Last but by no means least, I wish to record my gratitude to my editor, Cathie Brettschneider, and to Ellen Satrom, both at the University of Virginia Press, for their patience and assistance in readying the manuscript for publication, and to Joanne Allen for her thorough reading of the manuscript and her keenness of eye.

A previous version of chapter 7 appeared as "The Chaguaramas Affair in Trinidad and Tobago: An Intellectual Reassessment" in the *Journal of Caribbean History* 40, no. 1 (2006): 92–116.

Eric Williams and the Anticolonial Tradition

Introduction

THIS STUDY examines the efforts of Dr. Eric Williams, the Trinidad and Tobago (Trinbago) Oxford University–educated historian and intellectual, much like Caliban's efforts with Prospero in William Shakespeare's play *The Tempest,* to use the knowledge he had acquired as a colonial subject and a historian to rail against—"curse"—the language of colonialism. Williams's efforts, along with those of other, similarly situated individuals, resulted in political independence from Britain for Trinbago in 1962 and, more importantly, the generation of a body of "new" knowledge or intellectual activity on his part.

Williams's anticolonial "cursing" occurred during three distinct but overlapping stages of his life as an intellectual. The first stage, as an *academic intellectual,* occurred between 1931 and 1948, when he was a student at Oxford University, in England, where he obtained a first-class honors degree and a doctorate in history; and at Howard University, in America, where he was a professor of social science. During this stage, Williams learned the "rules of the game," or the *habitus,* to use Pierre Bourdieu's term, regarding knowledge production and acquired what Bourdieu refers to as the *cultural capital,* or the *credentials,* of the professional historian.[1] Along with his knowledge of Trinbagonian pedantry, Williams was able to attack imperialism, enslavement, and other manifestations of the language of colonialism.

The second stage, that of being a *public intellectual,* began in about the late 1940s, while Williams was still at Howard University, and continued up to mid-1955, following his permanent return to Trinidad in 1948. During this stage Williams used cultural capital to acquire what Bourdieu refers to as *symbolic capital,* or the prestige and honor associated with being a professional historian, to obtain the *credibility* that allowed him to begin to teach and mobilize others against colonial oppression outside the university setting. Additionally, Williams's "cursing" of the language of oppression was undergirded by the use of his cultural capital to acquire *economic capital* (income) while employed at Howard University and, especially, at the Anglo-American Caribbean Commission (AACC), later the Caribbean Commission. Finally, during the third stage, the stage of most concern to this study, that of the *social-movement intellectual,* which began around mid-1955 and continued up to 1962, Williams utilized the techniques of knowledge production and knowledge dissemination that he had acquired as an academic intellectual, a public intellectual, and a teacher to continue to "curse" the language of colonialism and trumpet the *relevance* of Trinbago political independence.

THIS STUDY was prompted by a number of factors. First, as a diasporan academic intellectual and an outstanding historian with an international reputation, Williams has been the subject of a significant body of writings, particularly by historians about Williams the historian. These efforts include edited collections such as Barbara Solow and Stanley Engerman's *British Capitalism and Caribbean Slavery,* Heather Cateau and S. H. H. Carrington's *Capitalism and Slavery Fifty Years Later,* and Sandra Pouchet Paquet's "Eric Williams and the Postcolonial Caribbean," as well as Anthony Maingot's essay "Politics and Populist Historiography in the Caribbean," and Colin A. Palmer's *Eric Williams and the Making of the Modern Caribbean 1956–1970,* which uses archival data from the Eric Williams Memorial Collection (EWMC) and documents from the British Colonial Office and the U.S. State Department.

Studies that do not deal specifically with Williams the historian include the social psychologist Ramesh Deosaran's *Eric Williams: The Man, His Ideas, and His Politics,* which assesses Williams's personality; and the political scientist Selwyn Ryan's *Race and Nationalism in Trinidad and Tobago* and his political biography of Williams the politician, *Eric Williams: The Myth and The Man.* However, neither of Ryan's works has a discernible theoretical framework or makes use of archival documents. Additionally, Ken Boodhoo's edited collection of essays *Eric Williams: The Man and The Leader* and especially his *The Elusive Eric Williams* offer interesting insights into Williams's background, personal life, and personality. The latter study uses documents from the EWMC and is the only study of Williams that makes considerable use of interviews with individuals, such as family members, not necessarily involved in politics. Ivar Oxaal's *Black Intellectuals Come to Power* deals with the political-independence struggle in Trinbago. However, with the exception of interviews with knowledgeable informants, because of Oxaal's intention to limit what he describes as the "conceptual baggage," this effort disavows any specific theoretical framework and also does not make use of archival material.

Williams's political activities have also been chronicled in reports by various Colonial Office and U.S. State Department officials; in books by former cabinet colleagues, such as Winston Mahabir's *In and Out of Politics,* Patrick Solomon's *Solomon: An Autobiography,* Elton Richardson's *Revolution or Evolution,* and Donald Granado's "An Autobiography"; in annotated collections of Williams's speeches, such as *Eric E. Williams Speaks,* edited by Selwyn Cudjoe, and *Forged from the Love of Liberty,* edited by Paul Sutton; in various journal and newspaper articles; and in C. L. R. James's *A Convention Appraisal.* Lastly, Williams's own autobiography, *Inward Hunger,* sheds useful light on his background and his political life, as well as on his struggle against colonialism in Trinbago and abroad. However, it is written in the first person and pays scant attention to the contributions of other individuals to his intellectualism.

A second factor prompting this study was the tendency for the not inconsiderable literature on social movements to focus on them as forms of protracted collective action, primarily in Western countries. Thus there was less emphasis on the displacement of the challenged (e.g., the colonial power), located in other parts of the world, by challengers living in places like Trinidad and Tobago. Analysts of social movements generally have concerned themselves with specific explanatory frameworks rather than a conflated effort that seeks also to reflect, and fittingly so, what C. Wright Mills refers to as the imbrication of history and sociology.[2]

Third, approaches to the social production of knowledge have variously highlighted the relevance of social class, as in Karl Marx and Frederick Engels's *German Ideology;* religious phenomena, as in Emile Durkheim's *Elementary Forms of the Religious Life;* the activities of individuals in academic institutions such as universities, research institutes, think tanks, and political organizations, as in Robert Merton's *Social Theory and Social Structure;* and the intersectionality of race, class, and gender with respect to African American females, as in Patricia Hill Collins's *Black Feminist Thought.*

There is also a considerable literature on intellectuals in general and the West Indies in particular. The latter efforts include Gordon Lewis's *Main Currents in Caribbean Thought,* Denis Benn's *Growth and Development of Political Ideas in the Caribbean, 1774–1983* and *The Caribbean: An Intellectual History, 1774–2003,* and Anthony Bogues's *Caliban's Freedom* and Rupert Lewis's *Walter Rodney's Intellectual Thought,* both of which make meaningful use of the concept of biography. However, with the possible exception of Faith Smith's *Creole Recitations* and Kent Worcester's *C. L. R. James: A Political Biography,* which provides, among other things, a helpful statement concerning James and Williams's relationship between 1958 and 1960, both abroad and in Trinidad, there is usually no overtly stated theoretical framework regarding intellectual conduct. Finally, while the utilization of the character of Caliban in Shakespeare's *The Tempest* is to be found in the treatment of antihegemonic activity in the Caribbean in Paget Henry's *Caliban's Reason,* George Lamming's *In the Castle of My Skin* and *Pleasures of Exile,* Supriya Nair's *Caliban's Curse,* Aimé Césaire's *A Tempest,* and Silvio Torres-Saillant's *Intellectual History of the Caribbean,* the intellectual implications of this approach have not been specifically stated. In sum, there appears to be no study of Williams as an intellectual that is situated in a conflated theoretical framework privileging *biography, social-movement theory,* and *intellectualism* and that utilizes a methodology involving archival data normally employed by historians. This study hopes to fill this lacuna.

From a theoretical perspective, since no two individuals can have the same biography or lived experiences, the term *biography* is relevant especially because of its emphasis on the history of the individual or the agency factor. This includes webbed relationships with other individuals, or *biographical others.* Biographical others are individuals or groups with whom the actor interacts and who help to shape his or her thoughts and actions, subsequent identity formation, and political actions that conduce to intellectual activity. In other words, what Roderic Camp terms *collective biography*—family, education, and professional relationships with other intellectuals and one's relationship to the state—is directly linked with intellectual activity.[3] For Williams, biographical others include family members, teachers, university colleagues, publishers of books and scholarly articles, and especially fellow social-movement intellectuals and others involved in the political-independence movement. Biographical others also include British Colonial Office and U.S. State Department officials, as well as other detractors in Trinbago, such as opposition politicians and, sometimes, the local press. Again, the concept of biography allows us to contextualize and to compare and contrast the biographies of, and the relationships Williams maintained with, other exceptional minds who were involved in antihegemonic activity regarding oppression. Finally, the emphasis on biography, as will be seen, enables the pinpointing of "transformative" experiences, which are critical in understanding subsequent intellectual activity.

Early statements with respect to *social movements* tended to view this form of collective action as constituting an attack against civilization,[4] or the work of "sinners" and "misfits,"[5] or associated with "irrational beliefs."[6] However, the fact that the American civil rights movements and other movements, such as the workers' movement, for example, were led by members of the more educated stratum among the dominated has led to a rethinking of these forms of collective action as rational endeavors. Resource mobilization theory (RMT), for instance, emphasizes the manner in which resources are used by movement leaders to mobilize and educate their followers regarding social change. These resources might include time, energy, and knowledge of history,[7] as well as previously organized entities,[8] bridge organizations,[9] collective-action frames,[10] and an enabling political-opportunity structure.[11] Resources, however, do not arise out of thin air but are part of the sociohistorical experiences of the aggrieved, and their use reflects the scale of preferences of those who seek social change.

Cognitive-praxis theorists, on the other hand, point to the manner in which social movements open up opportunities for the performance of intellectual labor by movement participants. These theorists, therefore, tend to emphasize the production of "new" knowledge (intellectualism) resulting from these efforts.[12] "New" knowledge may include ideologies, strategies, tactics, in the case of a diasporan intellectual the debunking of myths that favor hegemonic control and new ways of viewing history that are relevant to the goals of the movement. With the possible exception of Ron Eyerman, no one has attempted to emphasize either the *social process* that undergirds knowledge production (i.e., history and culture) or the relevance of the biography of movement participants in explaining collective antihegemonic action. As Carol Mueller puts it, movement intellectuals appear to be "without a personal history or a gender, race, or class position within a social history."[13]

With respect to *intellectualism,* the literature is voluminous.[14] Lewis Coser, for instance, maintains that intellectuals "never seem satisfied with things as they are,"[15] while Seymour Martin Lipset and Richard Dobson contend that intellectuals also seek to engineer ameliorative social change.[16] Others view intellectuals as "critics of existing regimes [and] creators of social or cultural orientations and activities opposed to tradition" who, as part of the historical process, "generate new ways (ideas) of looking at society, and as human actors re-invent cultural traditions in different contexts."[17] Still others view intellectuals as providing "an interpretation of the world for that society [and whose] ideas are such that they challenge conventional wisdom or, at least, invite us to see the obvious in a new light."[18]

For still others, intellectuals, especially of the diasporan variety, are tasked with speaking the "truth," which Michel Foucault defines as "the ensemble of rules according to which true and false are separated and specific effects of power attached to the true."[19] This means not merely changing people's consciousness or even what is in their heads but reshaping the political and economic institutions that they embody. For Foucault, therefore, "it's not a matter of emancipating truth from every system of power (which would be a chimera, for truth is already power)," but one of "detaching the power of truth from the forms of hegemony, social, economic and cultural, within which it operates at the present time."[20]

This point is of special relevance to this study because the term *language of colonialism* refers not simply to the pedantry (English literature, Latin, French, colonial history) but also to religion and the sport of cricket and flows from what Jürgen Habermas calls the *system-lifeworld nexus.*[21] The *system* is the colonial structure of institutional arrangements, involving education, religion, race relations, economic exploitation, political disenfranchisement, and a cultural underbelly of fear, humiliation, and violence, which expresses itself in the everyday trials and tribulations, or the *lifeworld,* of the oppressed.

Others, such as Seymour Martin Lipset and Asoke Basu[22] and Dick Flacks,[23] point to the efforts of intellectuals to make their knowledge socially relevant, as well as transmissible and therefore available to their public. Railing against the system enables the intellectual to move issues of concern from the periphery to the center for more serious consideration and ventilation,[24] thereby creating space for "new knowledge" in the sociopolitical fabric. This is done usually by efforts "to make 'scientific' sense of the world," as well as by generating various theories of society that in turn make history. Social theories, therefore, as Flacks contends, "are levers intellectuals use to influence power structures, to facilitate political outcomes, to enable groups interested in exercising control to improve their [chances of doing so], to justify their ascendancy, to achieve their goals, or to advance their interests."[25] Finally, while the term *intellectual* has been used to include the intelligentsia (lawyers, doctors, writers, artists, and so on), Alistair Hennessy distinguishes between university lecturers, who merely regurgitate the thoughts of others, and those who examine the ideas and thought of others for the purpose of creating new knowledge.[26]

For the purposes of this study, intellectuals are viewed as knowledge entrepreneurs, who create a public (consumers) for their product, and by extension a market for their knowledge, by speaking to the *relevance* of their product. Furthermore, their knowledge is socially generated, that is, in terms of webbed relationships with biographical others; and historically situated, in the sense that "new" knowledge reflects that of the prevailing intellectual spirit of the age, or zeitgeist. Contextually, intellectuals *(a)* are never satisfied with the way things are; *(b)* make use of socially relevant resources to educate and mobilize oppressed "others" and thereby construct a "public" or collective identity among the aggrieved for antihegemonic activity; *(c)* construct specific settings for the transmission of the spoken and the written word dealing with antihegemonic knowledge; *(d)* create space for "new" knowledge by "selecting out" various ideas, theories, and so on, that represent the "truth" for movement into the public sphere; and *(e)* promulgate a body of "new" knowledge as being relevant, in this case regarding nationalism. More specifically, this study poses the following questions: First, what form did the colonial language of oppression take, and how was it transmitted to Williams and other Trinbagonians? Second, how did Williams, in particular, ráil against the language of oppression that he and various biographical others experienced? Third, what "new" knowledge resulted from Williams's antihegemonic railings, and to what extent did these activities constitute part of the diasporic tradition (zeitgeist) regarding anticolonialism?

Methodologically, the data for this study were garnered from three main sources: First, documents and Williams's personal papers in the Eric Williams Memorial Collection (EWMC), located in the West India Section of the University of the West Indies Library in St. Augustine, Trinidad, were critical in reconstructing Williams's lived experiences with colonial oppression in Trinbago and England. Second, archival data from the National Archives, London (formerly the Public Record Office) and the National Archives, College Park, Maryland, were used to shed light on the British and the American language of colonialism, respectively. Third, secondary-source data were obtained from national and political-party newspapers in Trinbago, scholarly papers, autobiographical and other statements of former cabinet colleagues of Williams's and other biographical others, and books and articles written by Williams and by others about him and his personal life. Many of these data, which are housed in the University of the West Indies Library in St. Augustine, provided key indicators of Williams's thought, especially regarding colonialism and political independence, as well as insights into his relationships with key biographical others.

CHAPTER 1 deals with Williams's experiences with the language of colonialism while growing up in Trinbago and how these were manifested in the private sphere of the household, the semipublic sphere of the school, and the public sphere of the wider society. I look at how these experiences and Williams's relationships with key biographical others influenced major decisions on his part, such as to study, and to become a teacher of, history, and also to why these decisions, arguably, undergirded his later anticolonial "cursing." In other words, Williams as an intellectual "with a history" is contextualized.

Chapter 2 discusses Williams's continuing experiences with what he perceived to be the language of racialized oppression as a student at Oxford University and how, despite being treated as an outsider within, he acquired the credentialism and learned the habitus concerning knowledge production as a professional historian. I make reference to his activities as a teacher and to his relationships with a number of exceptional minds, both at Oxford and at Howard, as well as to his use of specialized historical knowledge to delineate and to "curse" colonial domination. This use of specialized historical knowledge took the form of two published books, a number of scholarly articles, and two unpublished monographs dealing with education in the context of colonialism in the West Indies. Attention is also drawn to the inception of his role as a public intellectual by way of his connection with the Anglo-American Caribbean Commission as a researcher with expertise of the Caribbean and to his extrauniversity activities, which brought him in contact with individuals, in America and other countries, who were experiencing colonial domination.

In chapter 3 Williams returns to Trinbago and solidifies his role as public intellectual, which involves efforts on his part to begin to change the "rules of the game," from those associated with the production of knowledge as an academic intellectual to those more germane to the role of public intellectual and later social-movement intellectual. I therefore focus on a number of lectures he gave on colonial oppression and a well-publicized debate with another individual with an earned doctorate. These activities enabled Williams to continue to create a public, as well as space for his intellectualism in the society, especially following his departure from the Caribbean Commission, an organization that he felt discriminated against him because of his race and reflected quasi-imperialist practices.

Chapter 4 examines Williams's first definitive shift from public to social-movement intellectual and thus his ongoing efforts to make the rules of knowledge production more *credible* and, especially, *relevant* to his nationalist aspirations. This he did by promulgating the idea of the "University of Woodford Square" (UWS), or the "People's Parliament," as a setting for teaching and mobilizing his increasing public, in two senses: first, by investing various public spaces, such as the Trinidad Public Library and especially Woodford Square, a public space named after a former governor, with new meanings consistent with his *verbal* anticolonial railings; and second, by using the newspaper of the People's National Movement (PNM), a political party of which he was one of the founders, and the party press to transmit his *written* anticolonial railings. This enabled Williams to create more space, and a wider "public," for his historical knowledge and to move his "cursing" of the language of oppression from the semipublic sphere of the classrooms of Oxford and Howard Universities, to the public sphere of the UWS.

In chapter 5 we find Williams continuing to attempt, along with various biographical others, to use his *cultural* and *symbolic* capital as a historian to "curse" the language of colonial politics. This involved, in particular, the application of intellectual labor by Williams and by previously organized groups, especially teachers and females, in facilitating the PNM's emergence and in fashioning its philosophy and ideology. It also involved pariah intellectuals, members of a loosely organized aggregation of subalterns with a dissident subculture, who populated the crowds who listened to Williams's many lectures at the UWS. Also mentioned are Williams's attempts to portray the PNM as an innovative organization, rather than one that merely mimicked existing political organizations, and his exploitation of the extant political-opportunity structure, occasioned by the liberalization of the franchise and the prevailing tendency to vote for the individual rather than for the political party.

Chapter 6 deals with Williams's ongoing efforts as a social-movement intellectual–cum–teacher to create space for his views regarding political independence, which paved the way for his and the PNM's election to office in September 1956. Accordingly, I discuss the *relevance* of his views regarding economic reform, race relations, constitutional reform, political parties, and party politics in relation to nationalism, which facilitated his entry into formal politics as leader of the government of Trinidad and Tobago (GOTT). I also examine Williams's attempts to distance himself and the PNM from what he referred to as the colonial politics of "anything goes," which involved corruption and a tendency for politicians to say one thing and do another, among other things. The chapter closes with an examination of Williams's views regarding the role of party members, the party leader, and the party press, as a mechanism for knowledge production and transmission, regarding political independence.

In chapter 7 I look at the efforts by Williams and other social-movement intellectuals to create space for his views that the presence in Trinbago of an American base, which he described as the "hydra," or principal head, of colonialism, was incompatible with a politically independent Trinbago. I discuss how the base came to be sited in Trinidad in the first place and the strategy of non–decision making employed by the Americans to defend and preserve the base's presence. I focus in particular on the "death by a thousand cuts," or pinpricking strategy, of Williams in particular, designed to counter the U.S. defense of the base. This involved Williams's use of historical knowledge to educate Trinbagonians regarding the "truth," "selecting out" the existence of the base, in particular, for critical discussion in the UWS.

Chapter 8 attempts to situate Williams's antihegemonic renderings, especially as a diasporan intellectual, within the wider anticolonial tradition by way of a brief assessment of the work of Aimé Césaire, Juan Bosch, George Lamming, and Frantz Fanon. Also discussed are further implications of the Eric Williams Memorial Collection for the production of even more relevant knowledge.

The book ends with a brief discussion of the 1970 disturbances in the twin island against Williams's policies, which exposed the dilemmas of the intellectual in power.

1 Colonialism in Early Twentieth-Century Trinidad and Tobago

The Construction of a Socially Dishonored Status

TRINIDAD AND Tobago's early history, like that of other Caribbean territories, such as Guyana and Jamaica, reflects a struggle for contested space by various European powers. In Trinidad, for instance, the Spanish introduced a cedula of population in the form of a decree issued from Madrid on 24 November 1783; it was designed to increase the amount of labor on the island by way of a free grant of land to every settler who came to Trinidad with his slaves. Since a requirement of the cedula was that the immigrant had to be a Roman Catholic and the subject of a nation friendly to Spain, the settlers tended to be almost exclusively French, as only the French planters could meet the requirement.[1] Later, following clashes between French privateers and British ships and because the British feared that a Spanish-French alliance would imperil its war strategy and be a threat to several of its most valuable islands, a British striking force under the command of Sir Ralph Abercromby engaged a Spanish squadron in February 1797 in Trinidad. However, the Spanish position was weak, and after token resistance the governor, Don José Maria Chacon, surrendered on 17 February 1797.[2] In this manner, these European powers were able to overcome the Arawaks and the Caribs (from whose name the word *Caribbean* derives), who had previously inhabited the island.

In this chapter, therefore, I focus on Williams's lived experiences while growing up in Trinidad, with the *lifeworld,* or the everyday trials and tribulations, of the dominated and its connection with the *system,* the bureaucratic nature of institutional control that characterized domination. In other words, I focus on the social process by which legal norms, the views especially of members of the elite, and established practices were used in the social construction of difference to privilege the dominant and disadvantage the dominated. These bodies of knowledge, however, became institutionalized in the sense that they were disseminated throughout the society in newspapers and, important for our purposes, the household and the educational institutions in such a manner as to rise to the level of "truth."

ERIC WILLIAMS's early years in Trinidad have been variously described by Williams himself,[3] as well as by others.[4] However, my main concern is to isolate various aspects of Williams's biography that ultimately will help us understand the type of person he was and how this undergirded his intellectual activities. Contextually, it is worth noting that Williams's published autobiography was not originally conceived as a biographical statement but, as he put it some fifteen years earlier, in 1954, as "a political manifesto," a statement of his education and his fight with his then employer, the Caribbean Commission. Additionally, Williams noted in the unpublished version that the autobiography was very much a response to the racism he had experienced at Oxford University and to British attacks against him following the publication of his book *Capitalism and Slavery.* Since the autobiography was to be an account of his education in a broad sense, the title was originally intended to be *Caribbean Museum, the Education of a British Colonial Subject.*[5] Consequently, he notes that his aim in the biography and then the anthology, with the history of the Caribbean to come, was to "cash in, with something new, on the present BWI [British West Indian] popularity, and to see if I can get a bestseller which will allow me to retire and devote my time solely to writing and to West Indian education through that medium."[6] It is evident from the above that, lacking an independent profession like law or medicine at this stage, Williams was intent on converting the *cultural* and *symbolic* capital emanating from his specialized knowledge into monetary benefits, or *economic* capital.

In looking at the question of race, Erving Goffman's views with respect to stigma are useful. Goffman notes, for example, that originally the term *stigma* referred to "bodily signs designed to expose something unusual and bad about the moral status of the signifier."[7] The stigmatized individual was seen as a blemished person, ritually polluted and to be avoided, particularly in public places. Goffman further distinguishes three different types of stigma—the tribal stigmata of race, nation, and religion—which can be transmitted through lineage and thereby contaminate all the members of the family.[8] Since the question of stigma may be viewed in terms of social relationships, this suggests that the experiences of the stigmatized person are important facets of his or her biography, while those who view and treat the attribute—for example, race—as being blemished are a part of a coterie of biographical others. I will therefore refer to the manner in which the stigmata of race conferred on the non-White Trinbagonian was a socially blemished status and show how the process of this conferral became part of the knowledge base of the society.

IN ADDRESSING Williams's experiences in the family and in education in Trinidad and Tobago, it is helpful to view the organizational expressions of these institutions—the household and the school, respectively—as social spaces. Space, as Georg Simmel contends, in and of itself is a form without effect. Space becomes a social space insofar as it is filled with what Simmel refers to as "social and psychological energies." Indeed, what, for example, makes a city or a society is less its geographical location than it is the presence and interaction among human beings who populate that space, thereby embedding it with social meanings. Spatial forms, therefore—such as households, schools, and universities, which are also physically demarcated existential entities in the sense that they have boundaries—thus become social spaces to the extent that social interactions and relationships are woven into the fabric of a physical space. As Simmel notes, spaces are not spatial facts "with sociological consequences" but rather "sociological facts that are formed spatially."[9] As we will see, especially in chapter 7, relationships within a physical space like the foreign-controlled U.S. base in Trinidad, which might be converted into a locale for domination, can be perceived as disadvantaging the locals and privileging the Americans.

To contextualize further, as John Urry observes, the "house" is not to be seen as a purely physical object but as a space within which one's imagination and daydreaming can take place and be given full rein. Since the household may contain various objects, such as books, it also becomes an externalization of the self and the site of memorized events, "imbued with memory traces." Furthermore, since the duration of time spent in the household is itself dependent upon spatial specificity, a space such as a household "transforms time in such a way that memory is made possible [and] plays a particularly significant role in the forming and sustaining of memory."[10] It is in this context that the household as a physical space assumes special significance with regard to biography and relationships with biographical others, especially in terms of memorized events—space and time—and ultimately knowledge production.

It is also in the household that identities are formed that will later influence political action and intellectualism.[11] Finally, since, as Paul Gilroy observes, race differences displayed in the culture are reproduced in educational institutions and, above all, in family life, families "are not only the nation in microcosm, but they also act as the means to turn social processes into natural instinctive ones."[12] As will be seen in the chapters that follow, an understanding of Williams's experiences and the knowledge he acquired in physical spaces such as his father's house and the educational institutions he attended, some of which were transformative, is vital for comprehending his subsequent "cursing" of colonialism, especially the racial component.

Eric Eustace Williams was born on 25 September 1911, the first of the twelve children, one of whom died early, of Henry and Eliza Williams. One of his most important experiences as a child, regarding the social construction of difference on the basis of color, class, and access to education in early twentieth-century Trinbago, occurred in the household. Williams notes, for example, that since his father was "dark brown," he was automatically beyond the pale of social acceptance. This disability was aggravated, according to Williams, by the fact that his father's father, "a full blooded Negro," had eloped with and married one of the daughters in a well-to-do local White family that employed him in a menial capacity. Since this was the least pardonable transgression of the language, or *habitus,* of race relations in the eyes of the White ruling class—"a coloured man might marry an English, Scotch or European girl, never a local White"—his paternal grandmother was disowned by her family.

The application of this negative sanction exemplifies, further, the argument that oppression, especially with regard to economic capital—and such facets of social capital as access to important social networks, for example, a good job, and of cultural capital as a good education—is passed on from one generation to another within the context of familial relationships. Since, as is clear from Williams's recollections, his family did not possess significant social, economic, or cultural capital to transmit to him and his siblings, they were doomed to experience social disadvantages not confronted by White families. This explains why, having violated the norm with respect to the transmission of these forms of capital to the next generation, Williams's grandmother could not confer on her family the capital that exemplified White privilege.

The response to this normative violation on the part of Williams's grandmother is also of interest in view of the fact that White *males* who fathered children with Black women out of wedlock were not necessarily deprived of economic capital. Indeed, as Faith Smith has shown, the products of these relationships peopled a privileged stratum of mulattoes who consequently were in a position to enjoy certain "compensating privileges." These included a good education and concomitant symbolic and economic capital, which aided them and others with whom they were in "constant intercourse" in their intellectual activities.[13]

One wonders, therefore, how things would have been had it been Williams's paternal grandfather who was White: in that case, would his father have been the recipient of symbolic and economic capital that would have positively impacted his life chances, and what implications would that have had for Williams's career overall and for the course of history in Trinidad and Tobago? Moreover, as Joe Feagin observes, in the context of racist oppression in the United States, "The social inheritance mechanisms are disguised to make the intertemporal inheritance of resources, power and privilege appear to be fair, when in fact the White resources, power, and privilege typically represent the long-term transmission of unjust enrichment across numerous generations of oppressors and oppressed."[14] This helps explain the protracted nature of oppression and the difficulty experienced in railing against colonialism as a form of oppression.

In any event, the prevailing norms with respect to physical characteristics—color in this case—seeped into the Williams household. Williams's only paternal aunt, who kept a small private nursery school and who was most important in his early life, was "a strict disciplinarian, ascetic in countenance as my father, dark brown in colour, with long black hair," or what was referred to in Trinidad as "good grass." This was the ideal of colored Trinidadians, who were mortally afraid of "bad hair," especially of the kinky variety, which was maliciously compared to goat dung. Such was the importance of the color and hair criteria as a basis for social differentiation that light-complexioned children of mixed marriages with "bad light hair"—more often than dark children with "good black hair"—were ridiculed with the appellation *shabeen* and contemptuously referred to by young boys as "wire-heads."[15]

Williams's mother, on the other hand, who was ten years younger than his father, came from a prominent French Creole family, the de Boissières, was light-complexioned, and had four sisters and two brothers. According to Michael Pocock, who was related to the de Boissières, Williams's mother was related to Henry Boissière, a wealthy landed proprietor who lived on the Champs Elysées estate in Maraval. However, although Williams's maternal grandfather, Jules Arnold Boissière, and his maternal great-grandfather, John Nicolas Boissière, were both born out of wedlock, in sharp contrast with Williams's paternal grandmother, their fathers provided for them financially, and John Nicolas's father even arranged for him to be born in Europe to avoid the possibility of scandal. This enabled the family to pass on social and economic capital to successive generations.

This less than socially pristine pedigree notwithstanding, Eliza Williams "was considered, and considered herself of bourgeois French creole heritage." Additionally, she "had the French style and she thought that she was an aristocrat."[16] Ken Boodhoo suggests, however, that because "his [Williams's] mother was the more assertive of the parents, how the family perceived itself, and its perception of others, must have been largely influenced by how she viewed her status in the society." And although the family was highly regimented and both parents were strict disciplinarians, one of Williams's sisters opined that the mother "was the boss. She was the ruler. She gave the orders," while the father was generally regarded as a "peaceful, if firm, individual."[17]

Although he retained few memories of his maternal aunts, who were also light-skinned, Williams maintained that their station in life afforded additional insight into the nature of colonial society at the time. Unlike in the case of some Trinidadian families, especially in the upper socioeconomic echelons, there was no discrimination either inside or outside the Williams family against the darker-skinned children. This was partly because even the lighter-skinned children "were obviously coloured"[18] and partly because Williams, who was one of the darker ones, had achieved an intellectual status despite the odds.

When it came to marriage, however, skin color was regarded entirely differently, and Williams's parents were adamant. One of his aunts married a Negro tram driver and was generally regarded as "having lost caste." According to the tenor of the times, the light-skinned woman who had reached the drawing room might go back to the kitchen after marrying "dark" but was not expected to descend lower than the "professions." Another aunt, who was generally considered to be a "play girl," also married a Negro and was heard to say in the context of domestic violence that "she would use the ice pick on her husband." A third aunt, who worked in one of the big stores in the capital "for a few dollars a week," had a Negro boyfriend whom Williams described as "not undistinguished looking [and] always dressed in a waistcoat," at the time considered to be a "symbol of the professional class . . . taking salt in his coffee or tea—a solicitor I believe, he was."[19] Seemingly, therefore, the race of the boyfriend was assuaged by his social class. Finally, the fourth aunt had a White boyfriend who kept a small store in Port-of-Spain that served as a vantage point for the annual islandwide festival known as Carnival. Her situation was rendered more acceptable by the race of her boyfriend and his petit-bourgeois social class.

Having been irretrievably locked in the castle of their skin color, Williams's parents, like other Trinidadians at that time, passionately desired a higher social status for their children. As Williams put it, they had all the complexes of the lower middle class. Social status for them involved questions of color and hair, and for a period of time Williams's curls, or "good grass," were the pride of the family. Beyond that, connected as his mother was to the local White aristocracy, it was significant that his father's mother (who, as noted above, was local White) lived with them until her death, while connections were severed with his father's father, who had mistreated Williams's grandmother.

The philosophy of Williams's parents regarding color was as follows: "That one might come from Africa . . . was one's misfortune, but hardly one's fault, but there was no point in going back to Africa [as] that would be not only one's misfortune but one's fault."[20] Consequently, his parents thoroughly disapproved of the Negro associations of some of his aunts. In their view, while one had no control over the circumstances surrounding one's birth as far as race and color were concerned, with blackness being associated with "misfortune," compounding the problem by marrying or intimately associating with those close to the African phenotype was a matter of choice and therefore one's "fault." Not surprisingly, Williams's parents desired professional men, namely, doctors and lawyers, for the girls and lighter-skinned women for the boys; put more simply, they wanted education in the case of husbands and color in the case of wives, or in their unavoidable absence, a good education or a good family background.[21]

In addition to race and color, Williams's father's lack of sterling academic qualifications, his relatively weak economic base, and his large family, a consequence of his father's adherence to the tenets of Roman Catholicism when it came to birth control, all affected the family's socioeconomic status.[22] In the absence of social capital, his father was forced to pull himself up by his bootstraps, though he did not get very far. Given his father's comparatively humble social position and the almost biennial additions to the family, there was an ongoing need not only to acquire additional resources but also to husband those resources. Williams's father, for instance, found it necessary to audit the accounts of friendly societies on the island, in addition to his regular job at the post office, and Williams himself, who had some facility with figures, acted as his father's assistant.

This turned out to be beneficial to Williams in that the gratuities he received from his father after he was paid by his clients were, as Williams put it, "first earnings, and represented a valuable addition to the slender resources of a boy with an inordinate love of the sweetmeats, drinks and pies sold on the streets, whilst I acquired an abiding love of figures which leads me even today to make all sorts of intricate computations . . . whilst driving, sitting on a verandah or walking on the beach." Williams's mother's contribution to the family budget was typical of the Trinidad housewife, who was expected to be excellent in the kitchen. She made bread and cakes for home consumption and for sale to a number of regular customers, which, interestingly, Williams viewed as a "survival of a common custom in the slave society." In addition, Williams was involved in both the preparation and distribution of the products of his mother's baking. For example, for the dough he went to the bakery, where "I saw how literally our tasty penny loaves were made. . . . I made the complicated measurements called for by the recipes [the baker] followed. I whipped up the eggs, mixed the butter and even learned to ice cakes." And he also delivered orders on foot.[23]

However, Williams admits that while he was a willing participant in the productive process, he was a most "reluctant *marchand* [dealer or peddler]," as he was ashamed of anything suggestive of work or poverty, and he would "slink by in the streets hoping that he would not meet any of his school friends." The Black *marchands,* as Faith Smith notes, were the sellers of fish, "whose street cries marked the rhythms of their labor"[24] but whose distinctive speech pattern and conduct, one imagines, would clearly have been inconsonant with the status of an attendee of Queen's Royal College (QRC). This explains why Williams goes on to state rhetorically, "What on earth I would have done if I had had to tote the basket myself, I do not know. This was not a personal idiosyncrasy. It was the attitude of class"[25]—and, one might add, of social decorum.

Turning to another indicator of social class, Williams recalls that housing, or perhaps more accurately, adequate housing, was always a problem for the Williams household; in his twenty-one years in Trinidad before he departed for Oxford University, the family moved eight times. Here, as in other facets of his early years in Trinidad, the interpenetration of education or lack thereof, race, social class, and, very importantly, religious beliefs loomed large in Williams's existence, and all contributed to the weak economic position of the family.

In Williams's view, in order to live comfortably, it would have been necessary for his father to audit the accounts of all the friendly societies on the island, and for his mother to supply cakes for the entire population of Port-of-Spain, for the family to cope adequately with the consequences of not practicing birth control. Indeed, not only were his parents Catholic but his father was one of the leading figures in the erection of a new church in Woodbrook. As Williams recalled, humorously, with respect to the use of the condom, a schoolboy joke about birth control was that while the Lord sent the rain, he did not tell people not to wear raincoats. In Williams's father's house, therefore, "we simply got wet."[26] His parents, consequently, faced the dilemma associated with being children of the church but not being impecunious parents.

Williams also recalled living in a house with no electricity that had a front room called the "drawing room," with the dining room beyond that and two bedrooms beyond the dining room. At the back of the house were the kitchen, the toilet, and, interestingly enough, the servant quarters. The house also possessed two amenities restricted to urban areas, namely, a water closet and pipe-borne water. In those days, Williams noted, the smallest West Indian middle-class house had some sort of room for the servant, which in itself was "a visible and tangible symbol of the ascent of the family in the social scale by, at least, reducing the amount of work for the female members of the family."[27]

However, as the size of the Williams family increased, and circumstances evidently became more parlous, the family moved, and, it appears, not always to better conditions. The move in 1917 to Diego Martin, which by the time he was penning his unpublished autobiography had become a "highly-prized residential area," meant descending the social ladder. Life there was characterized by floods and by mosquitoes, frogs, wasps, and snakes, as well as an intermittent electricity supply, which rendered the oil lamp and the candle universal standbys. Beyond that, the hazard of the bush fire and the descent from a water closet to the cesspit proved to be intensely embarrassing; as the trucks rumbled by after cleaning out the cesspits, "the street loafers would apprise everyone by yelling out with gusto at the top of their voices, the nature of their cargo."[28] Following another move, Williams's father fell in arrears with respect to the rent, occasioning a visit from the bailiff, after which the rent was paid. Thus, the dread of eviction was added to the horror of the cesspit culture.

As a way of coping with the seemingly intractable nature of his social situation, Williams's father turned to two other solutions. His first turn was to the extranatural, by putting his fate in the hands of a spiritualist, a not atypical response of those among the oppressed who seemed unable to overcome the vicissitudes of their status. Williams recalls that his father would drag him and his younger brother along during his visits to an obeah woman, a skinny mulatto woman from St. Vincent, he believed, who lived in Laventille Hills. In keeping with the ritualistic requirements of the visits, Williams's father would provide a number of chickens. Matters came to a head, however, when one day his mother deliberately smashed an earthenware pot—a "tureen"—that the obeah woman had given to his father. As was his wont, Williams's father simply looked at his mother, said nothing, and went to work. The next thing Williams knew, his father had become one of the prime movers in the building of a new Catholic church named St. Theresa's.[29] In Williams's father's case, the brief excursion into the realm of obeah was necessarily temporary because it constituted a departure from his lower-middle-class status, as well as from the Catholic faith, which disavowed such activity.

THE SECOND solution to which the Williams family turned to cope with their seemingly immutable social situation was an emphasis on education, and with it a disciplined approach to life. As a reward for educational excellence, for example, Williams received a bicycle for having memorized the alphabet. In addition, he was the recipient of preferential treatment from his parents; since he was the eldest child, much was given, and as a consequence much was expected. As a result, there were times when he was fed curried shrimp and fish—which his siblings did not receive—presumably on the theory that fish was good for the brain. From an early age Williams was expected to help his mother take care of his younger brothers and sisters, as a consequence of which, in addition to the steps involved in baking cakes, he learned to cook and to clean, skills that he felt stood him in good stead later in life.[30] When one considers the amenities in the household and Williams's father's educational attainment and occupation, the family was solidly lower middle class.

Education, therefore, was regarded as being very important by Williams's parents. However, despite their adherence to Roman Catholicism, his parents did not send him to a Catholic school; instead they sent him, at considerable expense, to the state Tranquillity Boys' Intermediate School to help to prepare him for the college exhibition examination, which one took before the age of twelve. Success in the exam meant possible admission to various secondary schools, especially the prestigious Queen's Royal College and also the Catholic counterpart, St. Mary's College. It was therefore an important *rite de passage* in the educational system that led to a good secondary education and eventually to study abroad and good employment prospects upon return to Trinbago. Parenthetically Williams notes that while education was important to individuals of color like his father, Williams felt that it was "not fully appreciated by the Indian community." In any event, due to his success at the exhibition examination, Williams had the opportunity to decide whether he wished to attend the state-run QRC, which was in receipt of a government subsidy and stressed instruction in the classics, or the private Catholic St. Mary's College or the College of Immaculate Conception (CIC). He chose QRC. Williams recalls that when the parish priest called to congratulate the family on his achievement, he naturally assumed that St. Mary's College would be their choice. When he was told otherwise, the priest, with a look of consternation on his face, not only argued and remonstrated but also threatened Williams's parents with excommunication. Williams remembers that in the midst of the priest's efforts

> I remained curiously unmoved and the idea ran through my mind, that if anyone was to be excommunicated I should be. Was it an early inability to see any connection between religion and education, the school and the church? Or an early preference for state over private enterprise under West Indian conditions? Or the first faint glimmering of anti-colonialism? Or the first indication that religion was profoundly to influence my life? I cannot say. I know only that the decision to enter the State School was my own, and neither my father or my mother ever tried to influence me one way or the other.[31]

This revelation on the part of Williams is instructive in that it speaks to a specific event and an equally transformative moment in his life at a relatively early age—he would have been no more than eleven at the time—that was in fact an act of independence. Here, in addition to a statement about the canalization of religious beliefs in the making of a secular decision, the autobiography becomes what Paul Gilroy refers to as part of a process of "simultaneous self-creation and self-emancipation."[32]

In addition to its purely formal aspects, education for Williams also took on an informal dimension. Thus, not only was Williams physically punished by his father—with his buttocks bearing the brunt of his father's efforts at socialization—but Williams was given the authority to physically punish his younger siblings for socially disapproved behavior. Williams notes, for example, that on one occasion he gave a younger brother "the best hiding he ever got in his life" for calling him a liar when his brother knew that he had done something wrong, which in Trinidadian parlance was equated with "brazenness."[33] It is interesting that in referring to the onerous responsibility of surrogate parenthood, with respect to his four brothers, Williams would note that the task of keeping "the quadrumvirate at their lessons and inculcating in them some intellectual discipline was a wholetime one utterly beyond the capacities of a boy himself buried in studies who had his own friends and existence. The early habits of discipline which form the foundation of the character in later life became more and more tenuous in these younger children, and even as an adolescent I was worried."[34]

Doubtless, these experiences were instrumental in forming Williams's personality, which later influenced his relations with British and American officials and with other individuals and movement intellectuals who railed against colonialism. Also, these experiences constitute an interesting facet of the prevailing culture regarding physical punishment.

FROM A POLITICAL perspective, Williams notes that the Crown Colony government of early twentieth-century Trinidad and Tobago was designed to stifle political initiative. Moreover, any interest in politics was especially dangerous for the civil servant. Nonetheless, Williams recalls that two of his father's most respected friends eventually became active in politics. One was Charles Petioni, who resigned from the civil service and migrated to the United States in 1918. He studied at Howard University, where he qualified as a physician, and later became a well-known figure in Harlem politics and a member of the West Indian National Council. Looking back, Williams felt that Petioni had imbibed the bitterness of colonialism. Williams also stated that during a conference he arranged while he was a professor of social science at Howard, Petioni had given the British representative on the Anglo-American Caribbean Commission and later governor of Jamaica "a warm time."[35]

The other friend to whom Williams refers was T. A. Marryshow of Grenada, a journalist and one of the earliest advocates of representative government and the Federation of the West Indies. Marryshow later became editor of the *West Indian Crusader* and collaborated with Captain A. A. Cipriani, who had been born into a White French Creole family. Cipriani later became president of the predominantly Black, working-class Trinidad Workingmen's Association (TWA), especially after his support of Black troops against racism in the British West India Regiment, and represented Port-of-Spain in the Legislative Council (Leg Co) virtually unchallenged until his death.

Williams also notes that during a visit by Marryshow to the Williams household, the future legislator and lover of "flowery phrases" asked

Williams what he wanted to be when he grew up, to which Williams first replied, a policeman. Following his father's not surprising demurral and suggestion that instead he should choose medicine as a profession, Williams then mentioned being a teacher. While his written autobiography does not elaborate on the firmness of his decision to study history and possibly, as a consequence, to become a teacher, Williams does reveal that having cut his finger and fainted at the sight of the blood, he had decided that he could not become a doctor.[36]

Contextually, he also notes, with respect to becoming a teacher, that a German family who were their neighbors in Diego Martin lived in a "high house supported on wooden pillars which afforded much space for youngsters to play under the house."

> I recall now one of our favorite games under the house—playing school. I was always the teacher always the disciplinarian, satisfying not only a pronounced trait in my character but also, in the milieu I am describing, bearing rich dividends with pupils who, like most young girls of those days wore short dresses and no trousers, and who showed no reluctance whatsoever to being "benched" in true Trinidad school fashion—smacked on the buttocks which I insisted on baring, and derived as much pleasure from being punished as the teacher derived from punishing.[37]

However, as far as his future career plans were concerned, the matter seems to have been settled, although there was no indication that Williams's father was aware of his son's fainting.

Williams's decision was significant for a number of reasons. First, although Williams does not specifically mention that this experience contributed to his decision not to study medicine but to study history, he does state that after he won the island scholarship in 1931, this decision was influenced by the presence of a number of West Indian masters at QRC, whom he admired, and the fact that West Indian history was not taught at the school. Indeed, he notes rather matter-of-factly that despite the various artifices used by his father to get him to change his mind, he remained unmoved in his decision not to study medicine. Since it was he who had won the scholarship, not his father, Williams felt that his views should prevail.[38]

A second reason why Williams's decision to study history was significant is that the decision and the events leading up to it that involved Marryshow, a future political leader of Grenada, speak to the importance of elders in the formation of attitudes and identities during that period not only in Trinidad but also in the West Indies. Third, Williams's account points to another act of emancipation (besides the decision to attend QRC) that was part of his biography, in connection with two important biographical others, namely, his father and Marryshow. This also helps explain the formation of his political and intellectual identity as an independent thinker, likely to be unmoved by detractors once he had taken a position based on mature reflection.

IN ADDITION to race, class, and politics, education also functioned as a basis for social differentiation. Williams notes, for example, that a significant biographical other in this context, J. O. Cutteridge, the principal of Tranquillity Boys' Intermediate School, was an Englishman. The school curriculum stressed intellectual discipline and emphasized English grammar, spelling, dictation, arithmetic, and geography, which adequately prepared Williams for the college exhibition examination. But Cutteridge represented the language of oppression when it came to the education of upwardly mobile Trinbagonians like the Williams family.

Captain James Oliver Cutteridge was a product of a British policy between the two world wars of utilizing ex-officers of the armed forces as directors of education in the colonies, the idea being that pupils as well as teachers needed the iron hand of discipline as part of the educational diet. Upon his arrival in 1921, Cutteridge served as principal at Tranquillity Government Training School for just two years, after which he was appointed senior inspector of schools, then assistant director of education, and eventually director of education in 1934, although he did not possess a university degree. As part of his efforts to reform the twin island's education system, Cutteridge introduced a series of actions that earned him the opprobrium of a number of local constituencies.

The directors of education, according to the historian Carl Campbell, "were expected to be tough reformers, and to bring education practices in the colonies more in line with 'modern' developments in contemporary England."[39] While he was director of education, Cutteridge made efforts to convert the Tranquillity Training School into an English training college and the boys' school into an English-type intermediate school. Also, teachers were closely supervised and thoroughly subordinated by managers, inspectors, and directors. The child was viewed as a living personality with instincts to be developed, with the education system functioning as a catalyst for the development of all the intellectual powers of the mind and body. In addition, teachers' pay was based on results.

However, Cutteridge's tenure in the field of education was marked by controversy. For instance, he was criticized by Howard Bishop, the general secretary of the TWA and editor of the *Labour Leader,* the organ of the TWA; and also by Father English, the principal of St. Mary's College, who maintained that since Cutteridge did not have a university degree, he was not qualified for the position of assistant director of education.

Additionally, there were complaints that Cutteridge's textbooks, which were required for West Indian children, arguably a palpable effort to convert symbolic capital—relative to Cutteridge's social status—into economic capital, gave Cutteridge a monopoly over relevant knowledge as far as the children were concerned. This enabled him to make a fortune in the colonies in a novel way that was no different from that of the foreign plantocracy, which controlled the sugar industry. Moreover, his books were regarded as offensive because the drawings made "black people look like gorillas."[40] A correspondent for the *Labour Leader,* obviously intent on reinforcing the idea of Black consciousness, wrote in March 1929, "We want a full-fledged race conscious Negro to be the Director of Education's chief lieutenant and we must have one."[41] In September 1928 another writer for the same paper had described Cutteridge's West Indian *Readers* as being an insult to the Negro race, saying that his "nancy stories" sought to provide a misleading portrayal of West Indian folklore.

The Trinidad and Tobago Teachers Union, for its part, opposed the introduction in the Leg Co, in 1935, of a code of regulations for elementary schools that would *(a)* provide Cutteridge with the authority to send winners of college exhibition examinations to intermediate schools rather than to the traditional grammar schools; *(b)* reduce instruction in elementary schools to six years—this garnered the fiercest opposition; and *(c)* place restrictions on the entry of teachers in politics. To some of Cutteridge's critics, therefore, the fact that the man who had written nonsensical folk tales and had deemphasized the teaching of grammar now wished to give the principals of QRC and CIC the right to refuse entry to certain exhibition winners and to prevent teachers even to edit newspapers or write to the press on political matters was unacceptable. Viewing the 1935 code as not only "wicked and retrogressive" but inimical to the nationalist aspirations of the twin island, these critics "cursed" the language of oppression by raising the important question of knowledge relevance and dispensation.

As part of the construction of a socially blemished status for the colonized other, the mostly Black and colored children of the laborers, artisans, and peasant farmers found themselves the victim of fears of pollution on the part of middle- and upper-class parents, who did not want their children to mix with lower-class children in the rural areas. Also, by around 1900 a large proportion of the children of Indo-Trinidadian immigrants, who lived in the rural areas, did not attend the government-assisted schools.[42] In addition, apart from agricultural education for Blacks and the colored members of the population, there was always concern that exposing them to another level of education would generate socially unattainable aspirations, or, more accurately, "social pretensions," to higher positions on the social ladder, which in turn would threaten the positions of those who occupied, very often ascriptively, those privileged positions.[43]

The idea of providing scholarships for secondary education to bright Black and colored boys at government expense, therefore, was an important development. It was not without opposition from the elite class, however, because it meant that successful passage through these schools up to the level of completing the final exams, which were evaluated at English universities, would put these individuals in a position to compete for university (Island) scholarships. This would then mean the possibility of studying law or medicine, which in turn would mean financial independence. Besides that, whereas before 1872 all the winners of island scholarships were White, after 1872 non-White boys started winning island scholarships. The fear that the non-White winners threatened their White counterparts' hold on the scholarships is reflected in the view of the QRC principal William Miles (1872–1894), who felt that the "'free place boys' lowered the tone of the college."[44]

Similarly, the French Creole editor of the *Port-of-Spain Gazette,* in a comment that was illustrative of the racialized cant of the privileged class, maintained that the provision of scholarships at government expense in effect made the "upper and middle classes pay for the higher education of the children of the poorer classes three times for education, first for the higher education of their own children, secondly for the elementary education of the children of the poor and, thirdly, for the higher education also of the poor."[45] Moreover, to do this was in effect to foster ambitions (except in the case of geniuses), which nature itself did not intend. In the end, however, the anti–college exhibition faction was defeated, and the exhibition system was restored in 1893, with the annual number of scholarships increased to eight, but reduced to four per annum the following year.

As Faith Smith puts it, in emphasizing the prestige and honor associated with attending QRC and winning the island scholarship, "Queen's was the jewel in the crown of Trinidad's system, quickly establishing itself as an assembly line for Creoles who excelled in the Cambridge external examinations. . . . Since so few in the British Empire took these exams, Trinidadians delighted in the publication of the results, when they could see that a local candidate had placed favorably in a particular subject in relation to all the candidates who had taken the exam in England and throughout the empire."[46]

It is against this background of the interplay of race, religion, and social class and privilege[47] that Williams's sojourn at QRC, where he spent nine years, from age 12 to age 20, must be seen. These years were significant first of all because, as two of Williams's later cabinet colleagues, Drs. Patrick Solomon and Winston Mahabir, would observe, Williams was in his teens, a time associated with the transition from childhood, so to speak, to young adulthood.

Second, the QRC educational experience, which was suffused with social meanings that in a real sense were reflective of a raced colonialist ethos, directly and indirectly involved an effort on the part of the colonial authorities to inculcate those pupils who attended the school with a deep appreciation for the prevailing pedantry and the values and language of the colonizer. This included hard work, respect for the authority especially of the representatives of the colonizer, knowing one's place in the social-stratification system, and so on, while deprecating things indigenous to the territory, so that the resultant knowledge came to be regarded as truth.[48]

As Williams noted in adverting to the extant pedantry, Latin, which was his favorite subject, and he invariably obtained distinctions in it; he also enjoyed French and Spanish, as well as his "special" subject, British colonial history.[49] Immersion in the classics was important in Trinidad, where both classical learning and the classical curriculum were indicators both of a particular kind of learning and of social class. Beyond that, the ability to use classical references in speaking and especially writing was a sign of pedantic learning, which at the time was considered indispensable for intellectualism.[50] However, it was not until 1939, fully eight years after Williams left QRC, that West Indian history was included in the secondary-school curriculum, and even then it was only offered at the school certificate level, where it was expected to be studied "only by the 'weaker boys'; since a 'stronger' boy would, it was claimed, be distracted by it from the improvement of his foundation in English history preparatory to the more advanced history of the island scholarship class."[51]

In addition to the above, sport in general and cricket in particular were instrumental in undergirding the hegemonic process, which influenced the social placement especially of non-White Trinidadians. Cricket, as the historian Clem Seecharan notes, was introduced by the early English settlers and played by planters, the mercantile group, colonial administrators, Anglican clergymen, and visiting military personnel as early as the eighteenth century.[52] Initially, the participation of the enslaved in the game involved weeding the ground on which the game was played and throwing the ball from beyond the space (boundary) on which the game was played. Later, the enslaved were permitted to bowl to White batsmen—the art of batting was viewed as requiring more intellectual skills. Eventually, however, the enslaved were permitted to bat, which meant a step toward equal participation in the game on the field.

In the elite secondary schools, such as Queen's Royal College in Trinidad and Harrison College and later Lodge secondary school in Barbados, "muscular learning" was diffused in the form of cricket by the Oxford- and Cambridge-educated headmasters and teachers.[53] Herein lies part of the connection between Williams's experiences at QRC and Oxford, on the one hand, and his immersion in the classics and history, on the other hand. As part of Prospero's language the native learned, especially in the elite schools like QRC, where games were compulsory, the critical value of muscular learning, the unquestioned authority of the umpire (obedience to authority figures), the intellectualism involved in batting, bowling, and field placing, and sportsmanship. Moreover, as the reach of the game extended beyond the cricket field, or the "boundary," as C. L. R. James put it, segregation of cricket clubs and the choice of selectors and captains (leadership) were based on race and color. Moreover, like pedantry, excellence on the cricket field (distinction) was greatly valued. At QRC, as at other elite schools in the West Indies, cricket, at least on the surface, was a socially approved outlet designed to transform "rambunctious boys into honourable citizens."[54]

Beyond the above, values such as fair play, *esprit de corps,* and, in particular, respect for authority, regardless of the competence of the person in authority, were transmitted to those attending elite schools. Therefore, whether an umpire of a cricket match was right or wrong in rendering a decision that a batsman was out, or not out, in case of a "leg before wicket" appeal by a bowler or a catch behind by the wicket-keeper, the unfortunate beneficiary of that umpiring error was expected to take the decision stoically and not show any overt disagreement or anger, lest his action be assailed with the expression "It's not cricket." Since many of the critical authority figures in the wider society were White expatriates (including the principal of QRC and many of the masters who taught there), cricket "inculcate[d] into the mindset of colonial subjects an unquestioning and uncritical acceptance of the authority of Whites,"[55] as well as functioning as a metaphor for socially acceptable decorum.

A further aim of the language of cricket, C. L. R. James observes, was the internalization by the West Indians of the Puritan ethic of the English. The elements of that Puritanism included codes of acceptable conduct such as "the enduring reticence, the British self-discipline, the stiff lips upper and lower," in other words, "restraint"; and loyalty, which manifested itself in the support of both present and past QRC boys by their presence at the annual rivalry between QRC and CIC on the cricket (and football [soccer]) fields. The "social attitudes," James continues, "we could to some degree alter if we wished. For the inner self the die was cast."[56] Thus, he concludes, "cricket had plunged me into politics long before I was aware of it. When I did turn to politics I did not have too much to learn."[57] Like excellence in education, then, excellence in the sport of cricket was a mark of distinction, and exponents of this "art" form, especially in contests involving England, as James put it, were lauded and venerated as heroes.

Moreover, since excellence at cricket brought one respect, Williams represented QRC at cricket and captained the school's football team in 1929 and 1930. Indeed, Williams's interest in football is another example of his sense of independence. Williams's father, mindful that an injury could derail his plan and ultimate goal that his son win the island scholarship, forbade his son to play in the annual "Intercol" soccer match between QRC and CIC, the country's premier high-school soccer event. Williams not only disobeyed his father's instructions but eventually scored the winning goal, much to the delight and adoration of his teammates and QRC colleagues. Although his father disapproved of Williams's disobedience, he nonetheless was extremely gratified that his son had led his high school to victory.[58]

Williams's father derived a great deal of vicarious satisfaction from his son's accomplishments. Since he could not provide his son with "colour," the elder Williams was determined to provide his son with at least the opportunity to acquire two of the other social qualifications, a good education and financial independence, which he himself lacked. As Winston Mahabir, a future island scholar and minister of health in a PNM administration led by Williams, described the distinction associated with the island scholarship,

> In my father's mind, there was one burning ambition. One—any—of his four sons *must* win an island scholarship, the El Tucuche—the humming bird, the national bird—of academic achievement in Trinidad and Tobago, to which only a handful of Indians had climbed. I was the victim of the scholarship system in the sense that I developed a fierce but friendly competitiveness. Every game, we were taught, was to be played to win. To play it otherwise was to cheat. If you lost, you had to take it gracefully. The scholarship game was cruel and grueling. I developed a cult of perfectionistic detail and an addiction to knowledge (? education) as a virtue in itself.[59]

Similarly, for Williams "greatness, Trinidad style, was thrust upon me from the cradle. My father knew that what he had never been given an opportunity to achieve with his brains, he might with his loins. The island scholarship for his son became the dream of his life."[60]

While it is clear that cricket functioned to inculcate the values of team spirit, respect for doing one's best, whether in a losing cause or not—denigrating the losing opponent was discouraged—other facets of the QRC experience sought to emphasize and sometimes reinforce other values. Consequently, while team spirit was important, so were individual accomplishments and intense competition, and possibly a sense of superiority vis-à-vis students who attended secondary schools that were not as well equipped. To its credit, however, QRC did recognize that not every boy would be a shining example of academic excellence or other forms of individual achievement. Consequently, with the approval of Governor Sir John Chancellor, in 1918 the school's motto was written in Latin, as "Certant omnes, sed non omnibus palma" (All strive, but the prize does not go to all). As a consolation to those boys who fell short, Dr. Stephen Lawrence, a QRC old boy, offered the following poetic comment in a letter to the *Trinidad Chronicle* on 12 December 1918:

> If what shone afar so grand
> Turn to nothing in thy hand
> On again! *The virtue lies*
> *In the effort, not the prize.*[61]

This point is of some consequence, especially because of the understandable tendency at QRC to laud those boys who did well and to ignore those who either were average or in general had undistinguished careers. Indeed, a recent well-done book celebrating the centenary of the opening of QRC's Main Building,[62] lionizes the school's glorious tradition by way of the accomplishments of many island scholars and fellow travelers who subsequently became legal scholars, scholar athletes, international sportsmen, politicians, writers, top civil servants, university professors, and so on. The book does not, however, mention those who strove but did not win the prize and who for a variety of reasons might not have shone owing to sheer racial discrimination from expatriate masters. Furthermore, the mere fact that the school stressed excellence and a strong competitive spirit likely shaped the personalities of the products of this experience, notably in the direction of arrogance and intolerance of non-QRC attendees, who might have been successful in their own spheres of endeavor but nonetheless were perceived to be lesser mortals.

A final aspect of the QRC experience worthy of note is the application of physical punishment for socially deviant conduct, which was not unknown at the primary- and the secondary-school levels. Williams mentions, in this context, that at the secondary school he attended—obviously QRC, although he does not mention the school by name—the principal, an Englishman, whipped a "coloured boy" who had stayed away from school on Carnival day in front of one of the upper classes. In contextualizing the question of public humiliation and the manner in which the language of oppression was expressed in the semipublic sphere of the school, Williams recalls that

> the entire school was wrapped in silence as the lash fell, twelve, in a savagery which one could feel. On another occasion, I saw the savagery myself. Two fully grown coloured boys, one of them among the leading cricketers and footballers in the school, had thrashed a young White boy who had called them "niggers." The boy went home howling and complained to his parents, who reported the matter to the principal, a White clergyman. The principal assembled the entire school, called on two of the teachers, one of them notorious for his strength of arm, and gave the two boys a choice: public whipping or expulsion. They chose to be whipped, and got twelve lashes each.[63]

This type of sanction, which was part of the cultural underbelly of colonialism and likely a transformative experience for Williams, as he later put it, "reflected the policy of public humiliation and the fetish of the whip."[64] However, although Williams felt that public humiliation as part of the language of colonial oppression ranked higher than racial considerations, one might argue that as an aspect of social differentiation the practice of public whipping speaks powerfully and eloquently to efforts to teach the "coloureds" and other non-White races to "know their place," thereby preserving the space for White elites at the apex of the social structure.

In sum, as we look at the Trinbagonian society in the late nineteenth and early twentieth centuries, various points are worth reemphasizing. First, we noted the manner in which the household and the school as spaces were infused with certain social meanings that reflected elements of the social institutional matrix. This was especially evident in terms of the social differentiation based on race and color and actualized by way of ideas regarding the expected role of education and cricket in maintaining White elite hegemony and judgments as to who would occupy the non-White interstitial stratum between the White elites and the non-White masses by virtue of the attainment of excellence at QRC. As settings for knowledge production and in which meanings were constructed, therefore, the household and the school functioned as social spaces where the "other" were expected to "know their place." This explains why Williams's paternal grandmother was disinherited and the two non-White boys at QRC were publicly whipped. *Physical space* and *social place* assuredly combined to exemplify colonial oppression at the time. Also evident was the extent to which the recollections of Williams as a person "with a history" helped him understand the lifeworld of Trinbagonians, the autonomy and surrogate authority he was given, and how and why he made key decisions—of a transformative nature—such as to attend QRC and to study history and become a teacher rather than a doctor. Understanding these decisions is critical to understanding Williams's subsequent intellectualism. Doubtless also, the marketing of his mother's penny loaves, the fact that the family moved a lot, and the help he provided to his father in the auditing of the accounts of various friendly and burial societies in Trinidad all enabled Eric Williams to become acquainted with the island in a very unique way during that period.

2 Life Abroad

The Academic Intellectual and the Struggle for Credentialism

IN THIS CHAPTER I examine a number of factors that led to Williams's emergence as an academic intellectual and the inception of his role as a public intellectual toward the end of his relationship with Howard University. I will therefore turn my attention to his involvement in the habitus of knowledge accumulation, production, and marketing as an academic intellectual, which also involved the inception of his association with exceptional minds, arguably a key component of his intellectualism. The resources of energy, productive use of time, discipline, and single-mindedness of purpose that had characterized Williams's sojourn at QRC were pressed into service as he created space for his scholarship in the academic arena. This period of his life also saw the dawning of a change, on his part, in the "rules of the game" when it came to knowledge production, as his focus began to shift from colonial history to Caribbean history as a tool for social change.

Williams's sense of purposiveness manifested itself, it should be noted, even before he left for Oxford. Correspondence between Williams and V. J. K. Brock, the censor at St. Catherine's Society at Oxford University, which is to be found in the unpublished version of Williams's autobiography, is illustrative. In a handwritten, water-stained letter, parts of which are illegible, for example, Brock informed Williams that he thought he could waive the personal interview, which apparently was required of new students, and that Williams would have to bring his certificates to have them registered upon his arrival at the university.[1]

In a subsequent letter Brock acknowledged receipt of the testimonials sent by Williams and informed him that on the strength of the documents received, he would be glad to accept Williams for matriculation. However, Brock feared that Williams would not be able to compete for any of the exhibitions for that year, as the exam was at the end of June, which would be prior to Williams's arrival at Oxford.[2] In any event, by corresponding with Brock *before* he went to Oxford, Williams had taken the opportunity to make a favorable impression on an important biographical other who would be of much assistance to him when he arrived in England. This meant that when he presented himself to Brock in person, the censor might already have formed a favorable opinion[3] of Williams and his academic capabilities. For Williams, this was an important first step toward becoming an academic intellectual.

While at Oxford, Williams notes in his published autobiography, he experienced the tribulation associated with the tribal stigmata of race and nation. On one occasion during his first year, a "long nosed" colleague sought to question his intellectual capacity and, implicitly, his right to be at the university by inquiring whether English was spoken in Trinidad. This question in the mind of his would-be tormentor was prompted by the fact that while there were notations on the Latin examinations of the other students, there were none on Williams's. It turned out that this was because his tutor felt that since Williams's work was so superior to that of his classmates and he could do the required work "standing on his head," there was no need for him to continue with the class. This would not be the last time Williams experienced the racialization of the "other" while at Oxford.

Williams's recollections of these experiences are of further contextual relevance because, first, in addition to the public nature of the *space-cum-place* dimension, they exemplify the "outsider-within" status that is part of the lived experiences, or *lifeworld* and its inevitable connection with the *system,* of a member of the oppressed stratum, who may be accorded the opportunity to sit at the table but not be permitted to eat. Second, incumbents of this status nonetheless may obtain special insights into the mind of the oppressor, so to speak, and therefore be in a better position to contribute to a collective form of action that would lend itself, if not to the termination of the system, certainly to its emasculation. Third, although those who occupy an outsider-within status may be marginalized, they are, ironically, essential for the system's survival in that their position at the margin clarifies the boundaries of the social system and thereby validates its existence. But although they may possess, as Williams did, much knowledge about the system, occupants of the outsider-within status can never truly be part of the oppressor stratum.

Despite these and various other slights, Williams put to good use the self-discipline he had acquired at Tranquillity and the knowledge of Latin and history he had acquired at QRC, as well as, quite importantly, a growing appreciation of literature and art as "sources for the understanding, and appraisal, of historical development." History, then, "was not merely a record of dates and events" or even of the "follies and foibles" of individuals, but a record of the "development of humanity, of life, and of society, in all their various manifestations."[4]

IN ANY EVENT, in 1935 Williams continued to feel what he perceived to be the sting of racism and the peculiar manner in which it manifested itself in the British context. Following his graduation from Oxford with first-class honors in history, Brock congratulated Williams on a performance that was all the more admirable in view of his various health difficulties, mentioned that Williams's achievement had brought distinction to St. Catherine's, and applauded the triumphant manner in which Williams had overcome his difficulties.[5]

Three days later, however, Williams appears to have raised the question of race and color in respect to the award of fellowships at the university, to which Brock replied that those fellowships that "are given on examination are given quite honestly on the work of the candidates," presumably irrespective of race, and that he was pretty sure that a similar situation existed at All Souls College. Brock said, however, that the fact that Williams was not British "probably would go against him in trying for an ordinary teaching post at an ordinary college," as he would have to deal with "pupils with public school prejudices." Notwithstanding this, Brock opined that although Williams would not necessarily be handicapped in trying for a research or prize fellowship, competition was keen. The letter ended, quite significantly, with a discussion of the pros and cons of the possible options open to Williams, namely, the politics, philosophy and economics (PPE) degree, a diploma in education, and a doctorate.[6]

Accordingly, Williams accepted the suggestion that he pursue another bachelor's degree with the aim of applying for a fellowship at one of the colleges at Oxford, preferably All Souls. This, however, would have meant spending the next two years reading for the PPE degree, as well as satisfying the social requirements that involved exhibiting the proper etiquette, sartorial and otherwise, at dinner, or what Williams referred to as "trial by dinner." Since he would not have been able to apply a historical approach, or, for that matter, an approach in sympathy with the environment from whence he had come, in either philosophy or economics, despite a positive relationship with his tutor in politics, Williams decided to abandon the PPE degree. This meant giving up a chance for an All Souls fellowship, but it did not mean giving up the opportunity to pursue a doctorate in history.

Apparently, the last straw had come during an oral examination in French in front of a number of fellows, when a "horrible mistake" on his part led to a roar by those in attendance, which Williams concluded was directed at *him* rather than at the *mistake*. As he put it, "It sobered me at once, I lost all my nervousness, I looked all around the room, at one individual member after the other, until quiet had been restored. I felt like a schoolmaster upbraiding by looks a group of unruly pupils." When there was absolute quiet, Williams continued, but after reaching a passage about which he knew "neither head or tail," he declined to translate. Following three requests from the warden "to have a go at it," he told the warden that "I did not wish to give rise to another such guffaw as I had already listened to. He thanked me for my coming, and I took my leave."[7] Needless to say, that ended the humiliation. Williams remained convinced that his race had influenced the audience's behavior, especially when one of the fellows, upon meeting him in the street some days later, eyed him curiously and passed without speaking. This form of public humiliation, which was transformative for Williams, was another dimension of racial stigmatization visited upon him, as a nonperson and an outsider within.

In pursuing the doctorate, which he considered to be the second most important decision he made in his life—the other was the decision to read history in preparation for a teaching career—Williams's choice of a topic was powered by two main desires: first, to do some research on a topic that was germane to the West Indies; and second, providentially, to examine the prevailing view that the abolition of enslavement was due to the actions of a group of humanitarians whose activities had aroused the conscience of the British people and, ultimately, the decision of the British government to terminate enslavement. As a result of his research, he was awarded the doctorate in history in December 1938 for his thesis, *The Economic Aspect of the Abolition of the West Indies Slave Trade and Slavery.* Indeed, so high was the quality of Williams's work that one of the proponents of the position against which Williams had railed, in his capacity as one of the examiners, noted that were he to revise his own work on the subject, he would have to make fundamental changes based on Williams's work.

It should be noted, however, that Williams's path to the doctorate was not without difficulties, which Williams also attributed to his race. His last year of historical research, for example, was hampered by a serious lack of money, as his island scholarship had ended. When various remedial efforts proved to be abortive, and unable to ignore any longer the perception that race was a factor in his unsuccessful efforts to obtain financial assistance, Williams wrote a letter to the principal of his college on the matter. Although this led to some relief, Williams always believed that his impecuniousness and the slowness of the relief had been related to his race.

However, getting his doctorate would depend on funding, which apparently was not at Brock's disposal. In a letter of 25 January 1936 to his principal regarding his financial difficulties, Williams wrote that he could not qualify for an exhibition at St. Catherine's because his income was too large and that in any case the exhibitions were meant for poor undergraduates. He also stated that he "had great difficulty in even getting a grant at all" and that he was told "bluntly that money which in the last analysis comes from the British taxpayer cannot be used to subsidise a colonial." He felt also that he should have "as fair a chance at any opportunities, financial or otherwise, which are open to English students, more particularly because of my results last June and because my sole aim is to further my studies."[8]

Undaunted, Williams continued his efforts to obtain a measure of financial relief from various sources. For example, in comments on a copy of a letter written by Brock in support of an application by Williams for a Goldsmith's Fellowship, the censor wrote that he was inclined to believe that "they would probably prefer you to drop the PPE and go for Research, if you get a Senior Studentship."[9] Williams revealed that this suggestion turned out to be efficacious in that soon thereafter he was awarded a senior university studentship. He also mentioned that he had gotten a job coaching Siamese students at Oxford who were having difficulty with English, an assignment that had the unintended benefit of introducing him to the poetry of Victor Hugo, Alfred de Musset, and Alfred de Vigny, thereby adding to his intellectual development in the classics.[10] In any event, Williams's tenacity in seeking financial aid paid off, if only minimally, as on 3 July 1936 he received a letter from the clerk of the Leathersellers Company informing him of an award of fifty pounds for one year to be paid in three installments, provided he continued at Oxford.[11]

IN ADDITION to the above, Williams sought to create space for his knowledge as an academic intellectual by establishing contact with a number of individuals with well-trained intellects, in this case senior scholars, who would be of assistance to him later in his academic career. These included Professor D. W. Brogan, of Oxford University, who would later write the introduction to *Capitalism and Slavery,* describing it as "this brilliant essay in the economic interpretation of history. . . . It is characteristic of good books in that they are timeless and this book is as topical as it was in 1942." Williams was also in contact with R. Coupland, then professor of colonial history, who was one of the examiners for Williams's doctoral thesis, although Williams "deeply distrusted Coupland for his admixture of history and imperial apologetics. . . . Britain, Coupland urged, enjoyed a special tradition of responsibility toward 'weak and backward black peoples.'"[12] Coupland was also one of the proponents of the view that Britain had repented for its participation in slavery by voting "twenty million pounds sterling to the slave-owners for the redemption of their slaves."[13]

Williams apparently was also in contact with Cutteridge, his former principal at Tranquillity, who it seems had taken Williams on as a protégé.[14] Cutteridge wrote to Williams congratulating him on the Leathersellers award and informing him that Professor Coupland, to whom he (Cutteridge) had spoken regarding Williams's "ambitions, hardships and prospects," was a personal friend of Sir Claud Hollis, a former governor of Trinidad and Tobago and a member of the Leathersellers Company. Coupland in turn had written to Sir Claud on Williams's behalf. Cutteridge advised Williams to thank Sir Claud and not to "act rashly at the present juncture."[15]

Williams was also in contact with Learie Constantine, the famous Trinidadian cricketer, who later joined Williams in the struggle for political independence in Trinidad and Tobago. Constantine had known Williams when the latter was an undergraduate at Oxford, when Williams had spent part of his vacations with the Constantine family in Nelson. Constantine recalled that Williams appreciated a particular beer: "The kind of beer he liked was German, and this could only be obtained at Clitheroe, twelve miles away. So after my cricket practice was over, we used to jump into the car so that he could get to Clitheroe for his beer."[16]

Lastly, Williams was in close personal contact with C. L. R. James, his former tutor at QRC. In a handwritten undated letter to Williams that was partly illegible, the writer tells Williams that the fifty pounds from Leathersellers was merely an example of C (one imagines this was a reference to Cutteridge) trying to be magnanimous, not trying to maneuver him "out of the Goldsmith's." However, since one could not be sure, the writer advises Williams to see Coupland and hear what he has to offer, which can do no harm, but not to commit himself. Williams was also advised to work toward a bachelor of letters or to concentrate on his book but to leave that vague when he saw Coupland; and when he wrote to "C," he should thank him "with dignity and restraint" and thank (Sir Claud) Hollis "with qualification." The letter ends on a poignant note with the comment, "I exist here. But I have peace I can work. Alas, peace is not mine hitherto," and the request that Williams sell the writer's copy of *Warning from the West Indies* and send him a ten-shilling note.[17] Finally, it should be noted that while the letter contains references to "C." and "C.d" (presumably a reference to Coupland), it is signed "N," short for "Nello," the name by which James was known.

While Williams does not mention James and his contribution to his intellectual development in the unpublished and published versions of his autobiography, the two, according to James, had a lengthy personal relationship while Williams resided in England and also in America. During this time James appears to have viewed the younger Williams as a pupil, a role that Williams seems to have acted out even after he became premier of Trinidad and Tobago and James became the editor of the paper of the People's National Movement, the party headed by Williams. James had left Trinidad for England in 1932. In an interview at the University of Texas, Austin, when asked, "There are apparent parallels in political theory between *The Black Jacobins* and Eric Williams's *Capitalism and Slavery.* Did you help him to write his book?," James responded: "Williams used to come to my house in London and spend his vacations with me. When working on *The Black Jacobins,* I went to France to do work there. . . . Williams would go with me. He is a marvelous man at getting documents and keeping things in order."[18]

Regarding his role in Williams's intellectual maturation, James stated that Williams would send him "his papers from Oxford on Rousseau, on Plato and on Aristotle for my comments." James recalled that after Williams passed his bachelor's examinations, which James was sure he would do, Williams came to James, "as he usually did," with the question, "I am to do a doctorate, what shall I write on?" James responded, "I know exactly what you should write on. I have done the economic basis of slavery emancipation as it was in France. But that has never been done in Great Britain, and Britain is wide open for it. A lot of people think the British showed goodwill. There were lots of people who had goodwill, but it was the basis, the economic basis that allowed the goodwill to function."[19] According to James, Williams then asked, "Do you think that will be good?," to which James responded, "Fine." When Williams then asked what he should say, according to James, "I sat down and wrote what the thesis should be with my own hand, and I gave it to him. He must have copied it down, and took it to the Oxford authorities. Later he told me they said it was fine. And he went on from there. I saw the manuscript quite often, I read it about three or four times. The facts themselves and the road he was to take, I wrote that for him. I don't see why I shouldn't say that now, it isn't a crime on my part."[20] James's recollections are contextually relevant for at least two reasons. First, they point to his contribution to Williams's intellectual development at the time. Second, they raise some troubling questions regarding Williams's intellectual integrity, as well as his character and personality, for failing to adequately recognize James's help, particularly in the preparation of *Capitalism and Slavery.*

James left for the United States in 1938, and Williams arrived there in 1939. In America, the two continued their relationship. This is attested to by James's comments in the many letters he wrote to Constance Webb,[21] the young White southerner whom James courted for five years before they married, briefly, in June 1946. The letters not only contain many personal references to Williams—for a period James's correspondence was sent in care of Williams at Howard University—but reveal, ironically, that James continued to consider Williams, as well as Webb, to be his pupil.

The letters also reveal that James had read the page proofs for *Capitalism and Slavery,* which he considered to be a "masterpiece." In a letter to Webb dated 10 July 1944 James writes, "You know I have three special 'pupils'. There is Bill Williams. He is a Ph.D. of Oxford. He had already written and published some brilliant work and fall will appear a *superb* work in *Capitalism and Slavery.*" And waxing nostalgic, James writes on 28 October 1944, "In the old days, I listened to music with a friend, went to see my friend Bill Williams and his wife. It acted as a kind of poultice."[22] In another letter James writes, "Bill was up for the weekend. Already he has a superb piece of work done. All we need now is revision. It is about the ideas of a University for the West Indian people." This was a reference to Williams's paper "The Idea of a British West Indian University," which he had delivered in Atlanta in April 1946. Such was the nature of the relationship between Williams and James that James asked Webb to enlist Williams's aid in James's efforts to obtain a Reno divorce from his first wife, Juanita, whom he had married before leaving Trinidad for England.[23]

Thus, as stated above, by establishing and maintaining contacts with a variety of academicians and nonacademic biographical others, Williams was able to create space for his knowledge in the intellectual world of academia. To be sure, the actual process, which conceivably was influenced by the peculiar nature of his experience, contacts, and willingness to take chances usually is not evident. The same may be said for the stages, the methods of communication, and the type of interactants, which are also essential ingredients of intellectual activity, in this case of an academic nature. In other words, the intercourse with exceptional minds and the habitus, which seeks to reproduce the power of the dominant as gatekeepers of relevant knowledge, are usually hidden from those seeking to reconstruct the process that culminates in becoming an academic intellectual.

After being told by the dean of his college at Oxford that he should return to Trinidad because he was no different from other West Indians, who were all "keen on trying to get posts here which take away jobs from Englishmen," and with the prospect of academic employment unlikely and war clouds beginning to gather, Williams departed for the United States. There he would spend almost a decade teaching at Howard University, at the time considered the leading Negro institution of higher learning, where, in addition to colonial history, he would develop programs in West Indian history and West Indian affairs, do work on Caribbean affairs that resulted in employment with an international organization, develop proposals for a West Indian university, and conduct research on colonial questions in general.

Landing in New York on 7 August 1939, Williams spent some time in Harlem, where many West Indians lived, soon becoming acquainted with "the congestion, dilapidation, and squalor to which Negroes [were] subjected."[24] But Howard University was no ordinary university. As Tony Martin points out, for example, since African Americans were denied opportunities to attend majority institutions of higher learning because of racial discrimination, the Howard University of 1939 was a place where many of the top African American intellectuals had gathered.[25] Also, according to Linda Heywood, long before his employment at Howard, Williams no doubt had been aware of its status as the premier black university, a "haven for thousands of African-American intellectuals and students excluded from the White academic environment because of their race."[26]

At Howard University Williams continued to make a name for himself as an academic intellectual. As he had done before studying at Oxford,

Williams had made contact with a number of significant intellectual biographical others before he arrived at Howard. These included Rayford Logan, Abram Harris, Alain Locke, and Ralph Bunche, with whom he had carried on a three-year correspondence and whose efforts had made it possible for Williams to obtain the teaching appointment at Howard. All of these individuals were outstanding, internationally respected African American scholars. Locke, the first African American to win a Rhodes Scholarship, was also an Oxford graduate. Bunche, who headed the Department of Political Science, would subsequently enjoy a distinguished career as a diplomat and U.S. ambassador to the United Nations. And Harris, a young radical who chaired the Department of Economics, would also contribute to Williams's burgeoning radicalization as an intellectual.

In recommending Williams for the post, Bunche stressed the social-science division's need for a scholar in the "foreign field" and noted that Williams was well prepared to assume this role, having expertise in the areas of European government, foreign relations, international law, and the West Indies. Williams did not disappoint those who had recommended him. He taught a total of seven courses in the political science department and was responsible for inaugurating a social-science course that was a general-education requirement for undergraduate students; he also taught one course each in the social sciences, the humanities, and the physical sciences. In approaching this task with his customary gusto and thoroughness, Williams not only developed the syllabus that would illustrate the development of civilization from primitive man to the present but met with hundreds of students in the usual format. He would later write that in contrast to the small tutorial sessions characteristic of Oxford, the large classes he taught at Howard gave him invaluable experience in "the mechanics of mass education." As Heywood contends, "Undoubtedly the success of his populist lectures at the 'University of Woodford Square,' which set him on his political career, owed much to the Howard University Social Sciences survey course."[27]

In addition, teaching courses that introduced students to materials and topics in which they had a special interest, not excluding sex and race, according to the African American historian John Hope Franklin, would be "one of the most important contributions that Williams made to the intellectual and educational life of Howard University, in that it touched many hundreds of students while it set an example to his colleagues of how it was possible to be *creative* at an institution that was, in so many ways, stultifying to the creative impulse."[28] Franklin's reference to the "stultifying" impulse in the context of Howard is notable not merely because it adds to the significance of Williams's achievements but also because it speaks to the negative intellectual underbelly of Howard and, conceivably, that of other black institutions of higher learning in America.

Indeed, Williams himself referred to this condition when he spoke of the "administrative blocks which even the most committed individuals seeking to secure a position at the 'Negro Mecca' faced." Moreover, as Franklin later stated, although black universities contained a number of distinguished faculty, they were often unable to gain recognition by White faculty in majority universities, and the "energy expended in what Williams called campus feuds and politics was, perhaps, greater than that expended on research, writing, or even teaching." However, according to Franklin, this did not mean that at Howard "nothing constructive was underway":

> One needs only to examine the publications of the Division of Social Science to appreciate what these inestimable scholars were doing. It is, however, to say that a disproportionate amount of time and energy were expended in petty squabbles and unbecoming rivalries of one kind or another. One wonders what remarkable research might have been done and what important contributions might have been made to their respective fields had the members of the faculty at Howard University been able to enjoy unfettered freedom to live and work as others were free to do in the city of Washington.[29]

It was not only in the field of teaching, however, that Williams distinguished himself. During his tenure at Howard he compiled a record as a formidable researcher and a prolific writer. His research interests covered the economic aspects of the West Indian slave trade and slavery, the rise of European capitalism, and West Indian society. Indeed, during the early part of his Howard sojourn, Williams received two Julius Rosenwald Fellowships, which allowed him to travel to Haiti, Cuba, and the Dominican Republic to do research for his book *The Negro in the Caribbean,* first published by the Associates in Negro Folk Education in 1942. Shortly after his arrival at Howard, Williams was invited by Locke to publish his book in the Bronze Booklet series. In addition to this book, the publication while he was at Howard of a number of scholarly papers, especially in the *Journal of Negro History,* and *Capitalism and Slavery,* in 1944, exposed Williams to critical facets of knowledge production as an intellectual. I refer in this context to the willingness to expose one's ideas to critical assessments by experts chosen for that purpose, the ability to successfully transmit one's thoughts, in this instance in a published form, to a wider audience, and to move ideas, as Williams had done in his doctoral thesis and in the book upon which it was based, from the periphery to the center of intellectual discourse.

While, of course, the publication of a book or a scholarly article in one's field, especially one that breaks new ground, is an important indicator of intellectual excellence in the academic world, very often we are not privy to prior and subsequent activities that contribute to its success. These include reviews of the manuscript before and after publication as a book and, perhaps even more important, efforts made by the author and the publisher to aid in its dissemination, such as book signings, public lectures, and other forms of publicity regarding the book, in some instances even before its publication.

Williams's experiences with publication provide further insight into his emergence as an academic intellectual. The latter part of 1941, for example, saw Williams writing to an official of the American Council on Public Affairs and enclosing a chapter outline and a specimen chapter of a planned book, as well as a copy of the manuscript for *The Negro in the Caribbean,* which he said would be published shortly.[30] In early 1942 Williams wrote to John Krout, a professor at Columbia University and managing editor of the *Political Science Quarterly,* noting that he had been unable to meet with him during a recent visit to New York and informing him that, at the suggestion of a Professor Westerman, he was enclosing a copy of an essay titled "Protection, Free Trade and Sugar." This was the last chapter of a book on which Williams was working—to be titled *Capitalism and Slavery: The Contribution of the Negro to Western Civilisation*—which he asserted was "amply documented" and had been written with a view to publication in a scholarly journal.[31] Roughly two months later, Krout wrote to Williams informing him that although the manuscript "greatly interests" him and was "worthy of publication," he would like it to be revised to "no longer than 25 of your present triple-spaced pages."[32] The subtitle of the proposed book, which did not appear in the published version of the book, is of more than passing significance, because it points to Williams's ongoing efforts to write history from the standpoint of the dispossessed Negro.

In any event, with his customary single-mindedness of purpose, Williams replied that he had shown the manuscript to no less an academic intellectual than Professor Lowell Ragatz, of George Washington University, to whom he had dedicated *Capitalism and Slavery* in 1964,[33] and whom he described as "the outstanding authority on the Caribbean." Williams also mentioned that Ragatz had not only been pleased with the current manuscript but thought that "in its present form it could hardly be cut any more." Williams, therefore, not only regretted his inability to stay within the twenty-five-page limit but very shrewdly enclosed a copy of *The Negro in the Caribbean,* which by then had been published, with the comment that he would "esteem it a privilege" if Krout would read it and give Williams his impressions.[34]

Williams's standing his ground turned out to be efficacious, as Krout later wrote to tell him that he would try to include the article in the December 1942 issue of the *Quarterly.*[35] This experience in creating space for his knowledge as an academic intellectual conceivably was not only transformative but indicative of the manner in which the habitus seeks to include, as Bourdieu observes, both a system of schemes of production of practices and a system of perception and appreciation of practices. It is also in this manner that the habitus "expresses both the social position of those who determine it and the social context in which it is elaborated, and is only perceived by those who are in a position to understand the codes."[36]

To be sure, Williams's scholarly activities at Howard were of such a high caliber that John Hope Franklin, who later became the James B. Duke Professor of History Emeritus at Duke University and the recipient of many honors, including the Presidential Medal of Honor, would write that what impressed him most about Williams was "his preoccupation with a variety of projects and his complete absorption with his teaching and research. I was greatly inspired by the manner in which he went about his work, and I have no doubt that my own ambitious program in research and writing was inspired, in part, by the example set by Williams."[37]

IT IS ALSO obvious that during this period of his life Williams recognized the importance of another facet of intellectual activity associated with constructing an audience for his knowledge as cultural capital, namely, marketing. Not only, therefore, did he send copies of *The Negro in the Caribbean* to a number of important biographical others in the academic world but he also purchased a number of copies of *Capitalism and Slavery* and was so instrumental in arranging for the sale of these copies that he was applauded by the book's publishers, the University of North Carolina Press. As a result, he was in a position to pay off the subvention required by his publishers in a timely fashion. Evidently, Williams the "reluctant *marchand*" of his mother's penny loaves had become Williams the willing *marchand* when it came to marketing his intellectual efforts.

He would continue this entrepreneurial activity both as a public and a social-movement intellectual.

This predisposition toward marketing his cultural capital for the purpose of obtaining economic capital, combined with his purposiveness, also found expression in Williams's quest for employment toward the end of his tenure at Howard University, as he sought employment with the Anglo-American Caribbean Commission.[38] His efforts to obtain employment with the AACC must be located in the context of his decision not merely to study history (as opposed to an independent profession like law or medicine) but to pursue a doctorate in that subject at a time when the University of the West Indies, for example, did not exist, which meant that the prospects for a job commensurate with his qualifications probably did not exist in Trinidad. With his characteristic purposiveness, therefore, Williams solicited the help of Professor Brogan, his former tutor at Oxford, who was then with the North American Division of the British Broadcasting Commission.[39] As he had done before, Williams also enclosed a copy of his book *The Negro in the Caribbean;* in his reply, Brogan thanked Williams for the book and requested that Williams provide him with a brief résumé.[40]

In his response to Brogan, Williams, it seems, broached the subject of employment at the AACC for the first time, though he was willing to do his "best in whatever field the Government is prepared to use me." In subsequent correspondence with Williams, Brogan informed him that he had been in consultation with a Professor MacMillan and that he intended to write to Professor R. H. Tawney,[41] who he felt might have some ideas as to how Williams might be used.[42] Williams also wrote to Tawney, introducing himself and enclosing a copy of his curriculum vitae and two testimonials from his superiors at Oxford.[43] Beyond that, Williams contacted Dr. Vincent Harlow, Rhodes Professor of Imperial History at King's College London, who had supervised Williams's doctoral thesis. Williams informed Harlow that he had been recommended for a position in the Office of Strategic Services—later the Central Intelligence Agency—and that he believed he was considered suitable for the appointment, except that he was not a U.S. citizen.[44]

Continuing his quest for employment, Williams also wrote to John Huggins, at the British Colonies Supply Mission in Washington, DC, requesting an interview and indicating that a joint letter from Brogan and Harlow had suggested that he contact Huggins in connection with employment with the AACC. For good measure, Williams also mentioned his intense interest in the future of the people from the West Indies and stated that his work was stimulated by "the desire to assist in their development and integration in the larger movements of society."[45]

A week later, Williams followed up with another letter to Brogan, informing him that he had met Huggins, who by then had been named a permanent British resident member of the AACC and who would later be appointed governor of Jamaica.[46] Williams's efforts eventually paid off, and after securing part-time employment with the British section of the commission, he was eventually appointed deputy chairman of the Research Council upon his return to Trinidad. Not surprisingly, since he was becoming known as an intellectual, reports of his appointment as secretary of the Caribbean Research Council, along with his picture, appeared routinely in the Trinidad press,[47] as well as in the press in British Guiana.[48]

WHILE WILLIAMS was teaching at Howard University, Williams the public intellectual began to emerge. This emergence took the form, among other things, of his involvement in two conferences at the university, the authoring of two documents dealing with West Indian education, and relationships with various biographical others, both individuals and organizations, not necessarily connected with the academy. In May 1940, for example, he was involved in organizing the sixth annual Conference on the Negro in the Americas, in which Williams and Rayford Logan were discussants in the "Negro in the Caribbean" and "Indian in Latin America" sessions. So impressive was Williams's performance in the conference that, according to Linda Heywood, the *Washington Tribune*'s account of the conference contained not only a picture of Williams but also extensive quotes from his remarks.[49]

Williams was also very much involved in a 1943 conference on the economic future of the Caribbean. At the time he was program chair of the Division of Social Sciences, had been at Howard University for four years, and was employed at the AACC on a part-time basis.[50] In contrast to the previous conference, sponsored by Howard, this conference was much more broadly based. The major themes of the conference included "mono agriculture," antiracism, and the need for some kind of West Indian federation. In any event, Williams apparently used the conference to put together disparate elements, to forge political alignments, and, perhaps most importantly, to create a number of contacts, enabling him to land a high-powered job with the AACC.[51]

Among those presenting papers at the conference were Sir John Huggins, now head of the British Colonies Supply Mission and a British member of the AACC, with whom Williams had been in correspondence; S. Burns Weston, the U.S. secretary of the AACC; and Dr. Charles A. Petioni, of the West Indies National Council, who, it will be remembered, was a visitor to the Williams household in Trinbago and a former associate of Marcus Garvey's. It is noteworthy that during the conference Petioni asked Huggins to explain why there appeared to be no qualified West Indians, Black or White, fit enough to serve on the commission, to which Huggins laconically replied, "I am afraid I cannot answer that question."[52]

Also while at Howard, Williams took an interest in the movement led by Jamaicans, Marcus Garvey and his wife, and noted that Garvey had recruited many of his lieutenants from the West Indies; Williams described those recruits as "people who, one may presume, would naturally have been political leaders in the islands had they found sufficient scope there."[53] Williams was also in contact with the well-known African American scholar activist W. E. B. Du Bois, who helped him to organize the conference and for whom Williams, as chairman of the Program Committee, helped to organize a testimonial dinner under the auspices of Howard University's Division of Social Sciences; and Paul Robeson, the African American singer, actor, and athlete. Williams's contacts with these activists must have raised more than the occasional eyebrow in the United States. As will be seen, he himself would be accused of being a communist. In addition, Williams spoke to various radical groups and sought to use his college learning for activist purposes. He also remained in contact with C. L. R. James and fellow Trinidadian George Padmore, then a leading figure in the International Communist Party, whom, along with Jomo Kenyatta, a future prime minister of Kenya, Williams considered to be a close friend. Indeed, Williams had accompanied James to Paris when the latter did research for his celebrated book *The Black Jacobins*.[54]

By 1943 Williams was also interacting with other African American activists, as his academic prowess at Howard, coupled with the anticolonialist tenor of his writing, appealed to this group of individuals.[55] In early July 1943 Williams was a panelist at the Chicago conference that transformed A. Philip Randolph's March on Washington Movement into a permanent organization and where major civil rights figures like James Farmer and Bayard Rustin spoke. Williams was introduced to Kwame Nkrumah, who would subsequently become president of Ghana, at James's apartment in New York.

Clearly, then, during his American sojourn there was a radical side to Williams's activities that transcended geography and race.[56] Moreover, he began to display a remarkable capacity for juggling different, seemingly incompatible political constituencies with an interest in the anticolonial struggle in general and in the Caribbean in particular. For Williams, the 1943 conference was therefore much more than a gathering of individuals with a scholarly interest in the area.[57]

In beginning his memorandum of March 1945 for the Committee of the Commission on Higher Education in the Colonies (the Irvine Commission), Williams used a seemingly innocuous quotation from the author of a history of Jamaica written two hundred years earlier: "Learning is here at the lowest ebb: there is no publick School in the whole Island, neither do they seem fond of the thing. . . . The Office of a Teacher is looked upon as contemptible and no Gentleman keeps company with one of that character." The quotation speaks to the complete disregard with which education and the teacher were held, probably in the West Indies. The connection that Williams later forged with the influential Teachers' Economic and Cultural Association (TECA) and its affiliates, as well as his connection with teachers in Trinidad and Tobago, is further proof of the importance he attached to the relevance of education and to the acquisition and production of knowledge, as tools for emancipation as well as for upward social mobility.

In 1945, for example, Williams expressed his interest in West Indian education by penning a document containing a number of proposals regarding a British West Indian university.[58] In that document he began by arguing that the university is a mirror of the society, and its "mission is not to transmit an abstract 'culture', but to impart to young men and women an education in conformity with the economy and constitution of the particular community which it is established to serve."[59] This contrasted with the Greek notion that education was designed for the development of individuals belonging to a leisured class.

In addition to the above, Williams maintained that a West Indian university should be research oriented and that the graduate should have a better understanding of his environment. Furthermore, he felt that a West Indian university must "eschew uncritical acceptance or slavish imitation of a curriculum developed abroad." Thus, the university should be an independent entity, thereby avoiding the "insidious dangers of imitation and affiliation," which were likely to occur when there was dependence on other countries, and it should be unitary rather than comprising a number of university colleges on various islands, with a curriculum specifically designed for the British West Indies. Finally, Williams maintained that a West Indian university should "from its highest to its lowest level, recognize and reaffirm the idea of the connection between education and democracy—democracy, not solely in the sense of abstract or concrete political rights, but also, and more important, in the sense of the participation of the great body of the people in all aspects of social and political life." Such a university, therefore, should deliberately regard education in its modern sense, "as meaning, more than anything else, the education of the people themselves as to the necessity of viewing their own education as a part of their democratic privileges and their democratic responsibilities."[60]

While at Howard University, Williams wrote *Education in the British West Indies,* which he completed in 1946 and which was first published under the auspices of the TECA following Williams's return to Trinbago. In his introduction to the book, De Wilton Rogers, the director general of the TECA, noted that Williams had dedicated the book "to the great masses of the British West Indian people whom all proposals for education must serve, and whose development will serve education." In his prefatory comments Williams noted the twofold aims of the book as being, first, to "stimulate attention among those in Great Britain and the United States who are interested either in education or in the British West Indies" and, second, "not only to bring to the British West Indian people themselves some information, but also to encourage them to consider how far a British West Indian University affects them, and to what degree their interests can affect what is about to be undertaken." Also, in a further reference to what a British West Indian university should entail and the question of relevant knowledge, Williams repeated the need for people to view education as part of their "democratic privileges and their democratic responsibilities."[61]

Turning to the existing curriculum, Williams noted that it was based largely on the foreign (British) experience and was therefore an essential part of the colonial scheme of things, which required that a local stratum be able to carry out the policies of the colonizer. In other words, the educational experience was illustrative of the language of oppression. Thus, in addressing the question of external legitimation as part of the educational diet of colonial subjects and, as a consequence, to the question of relevant knowledge, which are important facets of the production of knowledge, Williams noted that instead of the curriculum's determining the examination, the examination determined the curriculum. Additionally, with attendance proving to be problematic and because Indian parents in particular preferred to keep their children at home so that they could work on the plantation, the illiteracy rates tended to be high. Touching on the question of dual control in the field of education, Williams observed that because the British West Indian community was a religious community, "all proposals for educational reform have to take into account the fact that "large numbers of schools are church owned."[62] In such circumstances, the educational system must safeguard the right of the community as a whole to determine the general trend of education. And while he hastened to note that this did not mean that the religious sentiments of the community should not be "scrupulously respected," it was not a question of religion but one of an "elementary democratic right." In other words, the political rights of the community should supersede those of the church or the mosque or the temple when it came to the pedagogical content of the educational experience.

Clearly, then, Williams envisaged the educational diet for decolonization as emphasizing the needs of the masses in contrast to those of the colonizer, which suggested a subaltern approach to relevant knowledge. He inveighed against the power of the pandit and the priest in favor of the power of the people to determine an educational diet that was relevant to the masses and not in the interest of the upper strata. These proposals did not sit well, especially with the Indian community and the church in Trinidad and Tobago. It is quite evident, therefore, that by the time he returned to Trinbago in 1948, Williams had begun to use the knowledge he had acquired as a student of West Indian history to "curse" the colonial enterprise. In other words, he framed education not only in terms of content but also with respect to its relation to colonialism and its implications for democracy and nationalism. As Erving Goffman might put it, the term *frame* was being used by Williams to refer to a "schemata of interpretation . . . that allows its user to locate, perceive, identify, and label a seemingly infinite number of concrete occurrences defined in its terms."[63] How these and other facets of Williams's intellectual activities would be applied in the service of political independence is addressed in the chapters that follow.

3 The Native Son Returns

The Public Intellectual and the Quest for Credibility

IN THIS CHAPTER I examine Williams's efforts to consolidate his role as a public intellectual, or as Jerzy Szacki might put it, to fail to "mind his own business," in this instance by coming out of "the libraries and laboratories into the political market-place" and thereby into the forum of public life. This sense of mission embodied in the right to act on behalf of the masses, Szacki stresses, is "intrinsic to the consciousness of the intellectual."[1] This Williams did by using his knowledge of history as a resource to pontificate on, and to educate his public regarding, issues that spoke to the lifeworld and were germane to the interests of Trinbagonians, in other words, to begin to use popular education to "curse" colonial oppression. I will therefore discuss lectures he gave that were open to the public; a well-publicized debate with Dom Basil Matthews, a Roman Catholic cleric who, incidentally, had attended the 1943 conference on the economics of the Caribbean; and finally, a speech Williams made when he announced his departure from the Caribbean Commission. These events will be examined in the context of his ongoing transition from academic intellectual to public intellectual, as he continued to construct a public for his deliberations regarding colonialism.

Even before his permanent return to Trinbago in 1948, Williams had given a number of lectures that made him known not only in Trinbago but also in the rest of the Caribbean and in America and Britain. He thus had begun to seek space on the twin island for his knowledge by transforming his symbolic capital as an academic intellectual into symbolic power. During a lecture on 3 April 1944 titled "The University of the West Indies," delivered to a packed house at Queen's Royal College, Williams remarked that "I am glad to remember what you gave to me proved not only adequate but rich for understanding and grasping the possibilities, opportunities and ideas of a world much greater than ours."[2]

A lecture delivered on 19 April at the Trinidad Public Library titled "The British West Indies in World History," which Williams described as a preview to his book *Capitalism and Slavery,* was significant for a number of reasons. First, it was also delivered before an overflowing audience. As Williams recalled, "The pandemonium was unbelievable. A hall, under repair, meant to accommodate 300 had perhaps two persons in every space intended for one. They stood on the stairs, they listened outside the building."[3]

Second, the correspondence between Carlton Comma, the librarian at the Trinidad Public Library, and Williams regarding this lecture reflected Williams's ongoing efforts as a willing *marchand* to market his knowledge. For example, Comma enclosed in a letter to Williams a copy of the proofs of the lectures given by Williams with the suggestion that they be sold in the form of a pamphlet for twelve cents or a shilling in order to defray production costs. Comma said that it should be possible to print three thousand copies, the proceeds from which "could be donated to the purchasing and developing of our section on the West Indies in the library." He ended with a postscript requesting a list of biographical others to whom copies of the pamphlet might be sent, as well as a fairly large picture of Williams for "our picture collection at the Library."[4]

In his typewritten response eleven days later, which speaks to the esteem in which an educated individual like Williams was held, Williams requested that Comma delete "on the cover and title page the Dr. and the Howard [University] rank . . . because there is too much damned snobbishness here about these things and my impression is that they denote nothing. Please delete them, therefore. If any questions are asked you are authorised to say that it was done at my request. I have naturally left out the Dr. in your Foreword." Williams goes on to ask that Comma add "preferably at the end of paragraph I of your foreword (which is incidentally excellent) the following statement: 'With the approval of Dr. Williams, the proceeds from this pamphlet will be devoted to purchasing books on the history of the West Indies for the West Indian Section of the Library.'" He also requests that Comma collect some opinions on his broadcast talks, or "better still," that he "get some listeners to write to me critically about them"; provides an update on the publication status of *Capitalism and Slavery;* and states his intention to send "for the West Indian section of the Library, autographed copies of all my writings that I am able to locate."[5]

Williams's letter ends with a request for fifty copies of the printed form of the lecture and a comment that he was enclosing a list of individuals to whom presentation copies were to be sent. The list is significant because it speaks to the wide circle of biographical others who Williams thought might be interested in what he had to say. Thus, in addition to prominent academics, some of whom, like Professor Dennis Brogan, had been instrumental in Williams's early development as an academic intellectual, the list included politicians like Jamaica's Norman Manley and Barbados's Grantley Adams; Negro intellectuals like America's Alain Locke and E. Franklin Frazier and Haiti's Price Mars; high-profile public servants; and Dr. Charles A. Petioni, the Reverend Brock, Professor Vincent Harlow, and Dr. Mordecai Johnson, the president of Howard University when Williams taught there. Williams also asked that copies be sent to a number of outstanding Negro papers in the United States, as well as papers in San Juan, Puerto Rico, and Cuba; and, finally, to Learie Constantine, who would be a member of Williams's first council of ministers after he became chief minister of Trinidad and Tobago in September 1956 and, later, Trinidad and Tobago's high commissioner to London. Evidently, Williams was using a marketing strategy similar to the one he had employed as an academic intellectual to create space for his knowledge, in this case as a public intellectual in Trinidad and Tobago, as he sought to expand his knowledge-disseminating activities to reach a wider public.

PERHAPS THE most important opportunity for Williams to establish himself as a public intellectual in Trinidad occurred during a celebrated debate in November 1954 with Dom Basil Matthews, a Benedictine monk with a doctorate in sociology from Fordham University. Contextually, at least two points are worthy of note. First, despite its undoubted significance, the debate seems to have received short shrift in the scholarly literature dealing with Williams. Indeed, Dr. Elton Richardson, a member of the study group that immediately preceded the People's National Movement (PNM)—the country's first mass-based political party, which Williams led—devotes a few brief comments to the debate in his book,[6] while Selwyn Cudjoe discusses its significance in terms of Williams's "real entrée into the public sphere" in just one paragraph,[7] and Ivar Oxaal devotes two pages to the debate.[8] Even more remarkable, Williams himself does not mention the debate in his published autobiography, *Inward Hunger,* but merely speaks of "my good friend, Dom Basil Matthews," in connection with a suggestion regarding possible disunity occasioned by religion in the educational system, in his speech titled "The Case for Party Politics in Trinidad and Tobago."[9]

Second, it may be asserted that intellectuals need to create the impression that they are not talking to themselves. Thus, the public intellectual, needs to create a "public," who will legitimate his or her status as an intellectual and with whom he or she can interact as an equal. By *equal* in this case I mean someone who possesses a certain amount of disciplinary knowledge, usually acquired at the university level. Disciplinary knowledge, as Jeffrey Escoffier suggests in referring to the bureaucratic structures that impact the production of knowledge as far as the academic intellectual is concerned, is "formal and regulated by the intellectual norms of already established disciplines, by the requirements of University curriculums, and by the power structure of educational institutions integrated within the larger society."[10] In other words, someone like Matthews, whose credentials, which were characterized by a demonstrated excellence in, and a concomitant strong loyalty to, a specific discipline, qualified him to engage Williams in what might be referred to as "the culture of critical debate."[11] As the possessor of a certain amount of cultural capital, Dom Basil, whose choice was hardly fortuitous, therefore proved to be the ideal foil for Williams's intellectual and, ultimately, political thrusts as a public intellectual.

Since the dialogue between Williams and Matthews was "clearly a major occasion in the intellectual life of the colony,"[12] in view of its focus on the usefulness of Aristotle's thought regarding the state, education, and slavery, it is helpful to place the exchange between the two "doctors," which was unheard of in Trinidad at that time, in a wider sociohistorical perspective. The contest was in a sense the culmination of discussions and efforts of members of a certain "public" that inhabited a physical space in Trinidad known as "Behind the Bridge"[13] regarding who was the more learned of the two "doctors."

There was a marked contrast between the two combatants. On the one hand, there was the man from Mount St. Benedict (Matthews), over six feet tall in his stocking feet. On the other hand, there was the man from Kent House (Williams), the diminutive soccer dribbler standing no more than five feet six inches and a considered recluse as far as the man in the street was concerned. Finally, the contrast was marked, perhaps more significantly from a cultural standpoint, by "the expressive equipment of a standard kind intentionally or unwittingly employed" by the two "doctors" during the performance.[14] For while Dom Basil "entered the arena with books that could have spanned the Ortoire river, Dr. Eric came in with a little piece of paper barely visible in his hand."[15] If performance may be indicated by efforts to get the audience to respond favorably to one's actions, then Williams created the impression that such was his command and grasp of the material (knowledge) that he needed nothing but a piece of paper as his "expressive equipment," a point that, most assuredly, was not lost upon the audience.

In keeping with the idea that *education is politics,* and based on considerable research, Williams had delivered a lecture on 28 September 1954 at the Trinidad Public Library titled "Some World Famous Educational Theories and Developments Relevant to West Indian Conditions." And even though he had previously given a number of lectures on West Indian history and social structure and was therefore well known in Trinidad and Tobago, the debate with a biographical other like Dom Basil was extremely instrumental in further underlining Williams's reputation as an academic–cum–public intellectual. During his lecture, Williams cited Aristotle and made reference to the latter's distinction between two classes of people in the Greek city-states—citizens and slaves—and his justification of slavery. However, in the course of defending his main argument, that state control of education was desirable, Williams was challenged during question time by Dom Basil, who disagreed strongly with Williams's representation of Aristotle's thought.

As noted above, state-controlled education was a familiar topic for Williams, and there had been previous discussion of the issue on the island. His observations regarding Cutteridge and his appointment as director of education, his dissatisfaction regarding the absence of West Indian history in the curriculum during his time at Queen's Royal College, and his abiding preoccupation with the establishment of a West Indian university were all indicative of Williams's deep and continuing interest in all aspects and levels of education in the colony, especially their relevance. So concerned, however, was Dom Basil with Williams's treatment of Aristotle's views on education that Matthews himself decided to respond by way of a lecture titled "Aristotle, Education and the State Control," which later took place on 9 November at the Trinidad Public Library.

The lecture, the *Trinidad Guardian* reported, had to be carried by loudspeakers to the hundreds who remained outside the library because its reference room could not accommodate everyone who attended. And when at a few minutes before 11:00 p.m. Chairman Ellis Clarke attempted to end the meeting during question time, there were shouts of disapproval from the audience.[16] During his lecture, Matthews maintained that to say that Aristotle believed that the aim of education was to produce a good Greek or good children (or, in our context, a good West

Indian) was to misrepresent his thinking. Moreover, those who did so were making Aristotle "the father of their favourite errors, and representing [him] as the enemy of truth, natural and divine."[17] This was in reply to Williams's statement during his 28 September lecture—interestingly, he was described by the *Trinidad Guardian* as "Dr. Eric Williams prominent sociologist"—that the present education system in Trinidad had many faults, the main one being that it did not do enough to produce the good West Indian, which was the greatest need of the day.

Continuing, Matthews suggested that the whole question of the state and education needed to be rephrased. He therefore maintained that one should not ask, what is education? Rather, one should ask, who and what is the state, what is its nature, and what is the purpose and meaning of life in the state? Only when one knew the answers to these questions, he contended, would he or she be in a position to determine "the prime content of education and what is the burden of citizenship." In a further reference to Williams's major contention, that is, the need to wrest control of education in Trinidad from the church, Matthews dealt first with the question of religion, which for Aristotle, he argued, was at the core of civic life. Furthermore, the meaning and the purpose of life in Aristotle's commonwealth was morality, not material well-being, Matthews noted, and although Aristotle's sense of morality referred to a social and a civic morality, "its final reference and ultimate sanction is deeply religious." Touching more specifically on Williams's argument, Dom Basil stated that for Aristotle, state control was, in the final analysis, "control in the name of the gods. It has little, if anything, to do with early state control of modern Socialists and Russian Communists."[18]

Dom Basil's portrayal of Aristotle's views had all kinds of implications for the debate as to whether the state or the church should have the last word regarding the content of the educational diet, not only of Trinbagonians but of the entire British Caribbean. The issue had been articulated in terms of dual control in what was then British Guiana. The government paid the bill for primary education, and the church, through various managers (of primary schools), who often were religious dignitaries, had a significant say in matters related to the educational content. These included whether teachers would be hired or fired because of their religious persuasion and whether children born to parents who were not married would be allowed to be educated in these schools. Indeed, as we saw regarding Williams's decision to attend Queen's Royal College, the priest obviously was an important figure, educationally and otherwise, in the lives of Trinbagonians.

However, it was Dom Basil's comment that "slavery was sometimes necessary for the common good but that you could enslave men's bodies but not their minds" that elicited the loudest shouts of disapproval from the audience, in particular from "an indignant Dr. Williams," who jumped up and almost shouted, "Aristotle never said that," as Dom Basil purportedly was quoting Aristotle. After giving what he said was the correct quotation, Williams later apologized to the chairman, Ellis Clarke, for his unrestrained outburst, soon after which Clarke adjourned the meeting. Since intellectuals have been known to ally the articulation of their views "with passion," it is conceivable that Williams's "outburst," especially toward the end of the evening's deliberations, which gave him the last substantive say, was hardly accidental. Since the whole atmosphere was charged with emotion and deep interest—the chairman had earlier appealed in vain for clearance of the passage outside the reference room, but the audience was interested in hearing more of the clash between the two PhDs—the debate clearly transformed the library from a space for reading, research, and reflection into an arena for argumentative debate and the clash of ideas. It was therefore another facet of intellectual activity that lent itself to knowledge production.

As it turned out, Williams had indeed been angered by Dom Basil's critical comments during his (Williams's) 28 September lecture and had intended to attack the Roman Catholic Church. However, since this was likely to be very problematic politically, he was persuaded to attack Dom Basil Matthews instead.[19] The dialogue, however, did not end with Dom Basil's comment and a subsequent lecture. Indeed, in a letter to Dom Basil dated 15 November 1954, Williams, in a manner and style reminiscent of an antagonist "inviting" another one to a duel at a particular time and place with the admonition, "be there," told Matthews that he intended to "reject your misconception of Aristotle's philosophy of education on Wednesday next, 17 November 1954, at the Public Library at 8.50 pm. I now invite you to be present and to sit with me on the platform, as you invited me to sit on the occasion of your lecture."[20]

In this manner the duel of the two "doctors" reached a crescendo, but not before another event occurred that further underscored Williams's quest to be a public intellectual and the whole question of argumentative debate. This was, surely, a cardinal feature of the democratic ideal as promulgated by the Greeks, who met not in the library but in an amphitheater or a square to discuss possible representatives and to make their selection. A similar point was made on the very day of Williams's lecture by the resident tutor of the Extra-Mural Department of the University College of the West Indies in Port-of-Spain in a letter to the editor of the *Trinidad Guardian.*

The letter commended the "recent remarkable manifestation of interest in the political teachings of Aristotle which took place at the meeting at the Public Library," which sought to ensure that controversial issues were brought into the open, where they ought to be, as such a process lent itself to "a healthy democracy." Mentioning him by name, the letter went on to say that Williams might now say, "Now we are getting somewhere," and it concluded with the suggestion that in furtherance of the democratic process it might be useful to undertake a systematic study and that it might be agreed that it was the proper function of the Extra-Mural Department to provide opportunities of this sort.[21] However, since Williams had thrown down the gauntlet, in the culture of Trinbago Dom Basil had no alternative but to respond.

In any event, the audience readied itself for the performance with such passion that by the time Williams arrived at the library to give his rejoinder in a lecture titled "Some Misconceptions of Aristotle's Philosophy of Education," reportedly "hundreds were storming the gates of the Public Library before Dr. Williams was due to reply at 8.30 pm, and when he arrived he had difficulty in getting through the hundreds at the Library. Also, some even suggested that he transfer the lecture to the Grand Stand at the Savannah or to Woodford Square."[22] In his lecture Williams seems to have concentrated on the subject he knew best, which he had previously described as "man's greatest inhumanity to man," namely, enslavement—more than likely the chattel variant—within the context of Aristotle's notion of the "ideal state." Williams noted, for example, that Dom Basil's enthusiasm for Aristotle's "ideal state" concealed "slavery, the exclusion of the workers from citizenship, the subordination of women, and imperialism." The object of the state, Williams observed sarcastically, was the best possible life, in which slaves could not share. Moreover, the master and the enslaved shared a symbiotic relationship: since the latter was an animate article of property, masters would only be able to do without slaves if each inanimate object were to do its own work on command or by intelligent anticipation, much as, to use Aristotle's actual analogy, if a shuttle were to weave on its own.[23]

Before leaving this topic, a number of other points relevant to the making of Williams as a public intellectual ought to be mentioned. First, according to Gordon Rohlehr, professor of West Indian literature at the University of the West Indies, much to the chagrin of the old ruling class of church and press, the debate had enabled Williams to create space and obtain a measure of recognition in a way that "resembled how the old stickfighters would violently confront each other for rulership of turf. The Williams/Matthews debate was a piece of intellectual stickfighting that was totally irrelevant to the concrete issues of Trinidad and Tobago, but totally necessary for the manifestation of the intellectual charisma upon which the new party would convince a cross section of the deeply fragmented society of Trinidad and Tobago that it was worth the people's trust and faith."[24]

Given the sequence of events in the contest, with Williams's comments followed by Matthews's, which in turn were followed by Williams's responses, which were clearly designed to annihilate his opponent, the whole affair was reminiscent of the contests between two calypsonians, each intending to best the other in a form of extemporaneous repartee, much to the delight of an audience. While the content of the debate might not have been relevant, the execution was very Trinbagonian.

In addition, articles in the *Trinidad Guardian* carried a picture of a youthful Williams rather than of the forty-three-year-old he was at the time, while there was none of Dom Basil. In the absence of television, this helped make Williams a recognizable public figure to the person in the street. Second, in November 1954, at the same time that the debate was being reported, Trinidadians were transfixed by the daily comprehensive reports of the murder trial of another "doctor," the Indian physician Dalip Singh, who was charged and eventually convicted and hanged for the murder of his German-born optometrist wife. Daily, the *Trinidad Guardian* carried pictures of all the major players—the judge, the defense and prosecuting attorneys, the police investigators, and the witnesses in the trial. That the Williams-Matthews debate was able to compete with such press coverage is potent testimony to the significance of the activities of the two "doctors," but more so to that of Dr. Williams's efforts as a public intellectual.

Furthermore, as a result of the debate, a proposal was put forward on the night of the last meeting that drew loud applause from the hundreds inside the library, as well as from those in and around Woodford Square. The proposal, which was addressed to the Honorable Albert Gomes, who was the chairman of the Library Committee and who presided over the evening's deliberations,[25] was that every person attending future lectures at the library donate one penny to a Penny Fund, the proceeds to be used to purchase books for the library. Indeed, that very night 837 pennies were collected. Dr. Williams suggested further that the government be asked to match the public's donation "penny for penny," and the City Council with one cent (equivalent to half a penny) per penny. The money collected would then be used to buy books dealing with Aristotle's thought, to be selected by a committee made up of the librarian, Williams, and Matthews.

Lastly, following the debate, Williams reportedly posed *the* question: "Have not Dom Basil and I moreover been the humble servant for bringing out the best in the Trinidad community and positive evidence of the emergence of an active and enlightened democracy in Trinidad?" In addition, he declared, rather expansively, that though there were differences between him and Dom Basil, neither had been the winner, as the victors were "the people of Trinidad and Tobago." Williams also noted that the debate showed that the brain was a better weapon than the stiletto and that it was more respectful "to throw quotations than corrosive acid, and that differences of opinion need not degenerate to the level of the 'Jamette.'"[26]

Most interesting is that, according to reports in the *Trinidad Guardian,* Matthews did not state that the views he adduced regarding slavery's justification were Aristotle's and not his. Furthermore, for some inscrutable reason, neither Williams nor, especially, Matthews drew a distinction between chattel slavery in Trinidad and Tobago and slavery in the Greek city-states. Indeed, chattel slavery involved the tribal stigmata of race—unlike slavery in the Greek city-states, where mostly foreigners were likely to be enslaved—as a consequence of which the inferior status of a slave was automatically passed on to slaves' progeny. Indeed, in pointing to the peculiarities of chattel slavery, Williams had previously made clear the distinction between the "servitude" experienced by the predecessors of enslavement in the New World, that is, the White indentured servant, on the one hand, and the enslaved, on the other. Thus, he argued that while

> the servant's loss of liberty was of limited duration, the Negro was a slave for life. The servant's status could not descend to his offspring, Negro children took the status of the mother. The master at no time had absolute control over the person and liberty of the servant as he had over his slave. The servant had rights, limited but recognized by law and inserted in a contract. He enjoyed, for instance, a limited right to property. In actual law, the conception of the servant as a piece of property never went beyond that of personal estate and never reached the stage of a chattel or real estate.[27]

In any event, a new day had arrived in Trinidad and Tobago politics, with specific implications for nationalism and the forging of a collective identity among the followers of the social-movement leader and intellectual. The creation of a nationalist collective identity involved the construction of a *subaltern counterpublic,* a lower-level or lower-class aggregation of individuals whose lifeworld activities run counter to those of the rest of the society, and the transformation of spaces like the library and Woodford Square into what might be referred to as "parallel discursive arenas where members of subordinated social groups invent and circulate counterdiscourses to formulate oppositional interpretations of their identities, interests, and needs."[28] That hundreds came out to hear the debate and hundreds read of it in the newspaper no doubt was evidence of an alternative public upon whom Williams could draw for support in other forms of discourse. Conceivably too, the debate provided an opportunity for Williams to use the authority, credibility, celebrity commitment, and ethics[29] associated with the academic intellectual's possession of historical knowledge (cultural capital) to further legitimate his status as a public intellectual.

I HAVE mentioned that Williams was associated with the Anglo-American Caribbean Commission before his permanent return to Trinidad. Because of its relevance to Williams's intellectualism, the AACC's emergence and that of its successor, the Caribbean Commission, deserve more than a passing comment. The AACC came into existence as a temporary advisory body on 9 March 1942 as a result of a joint U.S.-U.K. communiqué. It was charged with making recommendations to both governments for jointly coping with the rapidly deteriorating economic and social conditions in the Caribbean in wartime.

These conditions, it was felt, presented a threat not merely to the political stability of the Caribbean territories but also to the security of British and U.S. joint naval bases.[30] The joint communiqué also stated that the AACC was being created for "the purpose of encouraging and strengthening social and economic co-operation between the United States of America and its possessions and its bases in the area known geographically and politically as the Caribbean, and the United Kingdom and the British Colonies in the same area."[31] The AACC was also viewed as a manifestation of the Good Neighbor Policy and a form of trusteeship, considered to be the opposite of imperialism, but with a military-security component. Thus, the trusteeship principle was also applied to those areas "needed as security points in a post-war security system."[32] U.S. interest in the area, therefore, was hardly motivated by altruism alone.

After the visit of the West India Royal Commission (the Moyne Commission), and its report on the deplorable economic conditions in the West Indies, "a destroyers for Bases" agreement of September 1940 between Britain and the United States gave the latter rights to establish bases on certain Caribbean islands. The agreement addressed the need for increased security in the Western Hemisphere because of German aggression during World War II. The Caribbean, as one observer noted, now acquired a more substantial meaning for the American public, and the area came to be referred to as "our sea of destiny" or the "American Mediterranean."[33] Echoing U.S. recognition of the magnitude of the problems facing the West Indies in the early 1940s and the even greater problems the region would likely face in the postwar years, Oliver Stanley, then British secretary of state for the colonies, noted in March 1943 that the British government expected *(a)* a real partnership between Britain and the West Indies, which could not solve its problems on its own; *(b)* an organization that would bring together the West Indies and the rest of the Caribbean territories; and *(c)* an effort to more closely connect the Caribbean area with the rest of the world so that the area could survive and prosper.[34]

From its inception, however, the commission was bedeviled by problems.[35] There was, for example, opposition from within the U.S. State Department to the commission and its American cochair, Charles Taussig, who was viewed as unqualified for the position. Again, it was considered unusual that an organization so closely allied with the State Department would report directly to the U.S. president. Then, too, there was resentment from naval authorities, then secretary of the interior Harold Ickes, and several State Department officials who had doubts about Taussig's plans to solve the problems of the Caribbean, about which the State Department had not been consulted.

Finally, there was a great deal of opposition from the supposed beneficiaries of the commission's activities—the English-speaking West Indians—who viewed the AACC as another commission that would visit the Caribbean but leave no visible benefit in its wake. As the historian Annette Palmer observed, it was difficult to understand the United States' insistence on assuming what was obviously an imperialist posture in the Caribbean by way of the commission.[36] This may explain Williams's subsequent conclusion that the AACC was established because the two powers "wanted a listening post in the British West Indies."[37]

While it is not known precisely when he came to this conclusion or whether he made this statement in a moment of pique, in fact the objectives of the Research Council of the Caribbean Commission, of which he became deputy chairman, meshed nicely with Williams's own intellectual agenda at the time. The council's objectives were "to promote scientific, technological, social and economic research for the benefit of the Caribbean Area" and "to survey needs, determine what research has been done, arrange for dissemination and exchange of the results of research, arrange conferences between research or extension workers and recommend what further research and co-operation should be undertaken."[38] However, as will be seen, when attention turned to establishing a U.S. base in Trinidad, the British and the Americans had cooperated, without Trinbago's involvement, even before the AACC and later the Caribbean Commission established a presence on the twin island.

The Caribbean Commission came into being in December 1945 with its Secretariat and Research Council headquartered in Trinidad. Its aim was to support and facilitate the social and economic development of the countries it served, as well as to provide technical assistance, either through its Secretariat staff or through experts on loan to it from national or international agencies. Moreover, as Herbert Corkran notes, the commission was a purely advisory body in that it could not force the acceptance or implementation of recommendations made to the governments it served.[39] However, article 6 of the 1946 agreement gave voting rights only to the four cochairs, of whom three had to concur on procedural matters, while all four had to agree on substantive matters. To the leaders of the Caribbean territories, concerned as they were with nationalism and pride in self-government, the commission, with its four cochairs representing the metropolitan powers—Britain, France, America, and the Netherlands—seemed to be not only more and more of an anachronism but a nagging reminder of the colonial presence that Caribbean leaders were so eager to remove. Williams's subsequent tenure and departure from the commission, then, cannot be fully comprehended without some understanding of this point.

In addition to the debate with Dom Basil and various other lectures, Williams's experiences at the Caribbean Commission provided another opportunity for him and his ideas to be ensconced in the political landscape, while educating the masses about colonialism, in this instance in terms of the presence of the commission. His association with that organization was another distinctive facet of Williams's biography. His connection with the commission provided him, as a member of the educated elite without an independent profession, with an opportunity to convert cultural and symbolic capital into economic capital by way of employment. This was in the absence of a West Indian university, the University College of the West Indies having come into being in 1948 as a satellite college of London University, which Williams had opposed. Employment with the commission also afforded Williams the opportunity to travel throughout the Caribbean, which allowed him to become well acquainted with conditions in the region and, therefore, with another manifestation of the language of the dominant.

After holding various posts in both the AACC and the Caribbean Commission, in 1948 Williams was appointed deputy chairman of the Caribbean Research Council and head of the research branch of the Secretariat. His tenure with the commission was a stormy one, with Williams once again taking what he felt were principled stands against what he perceived to be injustices based on racial preferences, which privileged so-called incompetent White expatriates at the expense of Black colonials.[40] This was because Williams's employment with the commission required that he refrain from overt political activity and that any proposed publication of his be approved by a commission official before publication. This, Williams clearly viewed as censorship by the commission of what he considered to be "relevant knowledge," especially in the case of his first book, *Negro in the Caribbean.*

Typical of his intellectual activity at the time, the book was relatively short and written in a nonvernacular style. Apparently, as a diasporan intellectual, Williams was more concerned with the content, getting the word out, and attracting as wide a public as possible than with the prestige of the publisher. Also, the book was another significant turning point in the transition from academic intellectual to public intellectual. In it, for instance, Williams used the term *Negro* in reference not simply to physiognomy but also to the structural position of colonized individuals, especially vis-à-vis external political control and the centrality of "King Sugar" in the economy of the entire Caribbean.

This explains his references to Haiti and Puerto Rico. Besides his usual attention to scholarly references and analytical thinking, Williams sought to demonstrate how one's relationship to the economy influenced, among other things, one's ranking in the society, opportunities for education, and one's life chances in terms of longevity and the quality of life. Sugar workers, for example, were prone to contract diseases associated with hookworms because they had to go about barefooted, and because the latrines were located some distance away, workers were likely to answer an urgent call of nature in the nearest available bush. This permitted the worm, found in human waste, to enter the body through the soles of the feet.

Additionally, Williams argued that the education of the colonized was deliberately being sacrificed by the sugar plantocracy on the altar of labor-power availability and hence profitability. Having Negro children work on the plantation would be preferable, therefore, to educating them. This argument by Williams was consistent with what social-movement analysts refer to as "frame bridging,"[41] whereby two components of colonialism—race and education—were linked together as a means of interpreting this form of oppression. Williams thus notes that as one planter put it,

> Give them some education in the way of reading and writing, but no more. Even then I would say educate only the bright ones; not the whole mass. If you educate the whole mass of the agricultural population, you will be deliberately ruining the country. . . . Give the bright ones a chance to win as many scholarships as they can; give the others three hours' education a day . . . if you keep them longer you will never get them back to work in the fields. If you want agricultural labourers and not dissatisfaction, you must keep them longer.[42]

"As long as this is an agricultural country," another planter asked, "of what use will education be to them if they had it?"[43] Significantly also, Williams stated that lighter-skinned mulattoes considered themselves to be superior to their darker-skinned colonized brethren. And in instances where an educated Black male married a White female, the couple received better opportunities because the system felt that the female should be able to live in the manner and style of a European. This was, of course, in contrast to the experiences of his father's parents.

The arguments in *Negro in the Caribbean* and *Capitalism and Slavery,* along with a document allegedly written by Williams that seemed to advocate the abolition of private property, appear to have upset the AACC. Consequently, the books' arguments were used by the United States as evidence that Williams was a "dangerous "leftist" who was unfit for employment in the commission. The U.S. State Department, while recognizing that Williams was "widely and, in general, favorably known in the Caribbean and is considered by West Indians as the foremost historian of the Caribbean," initially opposed his appointment as deputy chairman of the Caribbean Research Council. This opposition was based also on the State Department's assessment that the document in question was "fairly conclusive evidence" that Williams had "violated his duties to the Commission" in view of the fact that the position of deputy chairman required, "above all, careful and objective scholarship and research directed to the purposes of the organization."[44]

However, based on an investigation of his background and qualifications, informal conversations with responsible government officials whose judgment the State Department respected, more formal investigation of security agencies, and the staunch support of the other three commissioners and that of Norman Manley, the State Department withdrew its earlier opposition to Williams's appointment. This withdrawal was made with the proviso that should Williams be appointed, the U.S. co-chairman of the commission, Ward Canaday, might deem it advisable to suggest to the commission that his work be "reviewed by an appropriate technical group to correct any lapses in judgment of the kind that led to the Department's earlier letter" opposing his appointment.[45]

Some of Williams's concerns were later expressed in a letter of 17 June 1954 to Jamaica's chief minister, Norman Manley, justifying the political component inherent in the act of writing.[46] In addition to thanking Manley—once more, one imagines—for his intervention enabling Williams to get the job as deputy chairman in the first place, which he portrayed as a trope for colonialism, Williams also wrote of being put on probation and being persecuted, as well as the prospect of imminent unemployment. Significantly too, he seemed to be saying that given what he perceived as his current untenable position, an entry into the political arena was a real possibility:

> I am persecuted because of my writing; I think therefore I ought to write some more. This may not work out, but it can hardly make me more unpopular with the Commission than I am now. Since I cannot go back to Howard, I may be out of a job in a year's time. There are elections here next year, and already I have been asked to come out and join the ILP [Independent Labour Party], and the suggestion has even been made that I should be its chairman. I do not rule it out, and my autobiography will be a sort of party programme if I am forced to take this way out. If they do not want to deal with me at the level of an innocuous research worker, perhaps they prefer to deal with me as a legislator. If they insist on my being a hewer of wood and drawer of water for a metropolitan boss, perhaps they prefer a colonial-metropolitan relationship at the level of my joining in the demand for complete responsible government and the complete West Indianisation of the Trinidad Civil Service.[47]

This letter constitutes powerful evidence regarding Williams's plans to continue to make space for his intellectualism in the political landscape, especially in terms of his resolution to write more, as a form of political protest in the struggle against colonialism and its various manifestations. For him, therefore, the completion of his autobiography and, later, an anthology of Caribbean literature and a history of the Caribbean constituted the first component of a three-pronged "weapon" in his fight with the commission. The second would be an undertaking of an adult-education campaign, and the third would be to carry on the fight against the colonialist metropolitan enemy from within the commission and the Secretariat. The commission's posture could be effectively countered by recourse to carefully researched and thus informed knowledge as a collective-action resource, which would then provide a theoretical base for "cursing" colonialism, which he determined to be the enemy.

Notwithstanding the above, it appears that Williams approached his job as deputy chairman of the Research Council with seriousness.

> According to staff members who were at the Commission at the time, Dr. Williams devoted tremendous vigor and enthusiasm to his work, driving himself and his immediate associates to the point of exhaustion. Williams, single-handedly, wrote many of the Commission's technical and research papers. So forceful indeed was his application to his work that, according to one long time staff officer, the entire Secretariat came to be polarized around the Research Branch and its dynamic chief. The rest of the Secretariat in other words, became little more than a service and administrative appendage to the Research Branch.[48]

WILLIAMS'S RELATIONSHIP with the Caribbean Commission came to an end on 21 June 1955, when he was informed that his contract would not be renewed. While officials at the commission were reluctant to discuss his case, according to a former staff member, Williams had begun to dabble in Trinidad politics, in strict violation of staff rules and article 14, paragraph 5, of the commission's agreement, which stated that the staff "shall refrain from any action which might reflect on their position as international officials responsible only to the Commission." If that was the only or even the main reason for the nonrenewal of his contract, and if education is politics and the act of writing (and for good measure the dissemination of one's written efforts) is a political act, then the commission's assessment was correct.

However, the act of speaking also was vital to Williams's political activities. Kamaluddin Mohammed, a future minister of public utilities, recalls, for example, that his first meeting with Williams occurred in early 1955, when Williams was the guest speaker at a meeting of students at the Old Morvant Market Building and Mohammed was chairman of the St. George County Council. On another occasion, on 29 April 1955, Williams participated in a panel discussion before an audience of about six hundred people at the Naparima College Main Hall in San Fernando, sponsored by the college's Old Boys Association, whose president was Dr. Ibbit Mosaheb, and chaired by Gerard Montano, then mayor of San Fernando. According to Mohammed, Williams delivered a most inspiring address titled "The Economic Aspects of Caribbean Culture."[49]

In any event, Williams's widely circulated speech delivered on 21 June 1955, titled "My Relations with the Caribbean Commission, 1943–1955," dealing with his experiences at the commission and his dismissal, was his first public declaration of his transition from public intellectual to social-movement intellectual in the cause of political independence. As he put it at the beginning of his speech, "I stand before you tonight, and, therefore, before the people of the British West Indies, the representative of a principle, a cause, and a defeat. The principle is the principle of intellectual freedom. The cause is the cause of the West Indian people. The defeat is the defeat of the policy of appointing local men to high office."[50]

Not only was he stating his vigorous opposition to the gatekeeping function of knowledge production in the form of vetting and censoring of knowledge and to the restrictions placed on the mobility of qualified West Indians that was part of the commission's policy but he was making it clear that this could be the fate of other, similarly situated West Indians. Significantly, Williams also informed his listeners that despite the trials and tribulations, he had remained with the commission because it had brought him into "close contact with present problems in territories the study of whose history has been the principal purpose of my adult life, while association with representatives of the metropolitan governments enabled me to understand, as I could not otherwise have understood, the mess in which the West Indies find themselves today."[51]

Doubtless, Williams's time with the commission had provided him the opportunity to be immersed in, and therefore to "curse," what he considered to be another manifestation of the language of colonial oppression. Significantly too, the rules of the game (habitus) that characterized his knowledge-production activities with the commission would no longer apply. As Bourdieu put it, "The game is over when people start wondering if the cake is worth the candle."[52] Williams would henceforth place his knowledge at the disposal of the Trinbagonian people, and in a way that they understood. During the four months following his exit from the commission, he gave a total of 36 lectures throughout the twin island,

and according to Kamaluddin Mohammed, by 15 June 1956 Williams had delivered a total of 156 lectures all over the country, mostly dealing with facets of colonialism. The public intellectual had begun to transition to the status of a social-movement intellectual.

But Williams's dismissal from the commission was not the end of the story as far as the organization was concerned. Corkran notes that after Williams left the commission, the Caribbean Research Council never met again, although technically it remained part of the commission. However, after it was decided that the commission would become the Caribbean Organization and that it would be headquartered in Trinidad, the British section of the commission approached the West Indian federal government and requested that it accept the normal financial responsibilities of having the commission remain in Port-of-Spain (in Trinidad), then the federal capital. The federal government indicated that it could not afford to assume the financial responsibility and suggested that the government of Trinidad and Tobago (GOTT), now headed by Williams, should do so. The GOTT's decision not to do so then resulted in the commission's relocation to Puerto Rico in 1960. Williams, it appears, never forgave the treatment he felt he received from the commission and had made it clear that the commission, in his view, served no useful purpose. The GOTT's decision, considered to be one of personal resentment, was criticized both by Albert Gomes and the *Trinidad Guardian*, especially since the commission's departure meant not just a loss of jobs for Trinidadians but also a loss of prestige for Trinidad.[53]

4 In Search of Relevance

The "University of Woodford Square" and the Political Party Paper

> A little less than five years ago when I severed relations with the imperialist organisation known as the Caribbean Commission, I indicated publicly that I would let my bucket right down here in Trinidad, and that the only University in which I would lecture in future is the University of Woodford Square.
>
> —Eric Williams

REFERENCE HAS been made to Williams's efforts as a public intellectual to widen a "public" who received his thoughts and ideas, his use of the public sphere for discussion and debate regarding matters of concern to the society, and his views with respect to the creation of a West Indian university. However, he also had specific views concerning the university as an institution for instruction with respect to political independence, involving face-to-face interaction consistent with the *spoken* word and the use of the print media for transmission of the *written* word. In this chapter I examine the manner in which Williams continued to construct two settings for the transmission of knowledge regarding political independence as he transitioned from public intellectual to social-movement intellectual. The first setting was Woodford Square, a physical space that became known as the "University of Woodford Square" (UWS) or the "People's Parliament" and was reconstructed for the transmission of the *spoken* word. The second was the newspaper of the People's National Movement Party, which was used to transmit the *written* word.

The public sphere, Jürgen Habermas observes, is an aggregation of individuals who come together as a public in order to engage in a debate over rules governing relations.[1] These individuals are likely to engage the dominant group in a debate over the general rules governing relations between the dominant and the dominated. The public sphere, therefore, was to be viewed as the arena of discursive relations and as a theater for debating, deliberating, and moving issues previously located on the periphery into the open for discourse. This medium of political confrontation and the people's public use of their reason, Habermas continues, were peculiar and without historical precedent.[2] However, the "great public" that formed in the theaters, museums, and concerts was "bourgeois in social origin"[3] and comprised the salons and clubs and reading societies, which were not "directly subject to the cycle of production and consumption, that is, the dictates of life's necessities,"[4] and the press, which monopolized the literary public space and thereby the capacity to influence public opinion.[5]

But as David Harvey contends, the "idea of the 'public sphere' as an arena of political deliberation and participation, and therefore as fundamental to democratic governance," had a long and distinguished history. The "imagery of the Athenian *agora* as the physical space [like Woodford Square] wherein that democratic ideal might be attained has also had a powerful hold on the political imagination."[6] During the classical period of Greek civilization and by about 600 BC, for instance, every city had a public space in the center, surrounded by government buildings, which was known as the *agora.* As a public space, the agora was where markets and stalls were located, people bought and sold their merchandise, slaves were bought and sold, and slaves sold their services. Moreover, the agora was accessible to every citizen for the purpose of discussing new ideas, for example, regarding democracy. Indeed, it was said that intellectuals such as Aristotle and Plato led their pupils in this form of intellectual activity in the agora. The agora also was the public space where Greek *citizens* (which did not include women, slaves, and metics, who were aliens or foreigners living in Greece without citizen rights, none of whom were permitted to vote) participated in deciding judicial matters and in the political process by voting and electing city officials. In other words, the agora functioned as a public space for activity associated with the public sphere.

Despite its significance, the extent to which public spaces such as parks and squares were part of the colonial enterprise has only relatively recently begun to attract the attention of historians of the Caribbean. The historian Brian Moore notes, for example, that a public square in Georgetown, the capital city of Guyana, known as the Parade Ground was used for most of the nineteenth century as an arena for cricket matches. There, the cricket captain, commanding his men on the field of play, devised strategies, "on his feet" in the middle of a match, that were inculcated and honed and were especially vital in the colonies, where Whites were grossly outnumbered by potentially hostile non-Whites. Since the Parade Ground was used as a space for military training, it was located, not surprisingly, very near Government House, the residence of the governor.[7]

As James C. Scott reminds us, the public space has always been a venue for unauthorized assemblies by the dominated and for parades and other events during which the dominant publicly displayed their military power, as a deterrent to antihegemonic activity.[8] Similarly, David Trotman notes that the naming of public spaces also served as a reminder of the colonial presence and consequently was part of the colonial apparatus of domination.[9] Such was the case with Harris Promenade in San Fernando, named for Lord Harris, governor of Trinidad from 1846 to 1854, and with Woodford Square in downtown Port-of-Spain, named for another former governor of the island. Sir Ralph James Woodford had taken up his post as governor of Trinidad in 1813, when he was twenty-nine years old, and served in that capacity until 1829, the year of his death. However, the square itself had a somewhat checkered history. For example, after an abortive revolt by the enslaved in 1805, the leaders were hanged and their bodies left swinging on the gallows in the square.

This public display of the might—or, for our purposes, the language—of the colonizer was meant to be a reminder to those among the dominated who would run afoul of the legal norms that sought to protract the system. As the historian Juanita De Barros notes with respect to what was then British Guiana, the public space was used by colonial authorities to demonstrate the power of the colony's judicial-penal complex. Public executions, a throwback to the days of enslavement, were attended by a procession of government officials, such as the prison surgeon and wardens, police officials, the dispenser, and the executioner. They were clearly awe-inspiring spectacles designed to terrorize the masses, who also attended them.[10]

It might be noted that not only are the names of these spaces a reminder of the tragic colonization experience of the twin island, but so were the names of spaces named after the Amerindians. These names, which were modified by assimilation, include Arima, named after an Arawak chief, and Amerindian toponyms that represent the names of trees, plants, and animals, such as Chaguaramas, named after a palmist palm; El Tucuche, named after the nation's hummingbird; and cocorite, named after the cocorite palm.[11] As I will discuss in chapter 7, those Trinbagonians who were literally and figuratively involved in the efforts to ensure the departure of the Americans from the Chaguaramas base were involved in a historical act, namely, invoking the spirit of their ancestors.

Indeed, Williams himself noted that Woodford, whom he stated must be turning in his grave every time one spoke of the "University of Woodford Square," in 1824 had opposed the application of a colored doctor of medicine to practice on the island on the grounds that "his mother was a slave, and he had formerly been a slave himself." Furthermore, Williams noted that as far as Woodford was concerned, "the racial discrimination which prohibited intermarriage, banned certain professions to people of color, and limited the amount of property they could own, could not possibly be abandoned if in his words and in the language of oppression, 'the Whites are to maintain their ascendancy and Great Britain is to preserve her West India islands as colonies.'"[12]

If the squares and other open spaces were important facets of the colonial presence, so were the cities, particularly the political capitals (or towns, as they were called) in which they were located. As Claudius Fergus notes with respect to Caribbean slavery as an early manifestation of colonialism,

> If the plantation was the heart of the colony, then the capital . . . was its brains. The capital legalized relations of power on slave plantations and buttressed the plantation authority structure through coercive state institutions. The most influential planters met in town to engage in political intercourse with the colonial authorities and, by extension, the Crown. In time the town became a quasi-metropolis to which some planters retired, leaving their estates in the hands of managers and overseers.[13]

The town was also the meeting place of enslaved persons, and in this respect Port-of-Spain was typical. Some of these individuals congregated on Sundays to trade wares, provisions, and very important news and gossip, which were always fuel for collective antihegemonic activity, while others drifted off to rum shops, the most popular sites for recreational activity. In addition, the towns functioned as spaces for runaways, some of whom as skilled artisans were able to sell their labor power to prospective employers. It is in this context, therefore, that the choice of different open spaces—or colleges of the UWS, as Williams called them—for the education of Trinbagonians regarding political independence and the idea of the public sphere must be viewed.

As part of his change of the "rules of the game" as a public intellectual and a social-movement intellectual, Williams used the space in downtown Port-of-Spain known as Woodford Square as a locale for the politicization and systematic education of the masses. Topics ranged from Greek mythology and philosophy to the intricacies and subtleties of colonialism and American imperialism and, eventually, to the mechanics of West Indian nationalism and Trinidad and Tobago political independence. Moreover, Williams exploited what he considered to be the native and political intelligence of his listeners by not talking down to them. Rather, he sought to raise them to his level by disaggregating sometimes fairly complex ideas in simple, but not simplistic, terms so as to make them easily digestible. For example, in seeking to tether education as part of the public sphere and the public space, he used his historical knowledge to inform his listeners that their presence in Harris Promenade, a college of the five-year-old "University of Woodford Square," constituted "a positive manifestation of the capacity of our people to undertake all the responsibilities and enjoy all the privileges of democratic citizens."[14]

From a geographical standpoint, Woodford Square was close to the official parliament, known as the "Red House" because the building was painted red, and the square functioned as a locale for a good deal of "liming" (mostly males hanging out and indulging in repartee and "ole talk"). Moreover, a confluence of streets (including Charlotte Street, with the imposing statue of Captain Arthur Cipriani looking northwards toward the square) led right into the square. To the east of what was known as the "Dry River," which began northeast of the square and snaked its way southward, was a space known as Behind the Bridge (about which more will be said). As another group of biographical others, the inhabitants of the area were instrumental in populating the audiences of many of Williams's orations at the UWS. Woodford Square was within walking distance of places such as Belmont to the northeast and Laventille Hills, from which old ladies would leave early on foot so as to get a good seat to hear Williams "teach." Finally, the square was close to the Trinidad Public Library, where, as already noted, Williams did a good deal of his research. And the offices of the *Trinidad Guardian,* on St. Vincent Street, as well as the main police station, the courts, and Trinity Church, were in close proximity.

THE UWS began to take shape in July 1955, during a lecture titled "Constitution Reform in Trinidad and Tobago." In it, Williams intoned, "Somebody once said that all that was needed for a University was a book and the branch of a tree; someone else went further and said that a University should be a University in overalls. With a bandstand, a microphone, a large audience and slacks and hot shirts, a topical subject for discussion, the open air and a beautiful tropical night, we have all the essentials of a University."[15]

As he had written in his assessment of the criteria for a British West Indian university in 1946, for Williams, a university on the twin island should be cognizant of the indigenous factor as far as social space was concerned. Therefore, he determined that slacks and hot shirts would replace the academic gowns worn by students at Oxford University and the University College of the West Indies. Moreover, he opined that the bandstand in the open air should replace the coldness of the classroom in the austere buildings known as halls; and opportunities for higher learning should be provided for the common man, or the individual in "overalls," as opposed to those who primarily occupied the upper stratum that characterized the acquisition of higher education at Oxford University. The idea was therefore to transform and imbue Woodford Square with meanings that would be relevant to anticolonialism and the individual in the street.

In trying to recall a picture of Woodford Square, Williams noted that he remembered it as "a market for night-food. All transactions were done in the shadows. Women strolled about in search of male friends whom they had not yet known. Men sat on benches in the attitude of tolerable and even pleasing boredom. And there were always a few lunatics who had either avoided or escaped the attention of the state. Today, this same Woodford Square has become Mr. Everyman's Academy. The same people who used it appropriately, or inappropriately, as you like, in the past, now assemble there to learn."[16]

In addition, since he always considered education in general and political education for the masses in particular to be paramount, Williams contended that the university had an honorable place in the evolution of Western civilization and, through its teachers, students, and workers, had made enduring contributions to human progress and human liberty. Indeed, the foundation of London University and the emergence of various state universities in the United States had been instrumental in changing the social order and serving the needs of new classes.

To be sure, then, a new level in the evolution of the university as a concept was attained in Port-of-Spain on 21 June 1955—when Williams let his bucket down in politics—with the first of a series of public lectures on public issues in what was then known as Woodford Square.[17] "Christened a University two lectures later, on 19 July 1955," Williams continued, "the University of Woodford Square has in the past five years been a centre of free University education for the masses, of political analysis and of training in self-government for parallels of which we must go back to the city state of ancient Athens, or, in the modern world, to the political activity of Dr. Nkrumah in the Arena in Accra, Gold Coast, prior to the independence of Ghana."[18] And in reverting to the idea that education is politics, he went on to note in the context of political independence that the lectures at the UWS had dealt with

> constitution reform, economic problems, race relations, Federation and federal problems, the Bandung Conference, international affairs, the problem of Chaguaramas, the perspectives of independence. They have given the people of Trinidad and Tobago a vision and a perspective: they have given them an understanding of their own problems in the context of the larger world of which they form a small part, and they have reinforced their own aspirations by placing them in the context of the world struggle, past and present, for human freedom and for colonial emancipation. They have taught the people, what one French writer of the eighteenth century saw as the greatest danger, that they have a mind.[19]

It should also be noted that during a public lecture titled "The Bandung Conference," delivered at the UWS on 23 February 1956, Williams told his audience that from 18 to 24 April 1955 a total of twenty-one recently or soon to be emancipated nations had met in Indonesia for a conference that "cursed" and called for the end of colonialism. The delegates had not only denounced colonialism as evil and the subjection of peoples to an alien subjugation, domination, and exploitation that constituted a fundamental denial of human rights but called for a declaration of support for all colonized peoples; called on colonial powers to grant freedom and independence to colonized peoples; and condemned the racialism of colonial systems. As Robin Kelley observed, the conference of nonaligned countries, occurring as it did in 1955, was part of a zeitgeist of anticolonial activity that took the form of a number of writings by intellectuals between 1948 and the late 1950s, such as Frantz Fanon's *Black Skin, White Masks,* Richard Wright's *Listen White Man!,* and Albert Memmi's *The Colonizer and the Colonized.*[20] The reference to Bandung, which was reflective of the spirit of the times, or what might be referred to as a consciousness of kind, was vintage Williams the historian and teacher, who was again attempting to locate the Trinbagonian nationalist struggle within a wider international context.

In adopting an oratorical style, Williams went on to note that the UWS, as "the political forum" on the twin island, with exacting standards, was "highly coveted by aspiring politicians" and that many were called but few were chosen. By virtue of the fact that all were welcome to be educated, in contrast to the restrictive access to education that had characterized the society in which he grew up, the university had become "the great leveller in the traditional class society in Trinidad and Tobago [and] within its railings has emancipated thousands from the ancient shibboleths of class distinctions, the modern superstitions of racial discrimination, and the universal bugbear of inequality of the sexes and unfitness of the many for University training." And it mattered not, he asserted, whether one was black, brown, white, or yellow; Negro, Indian, European, Chinese, Syrian, or any of the permutations and combinations that made up the society; male or female, adult, adolescent, or child; factory worker, taxi driver, domestic servant, company director, store clerk, professional, or housewife. "The gates of the University are open to all and all besiege the gates on lecture night. It is the University in jeans and overalls. It is the nation in school."[21] This was heady stuff and a palpably political posture, and the audience roared in appreciation. Moreover, it was an effort to dismantle at least a facet of the system of social differentiation that had disadvantaged his father.

In addition to the UWS's location in the heart of Port-of-Spain, the act of reconstructing a space named after a governor who believed in, and actualized, the social differentiation of individuals based on the so-called inherent right of one race to govern and another to be governed as a space of "learned leisure" was previously unknown and no mere accident. It was perhaps the most dramatic of ironies, then, that, as Williams's daughter Erica Williams-Connell noted, while a colored doctor was not permitted by Woodford to practice his profession, years later another "colored doctor"—her father—would practice his profession as a teacher of history and a political-independence leader in the very square named for Governor Woodford.[22]

Finally, such was the transformation of Woodford Square that people listened there for hours in discomfort, when the loudspeakers meant they could sit and listen in their cars. Others did listen in their cars, parked at a discreet distance from the square so as to avoid being seen by powerful others who might wish to victimize them. These actions, as the Jamaican scholar and teacher Henry Fowler reported, were all definite indications of an intellectual hunger and evidence that Williams was creating a political movement.[23]

In sum, if West Indian history was being deemphasized, Williams the historian would use the *spoken* word (talk) in the context of the public sphere to teach it. This would be done in a way that "cursed" colonialism at the UWS, or, as he put it, in the "People's Parliament." This was because, as Habermas might argue, "only publicity inside and outside the parliament could secure the continuity of critical political debate and its function, to transform domination . . . from a matter of will into a matter of reason."[24]

Moreover, use of the spoken word to attack colonialism in this manner was all the more pertinent in view of Fraser's contention regarding Habermas's observation that the public sphere "designates a theater in modern societies in which political participation is enacted through the medium of talk. It is the space in which citizens deliberate about common affairs, and hence an institutionalized arena of discursive interaction."[25] Lastly, the ideas of "theater" and "talk" are synonymous with Goffman's dramaturgical analogy, which views behavior such as speeches as "on stage" performances by actors, in a setting that includes a "personal front."[26] In addition to his style, that valued personal Trinbagonian trait, Williams's personal front had taken the form of what Oxaal referred to as a trinity of props—hearing aid, dark glasses, and a cigarette drooping from his lips[27]—when Williams addressed various audiences as a public and a movement intellectual.

In addition to using the spoken word, Williams once again signaled his intention to use the language of the oppressor to attack colonialism, in this instance by using the pages of the PNM newspaper for the *written* word. In other words, the party newspaper would be used as a medium for the transmission of ideas and other kinds of knowledge regarding the political-independence struggle and especially for moving the PNM's policy regarding political education into the public sphere. As he observed, "We in the PNM have always placed the deliberate cultivation of West Indian culture, with emphasis on our West Indian history in the forefront of our national programme, and I shall continue to do what I can through the pages of *The Nation.*"[28]

This was important for at least three reasons. First, as Williams himself noted, writing was a political act. Second, while *speaking* involves a two-tiered process of knowledge transmission by way of mental organization and verbal enunciation of a thought or an idea, *writing* involves a different mental processing of information before transmission. This explains why some individuals speak well but do not necessarily write well, and vice versa. Third, while spoken words are like the wind once they are uttered, in the absence of reportorial bias the written word lives on as a portrayal of knowledge and provides an opportunity for later generations to peruse, critique, and regurgitate. This provides a basis for increasing the store of knowledge of a given society. What follow, then, are first a statement delineating the rationale for a party newspaper; second, Williams's vision of what the PNM newspaper should seek to accomplish; and third, some of the difficulties envisaged in articulating this vision.

The PNM activist Lynne Beckles recalled hearing a woman say during a public meeting at the UWS sometime in 1956 that "no newspaper ever told me how to vote." In expressing her disagreement with that declaration, which had elicited cheers from the audience, Beckles noted that in addition to providing news, newspapers, like other members of the media in their role as what has been referred to as the "fourth estate," are in a position to shape public opinion, not merely by what is said and the manner in which it is said but often by what is not said. This position was especially significant, Beckles continued, in Trinidad and Tobago, where there was only one daily newspaper, perceived to be unsympathetic to the views of the PNM and its political leader, Dr. Eric Williams. This explains why the first action of an organization, such as a political party, is to create a medium for information that will accurately and, of course, sympathetically reflect *its own* views on key issues connected to its policies.[29] As she put it,

> Above all, the PNM recognized that its aims and objects would of necessity conflict with the whole concept of foreign ownership such as was enjoyed by Trinidad's leading newspaper. This was never identified with nationalist causes and in the view of the PNM, it could not be expected to register objectively the social changes arising in the wake of the new nationalist movement. Because the primary objective of the PNM was to weld into some sort of national whole a people *of diverse origins . . . traditionally segregated and divided. . . .* Creating a national community called for the provision of a strong local bond, such as the PNM expected to provide, and a steady projection at all times of the social goals to be achieved. Nationalism was therefore a cult to be actively pursued and to that end, there would be research in Caribbean history, literature, art and culture.[30]

As can be seen from the foregoing, there was an implicit reference to the role of the party in forging a collective identity, or a "national community," in the service of nationalism. There was, however, an additional dimension to be considered. Since it was necessary to provide an international orientation to the struggle and the independence-oriented efforts of similarly situated individuals in Asia and Africa, which "meant little to the Trinidadian in terms of his own future," the PNM newspaper sought to carve out its own space in the sphere of print media. Thus, the paper was not designed to be a vehicle for "news" and to compete with the daily newspapers in this capacity. Rather, the party newspaper aspired to analyze "trends behind the news" on a weekly basis and to discuss what an independent Trinidad and Tobago would entail and what social changes were necessary "despite the heavy handicap of colonialist attitudes." It was with this in mind that the first issue of the *PNM Weekly,* which saw the light of day on 18 June 1956, expressed the party's determination to provide an independent voice in the society, since the existing media could not be trusted to reflect the views of the nationalist movement.

In outlining the scope and tone of the paper, as well as the relationship of the party press, the party, and the UWS as a space for knowledge production, in his first editorial, "A Movement Is Born," dated 14 July 1956, Williams pointed to the space the *PNM Weekly* would occupy in journalistic knowledge production in Trinidad and Tobago. He maintained that every political party "must have an organ for the presentation of its views. Every University must have textbooks for its students. Every country must have different points of view presented to its citizens and voters. The People's National Movement, which has given Trinidad and Tobago its own University of Woodford Square, now presents to the people the *PNM Weekly,* and through it a point of view not now available in the country's press."[31]

During an address on 24 September 1960 at the UWS marking the fourth year of the PNM's first term in office and two days before the general election, Williams contended that the *Trinidad Guardian*'s monopoly on the transmission of news, coupled with its influence on opinion formation, posed a serious problem for the PNM and its views regarding the struggle for political independence. To begin with, the newspaper "prostitutes freedom of the press. Its freedom of the press is freedom to attack the P.N.M. It omits the news which is favourable to P.N.M.; where it cannot omit, it distorts. So the P.N.M. has had, with its limited resources to counter the *Guardian*'s propaganda."[32] Thus, Williams announced that a new monthly bulletin that would report factually and without comment on the major events and developments at the governmental level was being distributed free of charge by the Information Service of the Office of the Premier.

Turning specifically to the *Nation,* the weekly party newspaper that had come into existence in 1958 and replaced the *PNM Weekly,* which had been launched with public support, Williams informed his listeners that the *Nation* had become the PNM's challenge to the *Guardian.* In arguing that the *Guardian* gave voice to the language of the oppressor, Williams said that what was needed in the current political climate was a powerful daily newspaper. It was not the *Guardian*'s anti-PNM stance that troubled him; rather, it was that apart from its being "so damned bad," the newspaper's "intellectual standards would not satisfy the Grade III School Certificate." Moreover, since the *Guardian*'s "ethical standards appear to be no higher," Williams maintained that because of the *Guardian*'s alleged anti-PNM's stance and low professional standards, the PNM's responsibility and one of the "highest priorities in the weeks ahead was to assist in the launching of a daily newspaper."[33] Williams's characterization of the *Guardian*'s reportage was somewhat apocryphal, as especially during the 1950s the paper had done a lot to showcase Trinidad and Tobago's literature (Sam Selvon, V. S. and Shiva Naipaul, and Derek Walcott wrote for the paper), and its culture (carnival, calypso, etc.) was featured. Williams's comments were clearly part of an ongoing effort to create space for the party newspaper, which would reflect the PNM's and his position on issues regarding political independence in particular.

Williams also sought to articulate even more clearly his views regarding the *Nation*'s vision. For example, during an address to the PNM's fourth annual convention, he thundered that under the able leadership of C. L. R. James the paper had become "the textbook of Independence [and] the people can see the West Indian Independence Movement in the stream of world politics . . . Constitution Reform, Chaguaramas, Federation—it hits hard week after week, mercilessly exposing the issues, pitilessly excoriating the reactionaries." And with obvious satisfaction he claimed that the paper not only had muzzled the *Guardian* but was "compulsory reading in the Colonial Office and the State Department, and had established relations with members of Parliament and Congress." Through the paper, he continued, "the PNM has what it did not have before, a public relations voice in the outside world."[34] However, while Williams's views regarding the *Guardian* possibly smacked of hyperbole, it is clear that he recognized the *Nation*'s capacity to influence opinion in the public sphere.

This, he maintained, was not all, however, for the paper was obviously capable of seeing more than one side of an issue. In a further comment regarding the *Nation*'s even-handed reportage, which spoke to the provision of political education for the people, Williams noted that if the paper "lashes out at the Colonial Office, it stresses the virtues of British culture, through its homage to British cricket it pays tribute to British literature, and holds out to the people the better and more harmonious relations which Independence will bring. If it attacks the obscurantism of the State department, it treats sympathetically and competently the virtues of the American civilization."[35]

In contrast to the *Nation*'s mission to provide balanced and enlightening information, the *Guardian,* Williams postulated, was determined that Trinbagonians should remain fundamentally ignorant of the issues, for instance, regarding federation and the position of Jamaica in this regard. In further contrast to the *Guardian*'s journalistic endeavors, and in echoing Beckles's earlier-stated view, Williams observed that in the pages of the party newspaper, "West Indian culture and history receive an attention they have never before received, whether it is calypso, carnival or Trinidad's or Tobago's historical development, or the poetry of Aimé Césaire or the novels of Naipaul, Selvon and Lamming. Emphasis on West Indian history and culture is a fundamental objective of the PNM."[36]

Turning more specifically to the party newspaper's vision, and in an obvious reference to another aspect of the *Guardian*'s monopoly as a daily newspaper, Williams revealed that he had urged the editor and the board of directors of the publishing company to increase publication to two issues a week as soon as possible. Furthermore, he stated that since transformation to a daily newspaper would require an enormous capital outlay, the party organization must recognize "a precise obligation to *The Nation* by distributing an agreed number of copies."[37]

Williams noted that the party newspaper was now being printed "exclusively by our own printing machinery and that this machinery was purchased in part from funds subscribed by party members to the Party's Development Programme." The PNM, it was felt, could now rest assured that whatever the political crisis, "we are now independently equipped to meet it and keep our public adequately informed." Finally, Williams revealed that the *Nation* hoped soon to enter "that virgin field which awaits the nationalistic cultivator—the publication locally of books and documents of vital concern to our nationalist movement for the education of the people, the encouragement of our writers and historians, and the elimination of the servile mentality in the West Indies which is nowhere more pronounced than in our continued dependence on European ideas and American popular publications."[38]

Williams's reference to the printing machine and its connection to writing by locally based writers, for whose work the printing machine would create space, was evidence of his understanding of the manner in which Caliban's antihegemonic activity, as far as the literary efforts of Caribbean writers were concerned, would contribute to intellectualism in the region. Williams recognized that their writing would also provide reading material for "students" of the UWS as well as continue to place ideas regarding political independence in the public sphere. Interestingly, however, he did not refer in his speech to the earlier efforts of the magazine the *Beacon,* with which James and Albert Gomes were associated. Nor did he refer to the novels of Alfred Mendes in the mid-1930s or to James's novel *Minty Alley*—about the inhabitants in the yards of Port-of-Spain, whose lived experiences add to the knowledge base of Trinbago—which was first published in 1936 in Trinidad, after his departure for England in 1932.

However, Williams's grand vision for the PNM's newspaper and its efforts to create space in the arena of journalism were not without various recognized problems. By March 1958 the paper had changed its name to the *Nation,* and it secured James's services as editor after his return to Trinidad on 18 April 1958. Notwithstanding James's assertion, on more than one occasion, that he was there to serve Williams and the PNM and never took any major decision without first consulting Williams, James's presence eventually proved to be problematic, as some members of Williams's cabinet felt that so strong was James's influence on Williams that it was working to the detriment of their own political future.[39] Although James did not occupy an electoral office nor, obviously, a cabinet position, he sometimes appeared to be number two in the party. In any event, as had others, James ran afoul of Williams and was later expelled from the party—more accurately, he was gotten rid of—on the false charge of embezzlement of funds, but not before he had resigned from his post as editor of the *Nation.*

James, it seems, had written two letters to Williams expressing his wish to be relieved of his position and had received a reply to neither. On 26 March 1960, for example, James wrote to Williams reminding him that he (James) had always said that given certain conditions, he would "walk out," and that he had reached such a point. James further expressed his respect and regard for Williams, which he said were "as great as I ever have had for anyone." The letter ended with two postscripts, one expressing an exhortation to "organize your Party, Bill, organise your party," and the other advising Williams to stay away from the office for a day or two in order to "penetrate into what I am trying to tell you" before talking.[40] In the second letter, written four days later, James gave "formal notice to the Board of PNM Publishing Company" of his wish to be relieved "as soon as possible of my post as Managing Editor of The Nation." He also expressed the view that he and Williams had "acted too closely together, excluding the Party from all we were doing and wished for *The Nation,*" and that Williams would be better off without him.[41]

In addition to James's emphasis on party organization, which he said often required long, hard work, of contextual relevance was his advice to Williams that the paper should be subordinate to the party and that Williams needed to diversify his activities, as it was not humanly possible for one person to be the chief minister and political leader of the party and also take an active part in the affairs of the newspaper. In his view, this was especially true in Williams's case since Williams "knows nothing about party organization," and would have benefited from a period in opposition.[42] Significantly, James also stated that the "secretary and the editor of the Party press should be elevated to a status not inferior to any legislator."[43] As he put it,

> Ordinarily the editor of a party organ is usually a member of the General Council, a member of the Executive or Management Committee and under ordinary circumstances shares with the Political Leader, the General Secretary and the Organising Secretary the effective leadership of the Party. That in the present instance the editor of a party organ is not a part of the leadership of the Party is a handicap, but the editor brings to the post experience, qualities and a long and intimate acquaintance with the Political Leader which it will not be easy to duplicate.[44]

James expressed the view that "without a deeply rooted party and a daily paper there was no popular movement in the social sense." And in drawing attention to the infrastructure that underpinned the production of knowledge in Western society, James wrote that behind the active politicians "are great universities and institutions of learning, great newspapers, serious journals, individual journalists and writers who probe into political life, philosophical, social, political, economic ideas, theoretical and political."[45] Ironically, if, as has been suggested, James ghost wrote the speech given by Williams titled "Perspectives for Our Party," in reality he and Williams were not too far apart on the issues concerning the role and function of the PNM. Indeed, Selwyn Cudjoe contends that many of the principles articulated in the document were not put into practice because so many of the ideas were James's.[46]

Among the challenges facing intellectualism and the development of the "great public," according to both James and Williams, was obtaining the finances necessary for publishing a daily party paper. All of these, however, presupposed the existence of a reading and buying public, essential antecedents to the production of knowledge that probably did not exist in Trinbago in the late 1950s, which was a reason why the great writers of the Caribbean, though inspired by the Caribbean, had published their work abroad and were based abroad.

It should be noted that in addition to providing employment for the party faithful, the *Nation* also permitted James—whose wife, Selma, also worked hard in producing the paper—at least for a time, to have a stage on which to make known his views on, among other things, the politics of journalism. Kent Worcester notes, for example, that James used the pages of the paper to advocate the appointment of Frank Worrell, a Black man, as captain of the West Indies cricket team, and to advocate in favor of West Indies federation, thereby placing the matter in the public sphere. With respect to Worrell, James wrote that it was the "constant, vigilant, bold and shameless manipulation of players to exclude black captains that has so demoralized West Indian teams and exasperated the people. . . . The more brilliantly the black man played, the more it would emphasize to millions of English people: 'Yes, they are fine players, but funny, isn't it, they cannot be responsible for themselves—they must always have a White man to lead them.'"[47]

Ironically, much the same sentiments had previously been expressed by Learie Constantine, with whom James was in close contact when they lived in England. Constantine had contended that the captaincy in the hands of a White man as a matter of custom rather than merit militated against the optimum performance of West Indian cricket teams. In referring to the 1930 West Indian team's tour of Australia, when the White West Indian cricket captain G. C. Grant went straight from Cambridge University and met the team in the West Indies before its departure to Australia, Constantine wrote:

> I think the time has come to speak out plainly what I mean in this matter of West Indian captaincy. It is not only what *I* mean—every coloured player who has ever turned out in an international side has been conscious of it, and it rots the heart out of our cricket, and always will until it is changed. The West Indies teams, mainly composed as they always are of coloured players, should have a coloured captain. . . . I venture to make a prophecy. It is that before I die I shall see a West Indian team, chosen on merit alone, captained by a black player, with a rubber against England.[48]

Interestingly, Williams previously had lauded James and his services in October 1958, referring to James as "Trinidad's brilliant son," whose name "when the story comes to be written of the fight in Trinidad and Tobago for full internal self-government and West Indian independence, with his editorials and columns in *The Nation,* will have its rightful place at the very top of the roll of honour."[49] Winston Mahabir recalls that even before he and his wife were formally introduced, at the home of a PNM supporter, to an individual whom he did not recognize and around whom a number of guests had gathered, he thought to himself that "whoever he was, that was the man whom Williams was imitating. That man was C. L. R. James. We met him later that evening. His manner of speech, his ideas, his mannerisms—they were all Williams magnified."[50] However, Mahabir suggests that Williams apparently dropped James when he became convinced that James's ideology

> was unsuited to the temper and needs of the West Indian times. But James' ideology was no secret. He had always been forthright and even boastful about it. Williams had sustained an active and passive association with this ideology for thirty years. Williams had kept in active touch with James throughout the years. He had consulted him on the first P.N.M. manifesto. It was Williams who brought James back to Trinidad. James was lionized by Williams who commandeered his services for the party newspaper which James rescued partially from its increasing insipidity. It was James who helped to develop the case for Chaguaramas.[51]

Alas, by considering himself to be the *master,* and Williams the *pupil,* in their relationship, James unwittingly may have contributed to his own political demise. For it is in the nature of the master-pupil relationship that once the pupil has reached a level of knowledge attainment, he is ready to become a master in his own right. In any event, not only were Woodford Square and the PNM newspaper instrumental in the formation of the "University of Woodford Square," as arenas for the education of the masses regarding nationalism, they contributed, significantly, to the continuing existence of the "great public" in Trinidad and Tobago. This included not merely individuals who, like Williams, produced and disseminated knowledge but others who attended, listened to, and discussed his views regarding political independence in various public spaces, such as the Public Library and Woodford Square, as well as in various schools and Behind the Bridge.

5 Exploiting the Political-Opportunity Structure

The Emergence of the People's National Movement Party

Magnum est PNM et praevalebit—Great is the PNM and it will prevail

The PNM Stands for Knowledgeism
—Unemployed seaman's phrasing of the PNM Party motto

IN THIS CHAPTER I focus on another facet of Williams's ongoing transition to a social-movement intellectual and his efforts to secure space for the role. He and other movement intellectuals sought to expand the nationalist movement through the establishment of the People's National Movement as a social-movement organization. The PNM, which came into existence on 26 January 1956, was the twin island's first mass-based political party. Accordingly, I will examine the manner in which the PNM's emergence opened up opportunities for intellectual labor, first, by utilizing previously organized entities; second, by promulgating a party philosophy that was unique to Trinidad and Tobago, and third, by recognizing and seizing the occasion, not previously taken advantage of, to enter the political system as a mass-based political party.

Analysts of social movements have defined social-movement organizations as formal organizations that emphasize and seek to achieve specific objectives related to the goals of a social movement.[1] The objectives of a movement like the political-independence struggle involved impacting major political decisions concerning a wide range of issues, such as universal adult suffrage; a bicameral legislature; meaningful participation in the economy; free secondary education for all who were capable of benefitting from it, regardless of race, ethnicity, class, or religious persuasion; and, as will be seen, the removal of unilaterally imposed foreign bases like that at Chaguaramas in Trinidad, to name a few. While it is true, as the case of Trinidad and Tobago illustrates, that these objectives might be most meaningfully articulated by a political party, in this case the PNM, it is also true, as John McCarthy and Mayer Zald maintain, that preference structures might be serviced by a number of other social-movement organizations.[2] These preference structures include voluntary associations, trade unions, and organizations that represent various occupational groups, such as those that represented teachers in Trinidad and Tobago.

Students of social movements have emphasized the importance of participants' forming a collective identity, or a sense of "we-ness," which separates them from others and links them to the preference structure of the movement and which in and of itself has a specific meaning for participants. This collective identity, according to Alberto Melucci, is facilitated by the existence of previously existing organized entities. These organized entities, which are "submerged" in the daily life of individuals, constitute part of the process by which actors produce meaning, communicate with one another, negotiate especially with the challenged, and make decisions regarding the goals of the movement. Submerged networks, furthermore, tend to be hidden, emerging only when a group of collective-action participants deem such to be necessary. And because members of a submerged network have previously worked together in pursuit of a common goal, a sense of collective identity will already have been established before the network surfaces.[3]

Previously organized entities, or halfway houses, as Aldon Morris calls them,[4] are only partially integrated into the larger society and therefore do not achieve national prominence. However, they may also enable a social-movement organization such as a political party to more easily mobilize individuals, and its leaders to forge a collective identity. Belinda Robnett suggests that previously organized entities may also function as "bridge" organizations, connecting the formal leadership of the movement with the community.[5] Thus, the intellectual labor of Williams and other movement intellectuals who held active membership in a number of previously organized entities was instrumental in facilitating the emergence of the PNM.

IN TRINBAGO, one such group was known as the Bachacs. According to Winston Mahabir, in late 1954 Williams initiated a weekly study group known as the Bachacs, the name given to "those fantastic ants whose characteristics include the ability to destroy apparently healthy plants—especially imported rose bushes—by a team effort involving a sophisticated communication system."[6] As the etymologist Richard

Allsopp notes, these ants carry pieces of green leaves to their nests to feed on later.[7] Apparently, the intent of the group was to reflect upon and later attack the existing colonial party system before replacing it with a variant more in keeping with the needs of the society. In other words, there would be an autochthonous dimension to anticolonial activity on the twin island by Williams and other movement intellectuals. Besides Mahabir, whom Williams had met while Mahabir was a medical student at McGill University in Canada, the group included Ibbit Mosaheb, who had first met Williams while he was a student at Howard University, and Halsey McShine, whom Williams had known at Queen's Royal College.[8]

Other members of the Bachacs included Norman Girwar, later associated with the Cane Farmers Association; Telford Georges, later to become chief justice of Tanzania; Claire Sloane-Seales; Dr. George Wattley, a leading island internist; Edward Lee, a former mayor of San Fernando; Gerard Montano; Donald Granado; and Dennis Mahabir, the brother of Winston Mahabir. According to Winston Mahabir, the group saw itself as "nibbling away at every plant—especially transplants—in the socioeconomic political order of Trinidad and Tobago[, which activity] by co-operative endeavor and understanding of communication patterns would build a symbolic nest of knowledge and competence."[9] As submerged networks are prone to do, the Bachacs, whose members provided "half of the first Party cabinet" (Williams, Granado, Montano, and Winston Mahabir), the first party mayor of Port-of-Spain (Dennis Mahabir), and the first party mayor of San Fernando (Mosaheb), dissolved once some members felt that enough had been achieved to warrant more positive action.

Consequently, after Williams's departure from the Caribbean Commission, at a late-night meeting with Elton Richardson, Mosaheb, and Winston Mahabir, who Williams had summoned to his posh Lady Chancellor Road residence, he asked what he should do next. Williams followed Richardson's advice that he replace his huge American Buick with a British-made "modest Vauxhall" car and change his residence to Woodbrook, a less upscale neighborhood. However, it was only following discussions that culminated with Williams's "first major, undisguised, public, political testament on the subject 'Why I left the Caribbean Commission'" that, for some, his political ambitions surfaced and the idea of a political party began to take shape.

Granado recalls that while returning to Port-of-Spain after a meeting with Richardson, the latter mentioned that he and Williams had been talking about the possibility of forming another group to take political education to the people of Trinidad and Tobago. Williams had requested that Granado be invited to join the group because of his varied background, popularity, and participation in so many different aspects of life on the twin island. Later, during a meeting attended by Richardson, Mosaheb, Granado, and David Nelson, who came to be a trusted associate of Williams's presumably because, among other things, he was employed by the *Trinidad Guardian,* it was agreed that Granado should form the Political Education Group (PEG) for the purpose of educating the people in politics.[10]

Still later, Wilfrid Alexander and his brother Felix, as well as the teachers De Wilton Rogers and John Donaldson, were invited because of their connection with another previously organized entity—the Teachers' Economic and Cultural Association (TECA)—to help organize the PEG's education program. In addition, Isabel Teshea, Kamal Mohammed, Cecil Alexander, Andrew Carr, Harold Duprey, Winston and Dennis Mahabir, Gerard Montano, and Eustace Piggott became members, by invitation, as the number of PEG members increased from the original nine to fifty. The PEG, which emerged out of the Bachacs, according to Granado, became the precursor of the PNM, and the Bachacs then became defunct. Meetings were held all over the territory, and it was only then, Granado notes, that it became clear to him that "the intention all along was to go into politics, and to form a Political Party. Such was my naiveté."[11]

The emergence of the PNM opened up other opportunities for the expenditure of intellectual labor. Wilfrid Alexander recalls, for example, that the PNM's entry on the political stage involved an effort to assess and reject various possibilities before agreeing on a particular position for the party, an effort that, conceivably, was more processual than linear.[12] This is important because the activities of previously organized entities, which tend to have an active political life of their own and to precede the emergence of social-movement organizations, are usually neglected by resource-mobilization theorists.[13]

Alexander contends, furthermore, that the PNM had its genesis in the activities and argumentative discourse of PEG members, not the Bachacs, which were taking place behind the back of officialdom. Moreover, the formation of the PEG was "neither deliberately conceived nor planned." Rather, it grew out of private discussions in the aftermath of informal gatherings and was to some extent inspired by Williams's series of public lectures and talks. Significantly, although the PEG was not a group of "intellectuals or for intellectuals"—it was a heterogeneous group of discerning individuals who were very much concerned with the social and political ills of the time—its activities were characterized by a certain amount of intellectualism. As Alexander asserts, while the PEG was not the only group with which the eventual leaders of the PNM were associated, it is misleading to claim, as others have done, that any other group was the immediate precursor of the PNM.[14]

From a programmatic standpoint, the PEG also found it necessary to devolve into various committees, concerned with its program and constitution, intelligence and propaganda, education, finance and economics, and elections. These activities involved a tremendous expenditure of intellectual labor directed toward whether the group should devolve into a new party or seek incorporation into one of the existing parties. Further, as the group's membership increased to one hundred and consequent upon the formation of various committees, the serious preparation for the emergence of a new party began, as the ideas and philosophy that eventually crystallized into the People's Charter and the constitution were developed and formalized.

Ironically, the momentous decision to form a new party, Alexander maintains, was approached with "tremendous hesitation." In the spirit of "argumentative debate," various ideas were entertained, and the constitution, philosophy, ideology, program, and prospects for success of every existing party, insofar as they could be ascertained, *"were all tested in the crucible of critical analysis."* It was no surprise, therefore, that "every existing party was found wanting. It was only after this definitive research, that with calm deliberation and scientific justification the final decision was eventually taken that the only hope for the country was the launching of a new political party."[15]

However, having decided to form a new party and having assessed the uncertainly of the political waters, the group concluded that the people needed to be politically educated. That is why, Alexander asserts, the PNM's slogan became "Political Education," which meant embarking on a resocialization process that involved not only *teaching for learning* but also *teaching for unlearning*.[16] Anyone, therefore, with even a nodding acquaintance with the subsequent activities of the party and the political-independence movement could not fail to recognize the hand of Eric Williams in the formation of the mantra of the People's National Movement.

The final stage of the PEG's political activities, according to Alexander, involved the preparation of a constitution and a program, which was entrusted to a special committee whose members included Ray Robinson,

Wilfrid Alexander, and Eric Williams. These individuals worked with unflagging zeal and energy to produce the original constitution and the People's Charter, despite many physical, emotional, and financial obstacles. Because of their importance and their deep relevance to the process involved in knowledge production and the creation of space in the political system, the production of the abovementioned documents, Alexander maintains, also involved the utilization of a great amount of intellectual labor. The "clash of ideas, ideals, of isms and ideologies, of doctrines and philosophies, the debates and discussions over forms and phrases that went into the making of these documents, and the fight over these things," which resulted in "at least four manuscript drafts of the constitution, and no fewer than three of the original charter," meant that no political party in the world could have boasted of "more democracy in its machinery."[17] The formation of the party, therefore, occurred in stages, and the process was dialectical in nature.

BECAUSE OF Williams's status as a professional historian and academic intellectual, it was decided that initially he should be the main speaker at public meetings but that others would also be called upon to speak as it became necessary. This was the inception of what Pierre Bourdieu calls the process of professionalization, in which the political means of production, that is, the means by which political programs, policies, and—the most obvious manifestation—political parties, with their own bureaucratic structures, full-time officials, and so on, are concentrated in the hands of professional politicians. Political dispossession, according to Bourdieu, is a two-step process that, apart from the establishment of a permanent office and a bureaucracy with paid officials, such as a political party, involves the provision of a mandate and a *mandataire,* the holder of the mandate, who speaks on behalf of the group—in this case Williams—to be distinguished from the mandator, who provides the mandate.[18]

However, giving an individual the right to speak on behalf of a group, which involves the consecration or canonization of the incumbent, Bourdieu notes further, is likely to divorce that individual from those who are most deprived of economic capital, in whose name the holder of the mandate claims to speak.[19] This is precisely what occurred, according to Granado, in the early stages of the PEG's existence. It had been decided that Williams "must submit a draft of any speech that he was to deliver in public before presentation."[20]

The draft could be done in outline form. Granado recalls that on one occasion, however, after the group had reviewed the draft of his proposed speech, Williams responded that he was not going to deliver the speech on the grounds that it was not "his speech," whereupon he was told "very definitely that it was precisely because it was not his speech that he was going to present it—'It is the Group's speech.' It was in this way that Williams, who did not always consult with members of the group, gradually gained ascendancy within the group."[21] Williams's action is noteworthy because it was a very early example of a predisposition on his part to defend an individual position at the expense of that of the group and a disinclination to adhere to the expectations of the group that provided him with the mandate.

Granado also notes that with all his academic brilliance, Williams was a neophyte in dealing with an ordinary crowd of people, although this was not intended to detract from his performance. Nonetheless, Williams "learnt quickly and decisively," and in the social context of Trinbago, where the ability to articulate one's thoughts orally was prized, he thrived mightily. Using the spoken word as a tool for educating the masses and articulating various concerns, however, did not mean that the audience always understood what Williams was saying. On one occasion, for example, when Williams had spoken before a "large crowd exuding interest and enthusiasm," the crowd had applauded while he was speaking, without hearing what he was saying. Williams, nevertheless, was moved to remark to Granado afterwards, "Donald, we have these people." Granado recalls, "I told him that half of those people did not understand one word of what he said, but he did not agree."[22]

Apart from the importance of the cultural matrix in which knowledge is generated and the social movement is located, as the above comment with respect to the crowd's enthusiasm illustrates, it is also important to note that the public response to the PEG was tremendous. This was because the public sensed that at long last some persons with know-how had so much consideration for the ordinary people—in contrast with the politics of "anything goes" and individual brokering—that they were taking the trouble to bring information to the people, information that they had never had and never expected to have. As a resource in the service of collective action, therefore, "Williams's analytical mind was exactly what was needed at the time," writes Granado, "and, with his professed dedication to Trinidad and Tobago, his abundant knowledge, his sincerity and his willingness to share his knowledge and experience with 'lesser' mortals, he was aptly qualified to be dubbed 'Messiah.'"[23]

The acquisition of the mandate was, for Williams, a critical stage in the transformation from public to social-movement intellectual and represented the use of cultural capital and symbolic power to achieve space in the political spectrum. As Elton Richardson notes, the reason why he joined the Bachacs and why Williams formed the group was that they hoped to gain knowledge, especially of a historical nature, by participating in the anticolonial struggle.[24]

However, as the political situation in the colony continued to change, the political momentum of the PEG increased, *pari passu,* as preparations were made for the upcoming general election, constitutionally due in June 1955. In September 1955, for example, the group helped sponsor and promote Williams's "Memorial on Constitutional Reform" to the secretary of state for the colonies. During his July 1955 speech on constitution reform, Williams proposed *(a)* the abolition of the single-chamber Legislative Council; *(b)* a lower house of elected members; *(c)* a second chamber of sixteen nominated members; and *(d)* that the majority leader of the house be appointed by the governor and the chief minister. He clearly envisaged a reduction in the power of the governor in favor of an elected group of legislators, among whom the chief minister would be paramount, and a role for business and religious leaders as nominated members. The Memorial on Constitution Reform met with such favor among the public that within thirty hours of its release for signatures, six thousand persons, including legislators and city councilors, had signed it.[25] Signatures were collected from all and sundry at the many lectures Williams delivered in various parts of the colony from July 1955 to 3 September 1955.

Not surprisingly, during the course of his lecture titled "The Case for Party Politics in Trinidad and Tobago," on 15 September 1955, Williams announced his and his colleagues' intention to form a new political party, which he said was modeled after the People's National Party in Jamaica and was the only party in the West Indies that based its policy on "democratic discussions and decisions of the people." And, while Williams did not then name the persons associated with him in forming the party or give the party's name, it was felt that because of his "good sense of timing," as well as his "flair for the theatrical," he would likely release further particulars at a moment he deemed more propitious.[26] By early December 1955 the PNM's constitution and the People's Charter had been drafted and were ready for presentation to the party's inaugural conference. Then, on 15 January 1956, Williams announced to a select group of associates and supporters the following elected officers of the new party:

Political Leader:	Dr. Eric Williams
Chairman:	Learie N. Constantine
Vice-Chairman:	Dr. Ibbit Mosaheb
Second Vice-Chairman:	Wilfrid. J. Alexander
Lady Vice-Chairman:	Mrs. Isabel Teshea
Education Secretary:	De Wilton Rogers
Public Relations Secretary:	Andrew Carr
Labour Relations Secretary:	Samuel F. Worrell[27]

As can be seen, the party leadership at that time sought to include various, but not all, constituencies in its makeup, and with the exception of Worrell, all of the elected officers had been mentioned before as being active in the formation of the party. Also, in addition to the inclusion of Mrs. Teshea, whose selection, as was noted, spoke to the recognition of the importance of women, the inclusion of Constantine, who had been helped by C. L. R. James in England to prepare for the entrance exams that enabled him to read law while he played league cricket in that country,[28] was a coup for Williams. This was because, despite many requests to align himself politically upon his return to Trinidad, the famous West Indian cricketer had "heretofore been on record as undesirous of engaging in politics."[29]

An Afro-Trinidadian who had risen from circumstances that were humble in every sense of the word, Constantine, who was born in Trinidad in 1902, had overcome the hurdles colonialism placed in his way and used cricket as a lever for upward social mobility. According to Frank Birbalsingh, spectators in England attended a match mainly to see Constantine field.[30] Moreover, Constantine's "was probably the most varied career of any Westindian cricketer: not only politics, diplomacy, writing, law and broadcasting, but the twin causes of racial justice and Westindian Independence, which he cherished most of all. If all this sounds too grand for a man to achieve in one lifetime, consider its grandeur as the achievement of the grandson of a slave!"[31]

While in England, apart from qualifying as a lawyer, Constantine also wrote seven books, six of them on cricket, including one that dealt with the techniques of the game and portended similar books by West Indian cricketers who followed in his footsteps. He was a member of Williams's government from 1956 to 1961, and he was the high commissioner of Trinidad and Tobago in London from 1961 to 1964. During his tenure as high commissioner, however, he made a statement deploring the Bristol Omnibus Company's policy of not employing "coloured bus drivers." As a result of his outspoken views and other actions, the company reversed its position. Constantine's actions apparently earned Williams's displeasure, and after failing to meet with Williams during a subsequent visit to Trinidad, Constantine returned to England and tendered his resignation as high commissioner.

Williams and the PNM were also able to attract the support of Jeffrey Stollmeyer, another former West Indian cricketer and a member of a prominent White Trinidadian family.[32] In a letter to *Time* magazine dated 9 October 1956 in which he in part explained his decision and which was published in the *PNM Weekly,* Stollmeyer criticized *Time*'s contention that Williams had formed the PNM along racial lines from among the polyglot colony's three hundred thousand Negroes. Stollmeyer observed that the ethnic and racial tensions to which the magazine referred were not of Williams's making and that with its polyglot population "in this small outpost we have a Heaven-sent opportunity to show the world how persons of different races, colours, and creeds can live together, as equals, in harmony. Moreover, under the leadership of such Movements as the PNM the opportunity becomes more easy of realisation."[33] Stollmeyer's decision was all the more relevant because, as a member of a moneyed, White family and therefore a "conscience constituent," he did not stand to gain directly from the attainment of the movement's goal of political independence. On the contrary, given the tenor of the times, he and his family stood to lose by his association with the PNM.

However, after a few finishing touches, on Tuesday, 24 January 1956, during a moment obviously deemed to be appropriate, the People's National Movement was presented to the people. This took place during a "solemn and historic launching ceremony" at the UWS presided over by the party chairman, Learie Constantine, before a crowd variously estimated at "from three to five thousand persons." It was, Granado recalls, the "largest crowd ever seen at Woodford Square, reportedly there was no room whatever, and even the streets were jammed with people."[34]

ANOTHER PREVIOUSLY organized entity that was instrumental in Williams's emergence as a social-movement intellectual and the PNM's emergence as a social-movement organization, according to De Wilton Rogers, was the Teachers' Economic and Cultural Association, of which Rogers was the director general and Wilfrid Alexander was the secretary general. Indeed, the TECA sponsored and published many of Williams's speeches. The accounts of Rogers and Alexander are particularly significant in view of the rather terse mention in Williams's published biography of their role in ensuring that all "these people" were present, for example, when he made his "let my bucket right down in politics" comment during his speech titled "My Relations with the Caribbean Commission" on 21 June 1955. This speech, it will be recalled, dealt with Williams's departure from the Caribbean Commission and was viewed by various individuals as his coming-out statement regarding his entry into formal politics and the leadership of the political-independence movement.

Although it came into existence in 1939, the TECA was not formally established until July 1942.[35] Besides Rogers, the other founding members of the TECA were John S. Donaldson, W. J. Alexander, A. A. Alexander, Cecil Alexander, and Donald Pierre, who were all young male Roman Catholic teachers. Among the aims of the TECA were "to co-ordinate and synthesise all movements for the economic and cultural advance of the teacher, to stimulate the social progress of the people," and "to promote functions, lectures, scholarships, and studies for the cultural advance of its members."[36] These aims were in harmony with Williams's role as a political educator. Later, a women's council of the TECA was established. Because of its concern with a broad range of women's problems, it held a number of meetings and rallies in support of, for example, equal pay for women teachers. As a bridge organization, therefore, the TECA, with its connection to teachers, who were not necessarily part of the formal leadership of the PNM, was in a position to contribute to the nationalist cause.

This effort on the part of the TECA was also facilitated by its connection with Tobago. John Donaldson, for instance, had spent many years as a head teacher in Tobago and was also a leader of the "island's social life in music and its politico-economic struggle among teachers and their forebears." Rogers himself had at one time been Tobago's representative in the Teachers' Union and, as a consequence, had paid regular visits to the island, where he was well known among the teachers and peasants. In a statement that underlined the potential for collective action that was part of Tobago's very existence and the mechanisms that were used to mobilize the teachers, Rogers noted that these men were "in the vineyard already where Donaldson had begun . . . garnering the widow's mite from the teachers there and showing the way towards the potential of a vast Teachers' Co-operative. It was not, then, by chance but by design that the People's Education Movement was first launched in Tobago."[37]

In reflecting on the salience of education, W. J. Alexander, then Rogers's deputy, wrote in a message to women teachers, "We are what our education makes us. . . . Excellent ideas in themselves must remain idle dreams as long as we are not taught a way of life and have not even the wherewithal to live! Only proper education will teach us to demand what we want. We are such sheep as our so-called education makes us." In commenting on why the teacher was best suited for the task in hand Rogers opined that "the teacher is strategically placed to move forward on the wave of unrest. The reason is there for everyone to see. The teacher as a concerted body rallying around a focal point is formidable. The leaven of womanhood is ever and omnipresent."[38]

In his published autobiography Williams gives very short shrift to the TECA's contribution to the mobilization of the teachers and to the existence of the TECA and its cultural arm, the Political Education Movement, or PEM, whose motto was "Whomsoever will may come." Williams also fails to mention the contribution of the various regional committees and secretaries, who, as bridge leaders, were instrumental in the creation of a dissident anticolonial subculture and whose activities therefore functioned as a launching pad for the formation of the PNM. In fact, Williams contends that with the experience of the British Labour Party in mind, the PNM party was "careful not to allow our Movement to be dominated by the trade union block vote," although provision was made for "affiliation of any democratic trade union, friendly, co-operative or credit society, professional, technical, cultural or sports association, or women's or youth group."[39]

Rogers recalled that on the night of the 21 June 1955 speech, dealing with his relations with the Caribbean Commission, Williams had turned to him and Donaldson and asked where the twenty thousand listeners had come from. This was perhaps when Williams began to recognize that as he transitioned from public intellectual to social-movement intellectual, there was an available "audience," or public, and that henceforth he would not be talking to himself about the relevance of his ideas and his vision regarding political independence. Rogers and Donaldson might have replied that while he was encamped in the manner of a recluse in Kent House or the Trinidad Public Library or the libraries of the world, they were laboring in the vineyards on his behalf and on that of social change. In any event, "No trade union then, nor now," Rogers continued, "could marshall such a host on its own steam."[40] It was due to the patient and unflagging organizing efforts of the TECA, its arm, and its members.

These observations notwithstanding, in his capacity as deputy chairman of the Research Council of the Caribbean Commission, Williams continued to be courted by the TECA. For instance, in June 1950 he had been approached by Rogers about becoming a consultant for the TECA, to which Williams agreed, his letter of acceptance testifying to his reasons for doing so, namely, the benefits of his association with the Caribbean Commission and the need to change West Indian complacency. In the letter, which dealt in part with the colonial mentality of some Trinbagonians, which Williams believed was in need of change, he noted that

> I have always had the view that the work of organisations such as the Caribbean Commission can very easily degenerate into a mere collection of papers and documents unless some vitality is injected into it by the people whom it is designed to serve. In addition, as you know, I am consistently fighting against that West Indian complacency which is prepared to sit down and await official pontification, to applaud publicly and grumble privately, and I feel that wherever possible, the people, the ordinary people should be encouraged and stimulated to look themselves into the problems of the area, discuss them and develop their own point of view. I am prepared to work with any organisation which has the same point of view. Within the limitation of my time, therefore, and subject to my official responsibilities, I shall be very happy to work with you.[41]

As a quid pro quo to his serving as a consultant, each member of the TECA was invited to pledge to sell to all teachers copies of Williams's book *Education in the British West Indies*. While this is not to suggest that Williams sought to gain financially from the sale of his book, doubtless this was another effort on his part to avail himself of the opportunity as an intellectual to disseminate his knowledge by way of a specific market, and to an audience that recognized the relevance of his ideas regarding education and nationalism. For example, a public lecture titled "Economic Problems of Trinidad and Tobago," which he gave at the UWS on 5 July 1955, was later published as a pamphlet under the auspices of the People's Education Movement of the TECA.

DESPITE THE significant contribution of women to Williams's becoming a social-movement intellectual, the story of their part in the mobilizing efforts of both Williams and the PNM within the nationalist movement has remained largely untold.[42] Indeed, that story has been omitted both by Williams in his published autobiography and by Rogers in his own effort, which he referred to as "an excursus and biography." Rhoda Reddock's account is therefore instructive because it describes the social structure of Trinidad and Tobago in the early 1940s and 1950s, which facilitated the efforts of Williams and the PNM. She notes, for example, that Mrs. Isabel Teshea, an early elected PNM member, was no stranger to politics on the twin island when she was elected to a leadership position in the PNM, having previously led the islandwide Federation of Women's Institutes, which was brought within the ambit of the PEM and, later, the PNM itself.

Further, as was noted, a major impetus for the emergence of the TECA was the dual-control system of education, which enabled the clergy to exercise great control over the professional activities of teachers, who complained of victimization if they strayed from the official line and if their religion differed from that of a particular denomination. The years 1946–51, therefore, saw a number of rallies held under the auspices of the Women's Council of the TECA, which drew hundreds of women teachers into a sphere of political activity oriented toward improving their condition. As a result of their activities, which were supported by Rogers and the TECA, the women teachers were eventually able to achieve parity in pay with their male counterparts.

No doubt, Williams, astute politician that he was, recognized the importance of garnering the support of women in the movement. Years later, in connection with the exposure of women to education, especially at the university level, he would write regarding the system of social differentiation that worked against women that in its "adult education programme, even more than on the undergraduate level, the University should have a special part to play in the education of women, who are still so heavily handicapped by their economic status and the traditional conception of the role of women in society."[43] Marilyn Gordon, a former PNM cabinet minister, in referring to the connection between women and the PNM and Williams's role, noted that

> in the early 1950s the large majority of women in this country were basically not involved in the politics of the country. Few of them dared to become involved, mainly because of the social environment of the time. Most of the women were housewives. Some were employed in the traditional professions of teaching and nursing. Others worked in the Public Service, in stores, as domestics, or seamstresses. There were very few female doctors. By 1956, with the advent of the People's National Movement, large numbers of women, particularly of the middle and lower socio-economic groups went to the University of Woodford Square to receive their political education from Dr. Williams. They got caught up in the excitement of the period and many of them became some of the most loyal and hardworking members of the People's National Movement.[44]

Additionally, Gordon notes that Williams sought to harness the potential and support of women by including in the PNM structure a women's arm, known as the Women's League, which comprised units from each constituency and whose membership was open to any female member of the party. However, only about half of the women chose to join the Women's League.

Although women were visible in the 1956 election as platform speakers, organizers of motorcades, and volunteer babysitters on election day and had assumed responsibility for checking electoral lists to ensure that the names of PNM supporters were included, the 1956 electoral slate of twenty-four PNM candidates contained no women.[45] Women were an integral part of the movement for political independence, which performed many tasks critical to Williams's and the PNM's success in winning a majority of seats in the important 1956 election. In fact, Reddock contends that "Williams's establishment and maintenance of this link with the 'grassroots women' was the main source of the party's strength and in fact the secret of its survival."[46]

Finally, it has been suggested that even Williams's small physical stature might have worked in his favor when it came to mobilizing and raising the consciousness of the masses, especially those on the distaff side. Because of his physical stature he was viewed, especially by females, as being "nashy," variously defined in Trinidad as "thin," "skinny," "small bodied,"[47] and, in Williams's case, as "in need of protection." Some of these women were known as the "fat ass brigade" because of the size of a certain part of their anatomy.[48] However, Williams was sometimes able to convert even the female detractors to his politics. For example, after a lecture on 27 January 1956 a "big, sturdy, sinewy, smooth Black female, wrapped him in her arms and enveloped him in her tresses so that for a moment he could not be seen" before uttering the words, "I love you Bad." When Rogers later asked how he had felt, Williams allegedly replied, "Mind your own business."[49]

NOT ALL aggregations that contributed to the emergence of the PNM could claim to have been organized, at least not in a formal sense. One such group that could not make such a claim was the habitués of another physical space in the capital of Port-of-Spain, the space De Wilton Rogers refers to as Behind the Bridge. This public space was located east of the "University of Woodford Square," near the confluence of streets that leads into the UWS. These individuals, who can also be described as a "bridge aggregation" with respect to the PNM, helped to expand Williams's "public" as he transitioned from public intellectual to social-movement intellectual and were also part of a dissident subculture that existed largely beyond the gaze of colonial officials. For example, the area had its own pharmacy, which provided a variety of folk and formally scientific remedies for the inhabitants and also brought individuals together; and the pharmacist acted as an adviser and healer and in many other capacities. As a physical space the pharmacy was "the hub of primary relationships with the pharmacist or druggist as the Public Relations Officer or propagandist." In fact, the apothecary's influence over his clients was even greater than the priest's influence over his parishioners.[50]

In addition, the area contained schools, a group of well-known teachers, many of whom were members of the PEM, and headmasters such as Ernest Quinlan and Robert James, C. L. R. James's father, who became legends in their own time. Then there were the "bad johns" and various other characters, such as Paulina, the man beater; Matil, who could butt like a cow; and the police sergeant, usually a six-footer. The area also served for a time as the city headquarters of Uriah Butler, the chief servant of the Home Rule Party. Finally, the existence of various unpatrolled sites such as rum shops, barber shops, and tailor shops, provided a locale for antihegemonic discourse regarding the colonial condition and the nutriment of a dissident subculture.

Most important, however, the area had its own culture of discourse, which took the form of open-air meetings in its own space, or its own "university," invariably under the lamplight. Participants debated who was the better lawyer, Gaston Johnson or L. C. Hannays, and discussed cricket and cricketers and, eventually, Eric Williams, at the time viewed as a mystery man buried in his Research Council of the Caribbean Commission. Indeed, especially after his famous debate with Dom Basil Matthews, Williams was described as the "most learned man in Trinidad today." He would later be elevated to the status of the sixth most learned man in the world, "better than Don [*sic*] Basil."[51] In fine, not only did the pariah intellectuals from Behind the Bridge have a discursive subculture that involved the lionization and mythologizing of individuals who were considered to be heroes but that discourse, from the perspective of Habermas, constituted a public space that was not bourgeois in origin.[52]

By the time Williams gave his speech "My Relations with the Caribbean Commission, 1943–1955," and consequent upon the mobilizing efforts of Rogers and Donaldson, "two teacher friends" to whom Williams had referred, a culture of argumentative debate had already been put in place in the Behind the Bridge area. This allowed Williams to educate the thousands who showed up for his lectures regarding the dynamics of colonialism and anticolonialism, which were given under the auspices of the PEM and enabled him to further construct a "great public" in Trinbago. Also, by the time Williams delivered the four other lectures in the series, from July to September 1955, under similar sponsorship and later published by the TECA, the topics of the Behind the Bridge discussions had changed from cricket and other matters—such as who was the better lawyer, Gaston Johnson or L. C. Hannays, both of whom had excelled in the practice of law; or which was preferable, the Trinity of the white man, comprising Pounds, Shillings, and Pence, or the Black man's Trinity, comprising Father, Son, and Holy Ghost—to public affairs and issues more germane to the condition of the oppressed. Williams, furthermore, had been transformed from the "mystery" inhabitant of Kent House (the official headquarters of the Caribbean Commission) to, in the words of one observer, the man who "taught me more about myself in one night than I knew in my whole lifetime. I dey wid him."[53] Since movement participants are more likely to be involved in collective action if they become convinced of the credibility and legitimacy of participation, the observation of the above Behind the Bridge inhabitant suggests that as a public intellectual Williams had achieved the required credibility and therefore legitimacy. The four lectures in question, about which more will be said in the next chapter, were "Economic Problems of Trinidad and Tobago," delivered on 5 July; "Constitution Reform in Trinidad and Tobago," on 19 July; "The Historical Background of Race Relations in the Caribbean," on 16 August; and "The Case for Party Politics in Trinidad and Tobago," on 13 September.

The activities of the lamplighters operating Behind the Bridge constituted another aspect of the hidden transcript, that of the antihegemonic discourse that takes place beyond the direct observation of power holders.[54] This was the case, first, because the activities of the Behind the Bridge inhabitants had occurred in a particular space and involved individuals qua confidants who shared similar experiences involving colonial domination. Second, these activities, coming as they were from an officially unpatrolled space, had permitted participants to express their discontent in an unreserved manner, whereby, in James C. Scott's words, "the unspoken riposte, stifled anger, and bitten tongues created by relations of domination find a vehement, full-throated expression."[55]

These socially marginal individuals were not only generators but also transmitters and, perhaps most important, *creators* and *innovators* of a culture that became part of the nation's cultural apparatus. As Jeff Henry notes, the inhabitants of Behind the Bridge, in preparation for Mas—the event that took place on Jouvay morning, the Monday morning that marked the beginning of Carnival—made all of the costumes used in Carnival. The Behind the Bridge inhabitants "learned not only the techniques of costume construction, such as collecting and stripping young bambu, bending wire, sewing, decorating and painting costumes," Henry informs us, "but were also taught where to go in the forest and what materials to search for in order to locate the right seeds or substances to mix paints." Nothing was acquired "from abroad," Henry assures us, and "most ideas and products came from the vision of ordinary men and women, not from the Shores of London, New York, China or India. The Mas nurtured a thriving cottage industry of young artists."[56] It is not too difficult, therefore, to comprehend the relevance of the geographical location of Behind the Bridge as a social space embedded with specific meanings. To be sure, these pariah intellectuals, Rogers notes, were instrumental in populating many of the audiences that attended Williams's anticolonial renderings at the "University of Woodford Square."

As OTHERS have stated, names that social-movement organizations adopt are important because names often seek to embody, if only programmatically, the ideals and aspirations of the movement. The importance of a name, especially the name of a political party in the context of nationalism, is all the more significant because efforts must be made to separate the social-movement organization from other organized entities, both past and present, in order to continue the construction of a collective identity that is distinctive.[57] Equally important is that the naming process may be related to some facet of the culture of the society and thereby becomes part of the cultural capital of a particular historical moment. Furthermore, the naming process lends itself to competition for discursive and political space for the movement, as societies "are imagining more than their present and future; they also imagine their pasts."[58]

Lastly, as will be seen, while selecting a name can generate strategic resources for the organization, the adoption of a name draws boundaries around the organization such that some claims become more meaningful, and others less so. Boundary delineation, therefore, lends itself to a them-versus-us affiliation-disaffiliation that, typically in the West Indies, serves to identify individuals politically and otherwise, with all the benefits and costs that such a distinction entails. In this manner, relationships with other relevant constituencies are defined, and both the name and the naming process remain important because they are reflective of the culture, as well as strategies and tactics used by movement participants.

Contextually, it was only after a number of suggestions had failed to gain acceptance by the committee saddled with the responsibility of coming up with a name for the PNM that, in a moment of inspiration, Dr. Mosaheb and Wilfrid Alexander "pieced together the hybrid—People's National Movement—a name which obviously owes something to various precedents."[59] Finally, that the PNM stood for "knowledgeism" and emphasized political education as a tool to achieve political independence was consistent with the party's efforts to occupy a distinctive space in the politics of the society.

The party sought to embody its distinctiveness not only in its name but also in its emblem. Reference has already been made to the manner in which physical spaces, like households, schools, and public squares, become social spaces by being invested with specific meanings by human beings. These spaces, I argued, characterize both oppressive and antioppressive conduct. The same may be true of objects, such as emblems, as Emile Durkheim observed in his study of religious behavior. Objects, including symbols, are used to represent whatever people in general think they represent.[60] Furthermore, as a visible object, a symbol may represent "to the mind, the semblance of something which is not shown, but realised by association with it."[61] As such, these objects can form the basis of collective representations, or the norms and values of a society, that are independent of the individual and also influence group conduct. Objects may also be in evidence during certain moments in groups' histories, when groups may experience a collective effervescence, or a heightened sense of collective exaltation, out of which ideas are born and which can lead to great social change,[62] like the various activities of Williams and others involved in the political-independence movement in Trinidad and Tobago.

In Trinidad and Tobago the balisier, a well-known indigenous plant recognized as indicating fertility of the soil, became the emblem of the People's National Movement. Indeed, the early French settlers, who were attracted to the island by the conditions offered to them, looked for growths of balisier to select what they described as good cacao lands. Again, since emblems can symbolize pride in certain beliefs or achievements, they can be used as a rallying point in the service of collective identity.[63] The PNM, therefore, adopted the balisier "as the symbol or emblem at one and the same time because of its [the party's] local roots and repudiation of external domination and of democratic association among its members rallying and supporting such definite principles propounded in its Charter as INTERRACIAL SOLIDARITY for the commonweal, aiming at POLITICAL EDUCATION for all sections of the community, NATIONHOOD for Trinidad and the Caribbean area within the British Commonwealth of Nations, Morality in public affairs."[64]

As the party's emblem, the balisier, according to U.S. Consul General Douglas Jenkins, was also meant to symbolize the PNM's commitment, as evident in its constitution, to the termination of colonialism and racialism throughout the Caribbean area and the world.[65] Therefore, when the formation of the party was announced on 24 January 1956, not only were the colors of the party described as being black, white, yellow, and brown, signifying Trinidad and Tobago's racial groups, but the bandstand at the UWS was decorated with the leaves and flowers of the balisier. According to the *Nation,* consistent with "the new and politically healthy spirit which was pervading the length and breadth of the twin island," and in keeping with the "decency, decorum and discipline" of the party, "the floral system of the Balisier was as distinctive among local flowers as the PNM is distinct among indigenous political parties."[66]

IN ADDITION to their concern with the manner in which previously existing entities forge a collective identity and facilitate the emergence of social-movement intellectuals, social-movement analysts are concerned with the manner in which the political-opportunity structure enables social-movement organizations to free up space so as to enter the political arena. As Sidney Tarrow notes, opening up access to participation is the first important incentive for collective action.[67] With this in mind, I will turn my attention to two factors of contextual relevance. The first is the nature of politics in Trinidad and Tobago prior to the emergence of the PNM. The second is an awareness that a political opportunity, such as the existence of personalized politics, existed in Trinbago. This point is important because before an actor can capitalize on a political opportunity, he or she must first recognize that such an opportunity exists, in this case in the quest for political independence.

An early opportunity for political action occurred as a consequence of the recommendations of the Moyne Commission regarding the need for universal adult suffrage in Trinbago and other West Indian islands. In Trinbago adult suffrage had arrived in time for the 1946 general election, and later it opened up space for the emergence of the PNM as a mass-based party. During the 1946 election, a total of 137,281 registered voters, or 52.9 percent of the 259,512 registered voters, exercised the franchise. The fact that at that time voters tended to vote for individuals rather than political parties meant that successful candidates who became ministers of government were able to practice the politics of patronage, rewarding supporters with jobs and other perquisites and punishing those individuals whom they viewed as their detractors, sometimes by seeing to it that they did not get jobs or were fired from their jobs. In addition, ministers of government, in the absence of party discipline and a meaningful parliamentary opposition, were free to follow their own policies, which were sometimes inconsonant with their own preelection promises, with impunity.

As the next election, on 18 September 1950, drew near, there was some movement toward removing restrictions on voting, as well as on qualifications for nomination to the Executive Council and as candidates for the Leg Co, though the power of the governor remained largely untouched. For example, a draft constitution order in June 1949 stated that in order to be nominated to the Executive Council, a person had to be a British subject, at least twenty-one years old, who had resided in the colony for a period of at least two years and was proficient in English.[68]

Significantly, the governor reported after the 1950 election—in which 189,628 people, or 67.02 percent, of a total of 282,962 registered voters (out of a total population of 603,000) had exercised the franchise—that a preliminary count had revealed that no party had a "clear majority" among the 18 elected members. Of the 9 incumbents who sought reelection 6 were returned to office. Of the 18 elected members, 7 were from the Butler Home Rule Party, 1 was from the Caribbean Socialist Party, 2 were from the Trinidad Labour Party, 2 were from the Political Progress Party, and 6 were independents.[69] Thus, not only was there an increase in the number and percentage of registered and actual voters compared with the previous election but the independents gained one less seat than the party that captured the largest number of seats. No political party, therefore, was able to form a government, and no party was the official opposition, when the PNM came into existence in January 1956 or, earlier, when Eric Williams formally entered the political arena in September 1955. This was part of the political-opportunity matrix at the time.

Also providing an opportunity for Williams, as a social-movement actor, and the PNM to create space for their ideas regarding political independence was the existence of personalized politics, from which Williams and the PNM sought to distance themselves. The historian Fitzroy Baptiste observes that in the early 1950s the major parties included the Party of Political Progress Groups (POPPG), led by Albert

Gomes, who it seems had organized this group following his expulsion from the West Indian National Party (WINP) in 1944, occasioned by his defiant involvement in Grenadian politics on the platform of T. A. Marryshow.[70] In addition, there were the Independent Labour Party (ILP), the Trinidad Labour Party (TLP), the West Indian Independence Party (WIIP), the Caribbean National Labour Party (CNLP), and the People's Democratic Party (PDP), led by the Indo-Trinbagonian Bhadase Sagan Maraj. However, despite a good performance in the 1954 municipal elections, the POPPG soon was wracked by internal strife, while the Democratic Labour Party (DLP) seemed to concentrate its energies on wooing the Indian vote.

During a lecture on 14 June 1956, Williams castigated Gomes, then minister of labour, industry and commerce, for claiming that the people of Trinidad and Tobago were, among other things, intellectually incapable of "self-government." According to Williams, Gomes "considered West Indians unfit to administer their own affairs except for their own benefit, . . . described adult franchise as a rotten fruit, . . . today advocates the continuation of the colonial constitution which he was principally responsible for inflicting on us [and] symbolizes the phrase he has made infamous, 'in politics anything goes.'"[71]

Dr. Patrick Solomon, who later became deputy PNM leader, in 1981 recalled the Barbados prime minister and federal prime minister Grantley Adams saying "some 20 years ago—half humourously, half seriously—that the greatest trick ever played on the West Indian world was that Albert Gomes had got the people to take him seriously." Solomon always regarded Gomes as a charlatan, a mountebank, and above all a supreme egoist, an individual to whom "ignorance meant nothing" and who was fond of doing violence to the English language.[72]

But although Gomes was not well regarded by Williams and other local politicians concerning his ministerial duties, the British government described him as "possibly the ablest of the five Elected Ministers." And although it would be incorrect to view him as in effect prime minister or the leader of the five elected ministers, "he has probably the strongest personality among them and his personal reputation has been enhanced by the part he has played in regional organisations as the champion of federation." Finally, Gomes reportedly had distinguished himself from his colleagues by his "breadth of outlook and his interests beyond the limits of the Colony. . . . [He] has a philosophic turn of mind enlivened by a keen sense of humour. His opinions are intelligent and well balanced . . . and though he was described as 'ebullient and noisy,' he is probably most effective when engaged with his opponents, particularly Mr. T. U. B. Butler."[73] However, it was also noted that there tended to be some contradiction between Gomes's public and private utterances.[74]

Gomes's published autobiography tells us that he, like Williams, was born in 1911; that he grew up among poor people, more than 95 percent of whom were Negroes; and that he was his parents' only surviving son. His mother had known poverty, his father was involved in business activities in which the Portuguese were dominant, and both parents were not very religious. Gomes himself spent long hours in his father's pharmacy, which was acquired after Gomes's return to Trinidad in 1930, following a two-year sojourn in the United States. His father owned various shops, but Gomes recalls that he never took legal action against his Negro tenants, even when they were months behind in their rent.[75]

Although Gomes had a Negro nanny and the household had a Negro maid, of whom Gomes was fond, his father was one of the founding members of a Portuguese association that "once maintained a rigid colour bar that excluded all coloured persons from its premises." As Gomes observed, "The Portuguese in Trinidad locked their colour prejudices in their minds so that their loins might be unaffected by them." They sought to "colonise in bed," and, paradoxically, many of the males had "coloured wives and concubines, and eventually coloured children."[76]

Gomes also recalls the ubiquitous cruelty in colonial Trinidad of "man to animal, of man to woman, of parent to child, of white housewife to Negro domestic, of almost everyone to the scorned and ostracized Coolie, of the ruling classes to the masses." However, it was the "Coolies," as the East Indian indentured laborers were called, who were the most stigmatized, according to Gomes. "Ragged, unwashed, and underfed, they swarmed the downtown area seeking escape from the peonage of the canefield and the chain gangs of the sugar estates"; they were the victims of a "constant barrage of jeers, sneers and obscenities from every side."[77]

As a trade-union leader, Gomes was largely responsible for the formation of the Federated Workers' Trade Union, of which he served as president-general from 1942 to 1944. As a politician, he was first elected a member of the Port-of-Spain City Council in 1938. In 1945, with the backing of the trade union, he was elected to the Leg Co. A year later he was elevated to the Executive Council, where he served as a member from 1946. He was appointed minister of labour, industry and commerce in October 1950.

In addition to his political involvement, Gomes became, with his mother's financial backing, editor and publisher of the magazine the *Beacon*, which emerged in 1931 and continued until 1933 and which he felt would occupy a literary space in the "vast philistine desert" of Trinidad. His literary pursuits led to his involvement with a group of individuals, including Alfred Mendes, C. L. R. James, and Ralph De Boissière, who were intent on addressing topical and controversial issues. Of interest also are Gomes's accounts of his efforts to edit the work of prospective authors especially with respect to "standards of writing and general literacy"—an essential facet of the written transmission of knowledge. As Mendes writes in a personal communication regarding the *Beacon* and intellectualism during the period in question,

> The *Beacon* was, of course, the best organ of opinion in Trinidad—and nothing touching it for intelligence, wit, satire and general excellence has appeared in Trinidad. . . . It created a furore of excitement in the island . . . and it set people everywhere thinking and talking as they had never talked or thought before. . . . *The Beacon* took anything in its maw that was fresh, good, intelligent—stories, articles on politics, race, music—reviews of books, of music recitals, of art exhibitions—controversial letters, stimulating editorial notes written by Gomes (Gomes was essentially a polemicist and not a politician or writer. He tried his hand some years ago at writing novels and failed dismally).[78]

Regarding the *Beacon*'s contribution to the existence of the "great public," it may be said that "the traditional prestige norms," that is, "those of the 'white' upper class," had been under attack since the 1930s. This was expressed in ways that included the "new writing, on native grounds of Mendes and James," and in the "growth of a nativist painting and theatrical tradition, institutionalized after 1945 in the form of the Art Society [and] in the long and bitter personal struggle of the *danseuse* Beryl McBurnie to foster West Indian dance."[79]

The existing anticolonial posture also expressed itself, Gordon Lewis notes, first, in the struggling obscure cultural clubs in which families like those of C. L. R. James educated themselves, by reading widely the magazines of the 1940s that contained references to many of the famous names of the later West Indian literary renaissance; and second, in the activities of well-known cricketers like George John and Learie Constantine, who railed against the pernicious organization of cricket clubs along color lines and in the transformation of individual skill into the game as a carrier of the dominant culture.[80]

Another political figure with a personal following was Bhadase Sagan Maraj, who used his membership in the Maha Saba to be elected to the legislature and as a launching pad for his later political aspirations. As the only member of the Leg Co to resign his seat in April 1955, in protest of the resolution to postpone the election scheduled for 1955 (about which more will be said), Maraj succeeded in fostering the impression of being a man of principle. In a comment on Maraj's political skills, for example, U.S. Consul General Jenkins noted that Maraj was able to parlay his resignation into political capital, in that this action was vindicated by his victory in a subsequent by-election, which enabled him to return to the Leg Co. However, during the election campaign Maraj was charged with assaulting Ranjit Kumar, a fellow Indian member of the Leg Co. Ostensibly in order to fight this charge and because of an unwillingness to bring the name of the Sanatan Dharma Maha Saba into disrepute, Maraj resigned his position as president-general of the approximately 150,000-member Hindu society on the grounds of ill health.[81]

Following his acquittal of the assault charge against him, Maraj continued to leverage political capital from the whole affair by remaining as head of the PDP and to show his political mettle by selecting and supporting winning candidates for county elections. Jenkins also reports that during the approximately three and one-half years that Maraj led the Maha Saba, thirty-one primary schools were established for the main purpose of giving Hindu children a (secular) primary education and instruction in the principles of Hinduism and that ten more primary schools were in the process of being constructed. Maraj was able to use his position as leader of the Maha Saba to further strengthen his personal popularity and to capitalize politically on the gratitude of underprivileged members of the Maha Saba, who had benefitted from his largesse in providing "personal loans and other handouts in the true manner of the lower level party politician."[82] These actions established Maraj as a personal power broker and a political force to be reckoned with, especially given his leadership in the Maha Saba and the PDP.

However, in the process of accumulating political capital, Maraj acquired a reputation of being somewhat of a "gangster," which made him unacceptable to the British and the Americans.[83] Specifically, various observers, including the acting governor, Mr. Dorman, and Carlton Comma, "had all expressed the view that Maraj was more dangerous than Williams, and that Maraj was Trinidad's No. 1 gangster, with an unexampled reputation and who is rumored should not stick at a murder or two."[84] During a visit to British Guiana, Maraj, the country's premier, Dr. Cheddi Jagan, and other Maha Saba leaders had spoken out against Trinidad and Tobago and British Guiana joining the West Indian

Federation. They feared that the Indians in the two colonies, being a minority, would not benefit from membership in the federation given the preponderance of people of African descent.[85]

Yet another exponent of personalized politics was the minister of education in the 1950 government, the Syrian Roy Joseph. As Selwyn Ryan points out, as the boss of the so-called eighth army, the political machine that functioned in the underworld of Trinidad politics, Joseph boasted that he could secure the election of any candidate in the municipality of San Fernando and also get jobs for individuals, in return for which he expected fierce and unadulterated loyalty. Since he was associated with no party or party policy, Joseph attracted attention to himself by being "socially ubiquitous" as the campaign season approached.[86] Joseph developed a reputation for being approachable, and indeed, it would not be an exaggeration to say that his home became the principal employment agency of San Fernando.[87]

Yet another prominent exponent of personalized politics who sought space in the existing political-opportunity structure was Tubal Uriah Butler. Born in Grenada in 1897 of African descent, he served for a time with a detachment of the British West Indies Regiment in Egypt. In 1920, owing to the growth in the petroleum industry in Trinidad and Tobago, many migrated to Trinidad; some, like Butler, found employment in a small oil field. In 1929 Butler suffered a permanent injury to his leg while working in Venezuela, for which he did not receive compensation. He later became involved with the Trinidad Workingmen's Association (TWA) and thereby with the problems of oil-field workers. Following the dismissal of some of the workers, Butler identified with their cause and was part of a delegation to the governor, Sir Claud Hollis, seeking some relief on behalf of the workers.

Butler's association with the workers brought him national attention, especially after the 1937 unrest, and following several public addresses laced with biblical references and strident denunciations of the colonial system, he was placed under surveillance. Butler also organized a strike in protest of the conditions of workers at the Trinidad Leaseholds Oil Company. Workers there had complained that they were often required to work overtime on weekends without compensation; that they were subject to immediate dismissal and lacked compensation for injuries sustained on the job; and that they were victims of the notorious "red books." These books contained records of workers' service, which companies shared with one another, making it difficult for dismissed workers to find employment elsewhere.[88] The mostly Black workers also complained that the White South African supervisors addressed them as "boy" and that less-qualified White workers were paid more than their Black counterparts. The strike in 1937 morphed into a general strike that turned violent and involved many fatalities, including the deaths of two policemen. Butler went into hiding but testified before a commission that investigated the unrest. He was later arrested, tried, convicted, and jailed for two years.

As a Baptist preacher and chief pastor of the Moravian Baptist Church, Butler used the church as a locale for his political mobilizing activities, and the monetary collections from the mostly female congregants as a source of income. Ironically, as Bridget Brereton points out, Butler never saw himself as a nationalist and, like Captain Cipriani, was "loyal to the British Empire and had faith in British justice." Indeed, Butler felt that he was "defending the rights of British citizens who had been betrayed by the unBritish behavior of local employers and officials" and conducting "a heroic struggle for British justice for British Blacks in a British country."[89]

Butler associated with another subaltern activist, the St. Vincentian–born Elma François, who worked as a domestic servant and became a member of the TWA, after which she started to speak at public meetings. Along with Jim Barrette, her companion, and Jim Headley, a ship's cook who had been active in the National Maritime Union and the young Communist League in the United States, where he had been in contact with George Padmore, François formed the National Unemployed Movement. François, who had only a fifth-grade standard primary-school education, was another one of the organic anticolonial figures on whose shoulders Williams would stand as a public and social-movement intellectual. Particularly interested in the condition of females in the TWA, François subsequently became involved in railing against the efforts of importers to increase the price of that working-class staple, condensed milk, which she contended would make it more difficult for poor mothers to obtain for their babies.[90]

Following his return to Trinidad on 2 August 1956, after an absence of eight months, Butler, the self-styled "Chief Servant," was met by a large, cheering, hymn-singing crowd. He soon set about abusing and threatening Williams, promising to oppose him in Port-of-Spain south-east or in any other constituency in which Williams might choose to stand. Williams, however, did not respond to Butler's "wild promises, bombast, vituperation and religious allusions,"[91] and it soon became apparent that the politics of the past, with which Butler was identified, was doomed to failure. This period, then, was a time of subaltern class and race consciousness, which was constructed and moved into the public sphere by Black leaders like the messianic Butler and François and Indian leaders like Cola Rienzi, another former TWA/TLP activist who had become disillusioned with Cipriani.[92]

In sum, Gomes's predisposition to the politics of "anything goes," Joseph's vote-brokering activities, Maraj's so-called unsavory reputation, and Butler's devalued political currency all provided an opportunity for Williams and the PNM to create space in the political spectrum prior to the 1956 elections. The emergence of the PNM constituted a "new, dynamic, organized political force" that offered a "middle of the road alternative" to the POPPG, which was dominated by the "predominantly white, reactionary, vested interests" and the "rabble-rousing, pseudo-socialistic demagoguery of Butler and his ilk."[93] By "cursing" colonial politics, Williams and the PNM created space for their ideas regarding serious party politics, and for the PNM, as an "innovative organization," or a producer of knowledge and a developer of shared cognitions, rather than an organization that merely mimicked extant political organizations.[94] However, while these activities were perhaps necessary for the attainment of political independence, it is conceivable that they were not sufficient to achieve that goal.

6 From Pedantic Visionary to Elected Politician

Nor are we an ordinary party in the accepted sense of the word. We are rather a rally, a convention of all and for all, a mobilisation of all the forces in the community, cutting across race, religion, class and colour, with emphasis on united action by all the people in the common cause. . . . Hence our name—The People's National Movement.

—The People's Charter

In this chapter I examine the manner in which Williams continued to create space, specifically as a social-movement intellectual, for his views and those of the PNM regarding independence in the political arena and, as a consequence, to formally enter the political arena as an elected politician. This was done by emphasizing especially the *relevance* of the ideology of the party, the economy, race relations, constitutional reform, and party politics, while continuing to capitalize on the existing political-opportunity structure and discredit the politics of "anything goes." Accordingly, I take a further look at how, as nascent political entrepreneurs, Williams and the PNM were able to launch the party as an "innovative organization." This was done by promoting the PNM as a party that broke new ground in the organizational milieu of political parties and personalities. In this manner, the PNM promoted a new organizational population with a different ideology, rather than acting as a "reproducer organization," which merely adds to the number of similarly situated organizational entities.[1]

In dealing with the question of ideology, Williams and other leaders of the political-independence movement generated a number of ideas that were transformed into ideologies and that not only served to forge a collective identity but perhaps, more importantly, were not unamenable to powerful others such as the British and especially the Americans.[2] This point is especially crucial because to the extent that the challenger's ideology is opposed to the ideology of the challenged, it becomes much more difficult for the former to achieve its goals.

As previously noted, a critical feature of collective action in general and social movements in particular is a belief system that powers collective actions. In an early statement on ideology, for example, Karl Marx argued that the ruling ideas in any epoch always emanate from the ruling stratum, which, as a consequence, becomes both the source of material wealth and the controller of intellectual wealth. This suggests that, generally speaking, the social class that has the means of material production at its disposal also controls the means of mental production. Ideas that are so generated then assume the level of an *ideology* because they tend to reflect the interests of the dominant groups.[3] It is likely, however, that in an effort to regulate the production of ideas qua knowledge, the dominant often find it necessary to restrict and otherwise control access to information that might conduce to a weakening of its hegemony. It follows, therefore, that for a belief system or ideology to be relevant, it has to adapt to the struggle for social change and to create space in the political system.

The thinking of Daniel Bell is also of relevance to our treatment of Williams's intellectualism and the creation of ideological space. Bell maintains, for example, that the analysis of ideology properly belongs to the intelligentsia and that what the priest was to religion, the intellectual was to ideology. Ideologies are ideas that are transmuted in such a manner as to rise to the level of "truth." These ideas not only serve the interests of a particular group but are converted into "social levers," in that certain ideas are *(a)* "selected out" for espousal and emphasis with a degree of passion by the social movement and, insofar as they can be simplified, *(b)* used to establish a claim to truth and a demand for social action of an ameliorative nature.[4] Social-movement intellectuals therefore seek to emphasize certain ideas germane to the movement in their quest for ideological relevance. Those ideas, which reflect the interests of the disadvantaged, moreover, are rooted in the sociohistorical experiences and the sociocultural fabric of the society.

One of Williams's earliest ideological speeches, titled "Economic Problems of Trinidad and Tobago," which also marked his transition from public intellectual to social-movement intellectual, was delivered on 5 July 1955 at, not surprisingly, Woodford Square. In that speech Williams categorically blamed the colonial government for doing nothing to improve the economy and advanced a model of economic development for a politically independent Trinidad and Tobago. Specifically, he maintained that since sugar and oil were the bedrock of the economy, because of the declining importance of sugar and its reduced capacity to provide jobs, it was necessary to diversify the economy. This was especially so in view of the increasing size of the population and the decline in the mortality rate, both of which meant that there was less to feed more people.

In continuing his intercourse with exceptional minds, and as a way of dealing with this problem, Williams turned to the Puerto Rican model and the views of the noted West Indian economist and future Nobel Laureate Sir Arthur Lewis regarding economic development, noting in the process that Trinidad had the advantage of oil, which Puerto Rico did not have. Born in St. Lucia in 1915, Lewis was an island scholar who had obtained a first-class honors degree in economics from the prestigious London School of Economics and Political Science in 1937 and a doctorate in economics from London University in 1940. Like Williams, Lewis was a teacher. The first Black to hold a chair at an English university, he was appointed Stanley Jevons Professor of Political Economy at Manchester University in 1948, after teaching at the London School from 1938 to 1948.

Williams maintained that the key to economic development lay in stimulating the modern sectors of the economy, such as tourism, so as to provide jobs for workers in more labor-intensive, declining industries such as sugar. In addition to tourism, he suggested that the industries holding out the prospect for greater development were hosiery, leather garments, footwear, china, paper, glass, and building materials. It would be necessary, however, to develop an infrastructure that would facilitate international trade, such as hotels and bath houses for those using the beaches. In keeping with Lewis's prescriptions, Williams emphasized the need to produce for export rather than for the limited domestic market, as well as the need for the British Caribbean territories to be united in a customs union. However, since industrialization was a costly business, beyond the means of Caribbean countries, Williams argued that the program should be based on appeals and incentives to established manufacturers in England and the United States. Moreover, since investors were likely driven by the profit motive and would only start businesses on that basis, Williams also suggested that it might be in the national interest for the government to intervene and start a business, which at the beginning might be unprofitable. In conclusion, and echoing Lewis's sentiments, Williams observed that British West Indians must find a way to put hope, initiative, direction, and an unconquerable will into the management of their affairs. This, he felt, was the hardest task of all.

In another lecture, on 14 June 1956, also delivered at the UWS, Williams noted that the PNM's economic program was "designed to achieve maximum use of our resources, physical and human, with emphasis on the reduction of our dangerous dependence on oil and sugar for exports and imported food and clothing for consumption."[5] This entailed encouraging the fishing industry, the small farmer, and the small artisan to produce more of the necessities of Trinidadians and Tobagonians, while expanding secondary industries with an emphasis on processing raw materials, encouraging investment, both local and foreign, and providing additional jobs. Williams and the PNM, then, were reiterating the need for a more indigenous economic activity designed to reduce dependence on oil, which was foreign-owned, and sugar, which he had previously described as weakening in dominance in the world market.

In addition to "selecting out" economic reform as an important plank in the PNM's ideology, Williams categorically maintained that philosophically the PNM was neither a subversive nor a communist organization but a party steeped in the basic principles of democracy. He also observed that the PNM had been "accused of using the tactics made familiar by the Russians and the Nazis, the Hitlers, the Mussolinis and the Stalins," and that in a recent address to the Party of Political Progress Groups, Albert Gomes, the minister of labour, industry and commerce, had allegedly informed his listeners that "they would not try to run before they could creep. . . . They did not want to make the mistake now being lamented by the people of British Guiana."[6] This was an effort to call into question the views of Williams and the policies of the PNM by comparing them with the actions of the People's Progressive Party in British Guiana, which in October 1953, after 133 days in office, had been ousted by the British government on the grounds that the party and the government were communist. Apart from the previously mentioned allegations that he himself was a communist, and armed with the knowledge that the West Indian Independence Party had declared its predilection for communism and that both the British and the Americans had made clear their distaste for communism and communists, Williams sought unequivocally to put an end to any allegations that the PNM was communist.

Thus, in his address of 14 June 1956 he dealt with what he considered to be the gravamen of the PNM's ideology:

> The P.N.M. denies emphatically that it is either communist, Fascist, Jaganist or Poujadist. The P.N.M. takes this opportunity of re-affirming its recent public pledge to institute legal proceedings against any person or persons seeking to defame it by alleging that it is a communist-inspired movement. The P.N.M. is a national party deriving its inspiration from the best in democratic theory, seeking to initiate the best in democratic practice, applying to the affairs of Trinidad and Tobago the intelligence, the democratic party discipline and the

> public morality which, in the opinion of the P.N.M. are lacking in the political life of our community.[7]

Perhaps mindful of the issue of communism, as well as the earlier-noted efforts by certain individuals to disqualify him from a position with the then Anglo-American Caribbean Commission, that Williams, during a conversation with U.S. Vice Consul Stanley Schiff about two weeks later, evidently found it necessary to again lay to rest any fears that he was a communist. Williams dissociated himself and the party from the communist or extreme left-wing element on the twin island, then represented by John Rojas, president of the Oilfield Workers' Trade Union, and made reference to the PNM's policy of industrialization by invitation. Schiff recalled that Williams, rather mischievously, had stated that it was common belief that the best way to get aid from the United States was "to have a communist problem or threat." However, Williams hastened to add that aid should not be contingent on the existence of such a threat, "otherwise a party in power might find it expedient to manufacture a communist problem."[8]

Williams also addressed the question of race, which had always been of paramount importance in politics in Trinidad and Tobago and especially in Guyana because of the colonial policy of divide and rule, which fostered racial discord between Indians and Africans. As early as 1944, in his book *Capitalism and Slavery,* Williams staked out his position on race—in that instance in relation to enslavement and the economy—from which he seems not to have departed. He maintained, for example, that the origin of Negro slavery was economic, not racial, and that it had to do not with the color of the laborer but with the cheapness of the labor.[9] Thus, following unsuccessful efforts to place the Indian in North America into servitude, Whites from Europe were recruited to take their place. These White immigrants fell into three categories: indentured servants, redemptioners, and convicts. The indentured servants were those who prior to their departure signed a contract binding them to plantation service for a stipulated period of time in return for their passage. The redemptioners arranged with the captain of the ship transporting them to pay for their passage and promised to repay the amount on arrival or within a specified period thereafter, failing which they were sold by the captain to the highest bidder. The convicts were sent out as a deliberate policy of the home government to serve for a specified period.

Like the enslaved Negro, these victims of servitude experienced the horrors of transportation and withstood the rigors of the plantation experience in the tropical climate in places like Barbados. However, the use of White immigrant labor, Williams argues, became less attractive to the planters only after they found that Negro labor was cheaper than that of Whites, and this was the decisive factor. Williams argues that *(a)* the money that procured a White man's services could buy those of a Negro for life; *(b)* the supply of the former's labor power was less forthcoming; and *(c)* escape was less problematic for the Whites than for Negroes, since it was more difficult to determine that a White was an escapee.

In a comment regarding the transportation of the enslaved from Africa to the Caribbean, George Lamming writes that during the six-thousand-mile voyage "on ship the slaves were packed in the hold on galleries one above the other. . . . The close proximity of so many naked human beings, their bruised and festering flesh, the foetid air, the prevailing dysentery, the accumulation of filth, turned these holds into a hell. . . . No place on earth, observed one writer of the time, concentrated so much misery as the hold of a slave ship."[10] Ironically, in creating a slave to support it, Lamming contends, the system also created Caliban the "monster, a child, a slave," bent on destroying it. This was the language of institutionalized oppression.

The purchase of the enslaved required both business sense and shrewd discrimination. As Williams observed, "An Angolan Negro was a proverb for worthlessness; Coromantines (Ashantis), from the Gold Coast, were good workers but too rebellious; Mandingoes (Senegal) were too prone to theft; the Eboes (Nigeria) were timid and despondent; the Pawpaws or Whydahs (Dahomey) were the most docile and best disposed."[11] To be sure, the slave trade, though risky, was profitable. The Negroes "were purchased; transported to the plantations, they produced sugar, cotton, indigo, molasses and other tropical products, the processing of which created new industries in England; while the maintenance of the Negroes and their owners on the plantations," Williams continued, "provided another market for British industry."[12] The rationalization for the exploitation of Negro labor power by the planter, then, was not "a theory," Williams emphasized, but a "practical conclusion deduced from the personal experience. . . . He would have gone to the moon, if necessary, for labor. Africa was nearer than the moon, nearer too than the more populous countries of India. But their turn was to come."[13]

During a public lecture titled "The Historical Background of Race Relations in the Caribbean," on 16 August 1955 at Woodford Square, Williams argued that historically, in addition to the racial and tribal stereotype, imperialism had also to justify its economic control by regarding the colonial peoples as inferior. Thus, their personal habits and social customs were despised, in essence denying their fitness to govern themselves, and they were described as a people without a history. As another part of the cultural underbelly of colonial oppression, this depiction of the oppressed involved the generation by the oppressor of a belief system intended to justify oppression of the "other," whose history, insofar as it existed, was to be located within the realm of discredited knowledge.

Moreover, the enslavement of the African and the indenture of the Asiatic were based on the hypothesis, expressed or understood, that the degradation of the laborer was essential to sugar cultivation. This led Williams to conclude that "the African or Asiatic worker in the Caribbean will never have a moral status so long as his economic status is envisaged in terms of working conditions which would not be imposed on white workers." For Williams, then, improvements in the political status of the African and the Indian in Trinidad and Tobago, which presumably would come with political independence, would improve their economic condition and their moral status. Much the same argument was made to mostly Indian sugar workers in an address delivered by Williams during a mass meeting on 25 September 1955, at the invitation of the executive committee of the All Trinidad Sugar Estates and Factories Workers Trade Union.[14] Clearly, Williams was not merely pointing to the paramount position of the sugar industry; he was also pointing indirectly to the similar structural position of the African and the Indian sugar worker.

Although there were various occasions when Williams stressed "interracial solidarity," involving *all* races, there was one instance when he seemed to find it necessary to locate the issue of race in the context of Indo-Trinbagonians and to select out the role of Indian organizations and politicians, whose actions he considered to be deleterious to the national interests and, perhaps more importantly, those of the PNM. During a meeting on 29 July 1956 at the "University of Woodford Square," Williams denounced the Maha Saba, characterizing it, in the words of U.S. Consul General Jenkins, as a "political organization in religious garb trading on the ignorance of the people and trying to use race as a weapon for political domination in Trinidad."[15]

On another occasion, during a speech on 1 April 1958, after the PNM had lost the federal elections of 25 March 1958, Williams criticized the Democratic Labour Party's appeal to the Indians to vote for the party, claiming that religion had figured prominently in the DLP's campaign. As he put it, "By hook or by crook they brought out the Indian vote—the young and the old, the literate and the illiterate, the lame, the halt and the blind, man and woman." Williams also referred to a letter purportedly addressed to "My dear Indian Brother" and signed "Yours truly, Indian." This was not the Indian nation talking, he claimed, but "the recalcitrant and hostile minority of the West Indian nation masquerading as 'the Indian nation' and prostituting the name of India for its selfish, reactionary political ends." These individuals, he opined, were a "danger facing the people of Trinidad and Tobago and the West Indian nation," and many of them were opposed to federation.[16] Williams also chastised and sympathized with "those misguided unfortunates who, having ears to hear heard not, having eyes to see saw not, who were complacent, for whom everything was in the bag, who had the D.L.P covered." Sparing none, he remonstrated with those who were "too tired or busy to vote," who wanted a car to take them to the polling station around the corner, who could still be fooled by the "loud-mouthed, empty ranting and vapouring of selfish politicians."[17]

This speech, admittedly one of Williams's most disputatious, was a source of much embarrassment to the Indian leaders in the party who were also on the platform, although Williams had ad-libbed that he was not referring to them, and it was criticized by various individuals.[18] For example, the former PNM minister of health Winston Mahabir described the speech as indicative of the "gross emotional instability of Williams."[19] Mahabir also mentioned that he and other Indians on the platform—Ibbit Mosaheb and Martin Sampath—as well as Walter Annamunthodo, a Guyanese compatriot of C. L. R. James's, had exchanged "horrified glances" during the speech. According to Mahabir, he, along with Kamaluddin Mohammed and Gerard Montano, went to see Williams that same night to express their displeasure with the speech and found him in a "gloating and triumphal mood." In what appeared to be further evidence of unwillingness on his part to heed the advice of other prominent individuals in the party, and adding insult to injury, Williams repeated the same speech the following night in San Fernando. Mahabir considered resigning from the cabinet but was talked out of doing so by the then colonial secretary, Solomon Hochoy, who reminded him that the cause was greater than the person.[20]

The speech is also relevant for other reasons. It is clear that Williams and the PNM favored a West Indian federation. And as we saw in his speech on economic reform, his views were premised, among other things, on the assumption that there would be a West Indian customs union. Seemingly, therefore, his apparent rant was directed at the DLP, which he noted was against federation, as well as individuals such as Albert Gomes and Patrick Bryan, who had jumped on the DLP bandwagon and whom he saw as frustrating his attempts to forge a national identity. Second, it is now known that the then Indian commissioner, Shri Badir Nath Nanda, had become very involved in the local political scene on behalf of the Indian population and had encouraged the antifederation posturing of Bhadase Maraj. Indeed, a Colonial Office draft report critical of Nanda's activities concluded that the Indian government "maintains a commissioner in the West Indies the result of whose activities, both innocent and otherwise, is to accentuate the Indian sense of separateness from the rest of the community and to encourage them to look forward to a position of political and economic domination." This in the hope that when Indians secured political control their sympathies "will turn towards India [rather] than the United Kingdom."[21]

According to Fitzroy Baptiste, Nanda had visited British Guiana along with Bhadase Maraj in late 1955, when he had met with Dr. Cheddi Jagan, the Indian leader of the People's Progressive Party, and had encouraged Indians in that country not to support the federation.[22] But Nanda appeared to have been sending mixed signals. American Consul General William Maddox states, for example, that "in the reports of the many speeches he gave during the British Guiana tour, Nanda was all sweetness and light—allegedly advising East Indians to be good Guianese, to cooperate with other races, and—to abandon any idea of repatriation." There were indications, however, that some East Indians were "not too happy about the crystallization of racial and cultural sentiments." Following a speech by Governor Rance, "who uses every opportunity to alleviate the friction [and who] had said something like this, 'Here we are—white men, yellow men, brown men, black men, all kinds of colored men—why can't we all be just West Indians together?,'" some East Indians "clearly implied their disapproval of Nanda's effort to strengthen the sense of cultural attachment to India." Again, in a private conversation with the consul general, Ashford Sinanan, deputy speaker of the Leg Co, revealed that "he had always favored federation but had not wished to vote for the Government motion without giving a public explanation. Being in the chair, he had to give first consideration to other members and the debate closed (at 4 a.m.) before he had an opportunity to speak. Hence he abstained."[23] I have argued that there invariably has been a certain purposiveness to Williams's activities. And it is more than likely that if he was not already aware of Nanda's and Maraj's activities in Guyana and Premier Cheddi Jagan's 1956 about-face on the federation issue, the Indians in that country made him aware.[24] Not surprisingly, the Indian government quietly withdrew Nanda in late 1955.

Williams's comments, it turned out, also moved the narrative on race from the margins to the center. Kamaluddin Mohammed, for instance, later contended that he had never known Williams to harbor racist tendencies and that with "the pressure he was under when the federal elections were completed . . . people must understand that when Williams talked about the hostile and recalcitrant Indian minority, he was replying to statements that were made about him. Don't forget it was said of him by those whom he criticized that he was out to inject the Indian women and make them infertile. He was going to inject the cows and the goats and make them infertile because he believed in family control and in those days it was a very strong issue."[25]

Additionally, as Kenneth Parmasad suggests, in his efforts to promulgate a national agenda Williams was confronted with a society with a high propensity for recalcitrant behavior and therefore, from his perspective, in need of discipline.[26] This is evidenced by Williams's comments on party discipline, honesty, getting something for nothing, and so on, to which reference is made later in this chapter. But Williams may also have reasoned that acceding to the Hindu population's demands for a space for their cultural heritage would only lead to similar concessions for other racial groups. This, coupled with a desire to maintain the support of the Creoles, placed Williams in the unenviable position of having to view certain elements of the Indian population as "recalcitrant," a term that Parmasad suggests might be used to describe the demand of Williams's offspring for "Black Power" during the 1970 disturbances in Trinidad.

As Brinsley Samaroo notes, the race question preceded the arrival of the PNM and the DLP and Rudranath Capildeo's assumption of the leadership of the DLP.[27] Also, while Williams was told that his speech was a "political blunder" and "that Indians may at one time have appeared to him as the 'recalcitrant minority,'" that, according to Patricia Mohammed, "should in no way serve to colour all of his efforts and accomplishments, nor his keen understanding of Indentureship."[28]

Finally, in adding his voice to the race narrative, Lamming argues, regarding the apparent failure of Williams's nationalist vision to embody the cultural differences in Trinidad and Tobago, that Williams, child of the Enlightenment that he was, had staked out his claim that race was an afterthought to the exploitation of the labor power of the African and the Asiatic. Furthermore, the application of *reason* and the utilization of empirical methodology should lead one to conclude that the best interests of the country lay in the construction of a national identity, which in the final analysis transcended cultural differences, especially since the Indians were part of the colonial experience. Possibly, this explains Lamming's contention that Williams's entire intellectual career was an unrelenting struggle against racism, which he saw as rooted in the economics of imperial expansion. Moreover, Lamming maintains that Williams was "the secular humanist with all the limitations of that specific western mode of thought which had conferred on its great intellectual achievements a universalizing authority that regarded the Other, in any of its forms, as an eccentricity which could be normalized by patient observation, study and interpretation."[29]

With such an orientation, Lamming continues, "it is not always easy to distinguish between national unity and national dilution. The Other's refusal to be diluted quickly becomes an example of recalcitrance; and recalcitrance soon becomes synonymous with disloyalty." However, although Williams was alert to the complexity of difference, especially in its manifestations of religion and modes of cultural affirmation, which required a whole new way of looking at the concept of nation, he recognized, possibly too late, "a truth about the great challenge of diversity and the diasporic adventure which should have been the fertilizing soil, the crusading rhetoric of the Party he had founded."[30]

In any event, during an address to the third annual convention of the PNM, in October 1958, Williams sought to locate his arguments regarding the significance of the Indian population within the democratic and nationalist aspirations of the PNM. He maintained that "we must not do to the Indian people the gross injustice of believing or even pretending to believe that those Indians who claim to speak in their name are their genuine political leaders." And, in an effort to carve out a particular political space that hitherto had not been occupied, he went on to say that the 1956 election had shown that a "large section of the population was waiting for people [by which he obviously meant the PNM and himself] to come forward so that they would turn their backs" on those who previously had led or misrepresented them.

It is more than likely that Williams was referring to the Democratic Labour Party, which was then led by Bhadase Sagan Maraj. Williams concluded that by being racially inclusive—including, that is, Africans, Indians, Chinese, Europeans, and Syrians—the PNM would show its commitment to democracy and, as it developed, encourage "genuine Indian leadership," further exemplifying the ethos of nationalism. Continuing,

Williams also noted that there had been a flowering of Caribbean literary activity, characterized by "quite astonishing inter-racialism among the cosmopolitan population." It was against this background, he maintained, that the PNM had been born and had crafted a policy that was deliberately interracial. Thus, he noted, the PNM cabinet contained two Indians, one European among its eight ministers, and one Chinese among four parliamentary undersecretaries, and never in the history of the country had racial tension been of so little consequence.[31]

Finally, perhaps remembering the saliency of race and color when he was growing up in Trinidad, in his 22 March 1961 "Massa Day Done" oration he noted that

> some of our most active and loyal P.N.M. members are indistinguishable in colour from our Massa. In recent weeks I, with several top leaders of the P.N.M., have had the opportunity to meet privately with many representatives of business and the professions in our community, and we have all been struck, notwithstanding a little grumbling here and a little dissatisfaction there, with the large reservoir of goodwill and admiration which the P.N.M. is able to draw upon. You members of the P.N.M. must understand once and for all that you misunderstand your Party and you do a great disservice to your national cause if you think that every White person or every Indian is anti-P.N.M. or that every black person is pro-P.N.M. You shall know them not by their colour or their race but their fruit.[32]

Having previously dealt with the question of personalized politics, Williams took the opportunity as a movement intellectual to address more meaningfully what he considered to be the undesirable state of party politics on the twin island. This was an attempt not only to "select out" a specific issue that was relevant to political independence and thereby to put more distance between the PNM and the existing political parties but also to further routinize Williams's charisma by shifting allegiance away from him to the party organization. A mere three months after what many felt was his formal entry into politics (21 June 1955), during a speech on 13 September 1955 titled "The Case for Party Politics in Trinidad and Tobago," which was published as a People's Education Movement pamphlet, Williams stressed the need for a viable opposition. He also issued a trenchant criticism of the government of Trinidad and Tobago, the cronyism and favoritism practiced by ministers of government, and the lavish promises made by political candidates during the 1950 election.[33] In outlining his case for party politics, as part of his nationalist vision he therefore emphasized, as the Political Education Movement had done, the importance of political education. This he felt must be accompanied by honesty, transparency, incorruptibility, adherence to the general principles of democracy in government, and especially the role of the individual in government, according to the Greek notion that "every cook can govern."

In addition, Williams deplored the incidence of raced politics, emphasized the role of capital and labor, and expressed a preference for state-controlled education for all in the society. During the speech, one of his most important concerning party politics and his opposition to personalized politics, he announced the intention to form a new party, repeating the statement that he had made in a letter to Norman Manley on 18 January 1955. The new party, he stressed, "should be openly the party of inexperience, inexperience in corruption, inexperience in kisgovernment [*sic*], inexperience in changing our views and decisions, inexperience in the determination to exclude reason and good sense from the conduct of public affairs."[34] Williams's speech also pointed to political fraud, which he claimed was not the sort of fraud the police could deal with and must therefore be dealt with by political methods. This, he felt, demanded the creation of an opposition so enlightened, alert, and relentless that "long before those eight months have ended our Legislators and our Government will be wishing that the Secretary of State for the Colonies had saved them from themselves. . . . We are going to do it right here in the 'University of Woodford Square.'"

Turning to the role of the opposition, and continuing to put distance between the extant political situation and the PNM's policies, Williams observed that it was essential that the party be "the organized expression of that overwhelming public opinion which is so flagrantly disregarded in prolonging the life of the present Legislative Council [and which] must be organized into an effective political party." In a further reference to the 1950 election and personalized politics, which he felt was clothed in the garb of party politics, Williams observed that although one party had contested all the seats, that party had been organized around the personality of a single individual, who had "advised the voters to vote for a frog if he told them to do so."

Moreover, since three smaller parties had limited their attention to the urban areas, the election had really been a contest involving "a horde of independent candidates." The nonparty candidates, Williams continued, had made all sorts of promises to all kinds of constituents. The aged, for instance, had been promised larger pensions, and while some candidates had talked of reducing the cost of living and about jobs, there had been no indication as to where the money would come from. Finally, Williams told his audience that the 1950 election campaign had produced many flattering self-portraits by candidates. Some of these individuals, he noted, had stressed their philanthropy, their social work, the trophies they had donated, the scholarships granted, and the years of free teaching they had provided.[35]

Clearly sensing that the opportunity had arrived for more meaningful party politics, Williams underscored the need for a coherent national program, not the personal thoughts of one man but the collective competence of the electorate. The program, which should be presented in the same form on platforms all over the country, should deal with national issues affecting the country as a whole, not sectional or parochial issues, and, in the final analysis, should take a national viewpoint. In addition, Williams suggested that "party members are members of a national team as in the United Kingdom, every member of Parliament has to sign the following declaration when he accepts appointment to a committee on a Bill: 'I swear that my constituents have no local interest in this bill and I have no personal interest in it.'"[36]

As a movement intellectual–cum–teacher and articulator, Williams intoned that the first goal of political education was to teach people to do things for themselves. In this context, he noted that after two months of intensive education, "the political intelligence of the masses," excluding those who stood to lose by it, was amazingly high; "their political instincts" were surprisingly sound; and, he added, probably with the UWS in mind, the masses were "the best and most vital students I have encountered in any University experience."

However, recognizing that the educational endeavor would be for naught if there were no mechanisms for transmitting knowledge, Williams conceived of the PNM as not merely a "vast educational agency," but one equipped with "an important research department." Data from this source would be presented in "simple language and an attractive manner to the people to encourage them to form their opinions," with a "party newspaper, party information leaflets and newsletters, and party pamphlets" to serve as a basis for intraparty group discussion. This was a recognition of the notion that to "educate is to emancipate,"[37] which in turn spoke to the liberatory nature of knowledge generated by Williams and the independence movement.

Clearly, Williams believed that education was the leaven needed for the bread of freedom and that a university education was the "great emancipator." He often wondered what would have happened had Britain established a university in the West Indies at the same time that it did in Canada.[38] In addition, since one of the gravest weaknesses of nationalist parties, in the West Indies in particular, was that they did not solidify achievements and establish traditions until they were in power, and even then not always, the PNM, Williams maintained, "must immediately seek the means to record in a book intended for the public in general its origin, its achievements and its perspectives."[39]

Continuing to educate his audiences, Williams noted that after political education the most important requirement for a party was honesty. Therefore, he inveighed against the prevailing "dishonesty and immorality," against graft, corruption, broken promises by politicians and squandermania of taxes, with ministers coming and going like "absentee landlords paying routine visits to the Caribbean to check up on their plantations, to hush up a scandal, to open up a big house, and to enjoy a little sunshine," in other words, behaving like Massas. This pattern of behavior, which Williams described as a disease, not only was spreading to the civil service but was a "poison seeping through the entire body politic."[40]

Turning his attention to what he felt were the cardinal principles of party democracy, Williams argued in favor of the "separation of Party Leader and Party Chairman, the supreme authority of the Party Conference, and the selection of party candidates by the party membership in the appropriate divisions being subject to the right of veto by the Party's executive." Second, he suggested that in order to reduce the likelihood of the party being dominated by specific interests such as big business, as was the case in America, the only solution was to have a mass party financed largely by dues-paying members and sympathetic individuals, with some of the revenue being refunded to the party and constituency groups, "rather than by undisclosed sources which might constitute pressure groups."[41]

Finally, since democracy, especially the Western variant, had been trumpeted as an antidote for communism, it was not surprising that Williams found it necessary to address this question also. The problem of modern democracy, he felt, was to find meaningful activities for the rank-and-file party members and to prevent the party from being overwhelmed by red tape, dominated by party bureaucrats, and overshadowed by party government. Returning to his favorite prototype—the Athenian model—Williams noted that the Greeks had faced no such problems in theory or in practice, as their democracy had been based on bottom-up citizen participation and, as noted above, on the idea that "every cook can govern." In other words, the Greeks had shown an extraordinary confidence in the capability of the "common man"—whether grocer, butcher, carpenter, sailor, or tailor, and whatever his education—to do the work required of him by the government and to hold office in divisions of the city.

Williams maintained that the electorate was also likely to judge the party he had in mind by its program. Space precludes an exhaustive treatment of his views that the party program should clearly and precisely indicate to voters what it proposed to achieve and how it intended to do so; it is sufficient to note that in Williams's view, the party's program should include an emphasis on infrastructure, which would involve the building of schools, roads, and bridges, providing jobs, as well as an emphasis on oil production, active cooperation of capital and labor, with the former providing jobs, and, lastly, a pledge to oppose racial discrimination in hiring.

Addressing the vexing question of religion, which threw into sharp relief the equally vexing question of education, Williams stated a clear preference for an indigenous solution to the issue of denominational schools. However, he also acknowledged the role of the church in providing education for the people of the West Indies when the state had deliberately refused to do so and that throughout history systems of state control of schools had had to face the fundamental difficulty that the state was considered by the people all over the country to be their principal enemy. Perhaps in an effort to reach out to Dom Basil Matthews, whom he referred to as "my old friend," and, evidently, the Catholic Church, whose disaffection he had acquired, Williams noted that Matthews had suggested to him "a few months ago" that the disunity possibly promoted by the present system "might well be controlled by a uniform curriculum coupled with rigid inspection of schools." This suggestion he regarded as an "honest and sincere effort to reconcile the wishes of the people with the attainment of our reasonable educational objectives."[42]

Going further, Williams observed that "the great Negro American scholar, Booker T. Washington, once said that if you want to keep a man down in a ditch, you must get down into the ditch with him. . . . The people of Trinidad and Tobago must either be kept down in the ditch in which they are or they must be pulled out of it. My colleagues and I lack the qualifications to keep you in the ditch. We believe we can pull you ot of it." The way to do this, he felt, was by organizing a party such as he had described, which would be a democratic party made up of "men and women of honesty and incorruptibility, all races, colours, classes and creeds, with a coherent and sensible programme of economic, social and political reform aimed at the development of the community as a whole, dedicated to its service, appealing to the intelligence rather than emotions of the electorate whose political education it places in the forefront of its activities."[43]

Additionally, in an effort not merely to build a collective identity but to reconfigure the notion of democracy, which in the colonial era had excluded the average Trinbagonian from even exercising the franchise, Williams stated that when party members were brought together at annual conventions, they were, first, "in effect, in our own small way, emulating the Greek practice of giving every citizen a chance to serve and an opportunity to be a member of the administration," and second, "creating a public assembly comprising a body of citizens who are personally familiar with the business of government."[44]

BUT INSTITUTIONAL change, while necessary, was not sufficient for the attainment of political independence. As a political educator, therefore, Williams also addressed the challenges facing the PNM, and in the process some of the shortcomings of the Trinbagonian "self," which he felt were antithetical to the nationalist endeavor. The party's financial difficulties, which affected the protractedness of a social movement, he noted, "were aggravated by the failure of many party members to do their duty to the party newspaper which not only endangers the paper financially, but also is an injustice to the party in that it limits its intellectual and political influence."[45]

During his address to the fifth annual convention of the PNM, in 1960, which had even clearer implications for relevant knowledge production and dissemination, Williams informed his listeners of the need for staff to type, stencil, and distribute documents, as well as to keep records and accounts and to maintain contact, both in person and in writing, "with the party groups and constituency groups." Also needed were "office space, filing cabinets, desks, chairs, paper, typewriter, etc.; and the payment of rent, and for light postage and telephone," as well as "staff, furnishings, and equipment, paper and normal office needs in respect of the Publishing Company," which was responsible for publishing many of his speeches and was in a "parlous state financially and editorially even in a worse state."[46]

Social-movement organizations, like political parties, also face the special responsibility, not merely of rallying the faithful and others who might benefit from the movement, but of providing a clear message concerning the legitimation of the movement and the need to adhere to the norms and values of the movement, as opposed, in this case, to those of the prevailing colonial order. This concern might have been fostered by the PNM experience in the March 1958 federal elections, in which, as noted, Williams accused party supporters of failing to vote. Consequently, while stressing the importance of the upcoming 1961 election and, more importantly, that of loyalty, Williams explained that since everything was of a lower priority than the elections, every act and every move must be seen in that context. Consequently, he intoned, no skylarking, sabotage, backsliding, disharmony, dishonesty, or intrigue could be tolerated.[47]

Williams warned against intrigue, faction, and *mauvaise langue,* which had reared their ugly heads in the movement. Individuals who sought to use the PNM for personal gain were, he stated, traitors to the party. Continuing, he noted, with party loyalty in mind, that this did not mean "ours not to reason why, yours but to do and die." Rather, as part of the notion of democracy, it meant "the fullest opportunity for expression of your views, on the policy when it is to be decided, and on the implementation and details of that policy, which, once a decision is arrived at by majority vote, must be supported and carried out by all."[48]

Continuing, Williams addressed actions that tended to hinder the nationalist movement, actions of persons whom social-movement analysts refer to as "free riders."[49] These are individuals who seek to benefit from a collective good, such as political independence, but decline to pay the costs involved, such as expenditures of dues, time, or energy, reasoning that even if they did not pay the costs, merely by being a member of the colonized stratum they would benefit from any outcomes associated with the movement. As a consequence, movement leaders may use various "selective incentives," such as benefits that accrue only to participants who are not free riders.

Williams appears to have attempted to deal with free riders by continually exhorting party members to support the party financially, especially since they stood to benefit cognitively, by way of a political education,[50] and by his anticolonial "cursing." And dues-paying party members were likely to be given preferential treatment when it came to government jobs or other jobs in the public service, as well as access to party leaders, especially in their ministerial capacity, and to Williams in particular.

However, Williams did not always operate in a democratic manner,[51] as people were sometimes able to bypass ministers of government and see him. Thus, certain party members were able to access opportunities for overseas travel on official business, foreign-service appointments, and invitations to functions, which carried a certain amount of prestige or symbolic capital because Williams, as chief minister, was likely to be in attendance. Finally, party leaders, and especially Williams, sought to advance the argument that while participation in the movement for its own sake was the right thing to do regardless of the accrued benefits, a politically independent Trinidad and Tobago was infinitely more desirable than a colonial Trinidad and Tobago.

This argument was advanced by way of exhortation and guilt inducement, which were resorted to by Williams during his addresses to party members and delegates at annual PNM conventions. Thus, it may be that selective incentives were not necessarily "financial" but were sensitive to cultural needs and the specific needs of the movement. As Myra Ferree notes, the "free rider dilemma appears to be largely chimerical. As is already well documented, mobilization begets countermobilization not by providing selective incentives but by highlighting the threat of collective bads that it would be difficult, if not impossible, to escape." Beyond that, there is also considerable evidence, Ferree notes, that "selective incentives are unnecessary or even irrelevant in many instances." Thus, movement leaders tend to expend available resources, in this instance resources such as time, energy, and printing materials, "in framing the issues and defining the affected community in ways that they perceive will give them strategic advantage."[52] This is exactly what occurred in the situation under discussion, where especially the threat of a collective bad, such as colonial oppression, was highlighted vis-à-vis the intrinsic value that was placed on a collective good, such as political independence, which PNM leaders, including Williams, clearly did.

Again, as the anointed one and the *mandataire,* Williams made it clear that the political leader of the PNM spoke with authority in the party, in the government, and in the country and had a very clear and special responsibility, which was directly related to the generation and transmission of knowledge. The political leader, therefore, was expected to be the main source of the party's ideals and its political attitudes. Moreover, he was to be free to develop these and to extend his knowledge in every sphere in collaboration with a cadre of capable individuals, all the while exercising "the all-important function of presenting these ideas in a manner that can be easily assimilated and grasped by the Party and the Public." Also, since the party paper was the principal medium of party education, the political leader had the special responsibility, with respect to the verbal dimension of intellectualism, to write a weekly article in the paper, which might be on a historical subject, foreign affairs, or any point of topical interest and which, "at difficult moments in the life of the party or in the life of a country, can be of immense value in educating and lowering or raising the temper of the party and the people."[53]

However, he continued, it was not "the writing of articles in the Press that is important. It is to lay down the lines along which articles should be written and to find and develop this talent in all sections of the organisation."[54] Williams reiterated that the only possible way to accomplish this was to organize the party in such a way that it not only had a political life of its own but did so as an indispensable complement to and in support of the legislators and the government.

He noted, also, that the party press, at least initially, should have its own cabinet and ministers in the central office, centering on the general secretary, who, like the editor of the party paper, would have a status "on a par with the legislative representatives of the Party." Knowledge production of documents presented to a convention therefore would involve not merely publication but circulation or marketing, which should be "at least twice what it is." And, in what was perhaps his most serious effort to underscore the habitus regarding knowledge production and the social-movement intellectual, Williams contended that the joint function of publishing and circulation must be related to the PNM's key function, which was political education.[55] It is conceivable that this was an effort to shift the focus away from the *priest* and religion, as the founts of knowledge and salvation to come in another sphere of existence, toward the *party* in general and *the political leader* in particular, with an emphasis on the rationalization of human conduct, not in a future existence but in the present one.

It should also be noted that the former party newspaper editor, C. L. R. James, who perhaps came closest to functioning as a professional fundraiser for the PNM, was also aware of the difficulties associated with the party as the organizational and intellectual expression of the political-independence movement. Indeed, after his expulsion from the party in September 1961, James wrote a damning indictment of the party's "top leadership," which he said did not know what it was doing and had scandalously and incompetently compromised the fortunes of the PNM. James's comments were particularly problematic for the "top leadership" because thousands had turned out to listen to Williams, and it was incumbent on the PNM to be a social and political organization operating in the vanguard of a new regime. As James put it, in regard to the intellectual function of the party in the context of political independence,

> In an underdeveloped country, particularly in the West Indies, only the mass-based democratic party can be the centre of the instinctive movement and need to fill the vacuum. If we do not produce new conceptions, organisations, etc., the old ones remain in bastard form, creating confusion and disorder. What are we going to teach our children in the schools? . . . They are rejecting the old and consciously seeking the new. . . . The party does not merely convey ideas, actions and projects of the political leadership to the masses of the people. It does not merely transform these ideas into shapes and languages that the people are able to absorb. A mass party of this kind is the sole means by which the developing consciousness of the people can be translated conscious, of what it is they want, of the possibilities and limitations of their desires. By this means the political leadership, the writers and the journalists, are made aware of the movement of ideas and the stages of development in the country.[56]

Obviously, not only did James feel that the party intellectuals had an obligation to bring out the true political potential of the masses but he reserved a role for other intellectuals, such as writers and journalists, in the production of ideas and "new" knowledge that would facilitate this process.

In addition, James emphasized the need for the party and the party's newspaper to transmit ideas to the masses, first on a weekly basis, later twice per week, and eventually on a daily basis, especially during an election. This would be done via manifestoes, pamphlets, leaflets, and other election materials of four to six pages. This, he felt, was possible in view of the arrival of a new linotype machine on the island and the employment of a former government printer as manager of the print shop, which meant that the press was "now equipped to do the work of the Party in any political situation, including a sudden election."[57]

It is clear from the foregoing that Williams and the PNM were intent on introducing a new, improved element into the political matrix in Trinidad and Tobago. The question that then arose was whether Williams could parlay his activities as a movement intellectual into a successful run for political office, given the hurly-burly of political life in the colony. Opinions vary as to why Williams formally entered politics. Indeed, a year before his departure from the Caribbean Commission, and as early as 17 June 1954, in a letter to Norman Manley, Williams had made a rather candid assessment of his employment prospects and had not ruled out the possibility of entering the political arena. As noted previously, Williams had told Manley that he felt he was being persecuted and that since he would likely be relieved of his position on the commission, he might, as he later put it, "let my bucket right down" in politics.[58] Williams had not only entertained that possibility; despite a hectic schedule of public and other lectures, he had thought that he would keep his "name before the public" as a possible prelude to entering "the political arena."[59]

Speculating on Williams's formal entry into the political arena, U.S. Consul General Jenkins opined that Williams's first "admittedly" political speech had occurred on 29 December 1955, during a meeting at the UWS. In the course of that speech Williams had reported on a mission abroad for the International Confederation of Free Trade Unions and had made, among other things, "significant disclosures, which spoke to the obtrusion of a new political party, and of letting his bucket down, in Trinidad politics." He also had stated that he had rejected offers of employment while abroad and would remain in Trinidad.[60]

Another, perhaps less charitable view regarding Williams's motivation for entering formal politics came from the former deputy prime minister and sometime PNM minister of home affairs Patrick Solomon. Solomon, who also had attended Tranquility School, where he had come first in the common entrance exams during his last year at the school, recalled in his autobiography that a notable addition to the school that year was "an undersized youngster not more than nine and a half years old, very bright, very cocky and hopelessly immature. His name was Eric Williams." Williams had not been successful that year, "but the next year he knocked spots off everyone else."[61]

Solomon claimed that Williams was a "grievance politician" and that Williams himself admitted that "his 1956 pre-election activities were originally designed with one object in view—to get Eric Williams seated in the Legislative Council."[62] Solomon also stated that Williams had entered the political arena in part out of pique but also because of a desire for revenge. His entry, therefore, was never well intentioned. Solomon surmises that "to the extent that [Williams] was proud of Trinidad and Tobago, it was merely as an extension of his personality; and if he could not mould it to his own image and likeness he would not stay and serve it. It had rather to serve him, to give him status and, above all, power. Should power be ever taken from him he would not remain in opposition. Equally, should he find the obstacles to his own personal ambitions being constantly frustrated despite his power, he would assuredly find excuse to quit."[63]

The Bachacs member Donald Granado claims that the group had decided that Williams would be the most suitable person to lead the PNM,[64] and De Wilton Rogers, as we saw, noted that Williams was courted by the TECA and asked to play an advisory role in the association's activities.[65] In like manner, Wilfrid Alexander contends that Williams was viewed as the best person to lead the PNM.[66] Moreover, it will be recalled that after the November 1954 debate with Dom Basil Matthews, discussions had begun regarding the formation of a political party, with Williams being given a mandate to speak on behalf of the party. Evidently, therefore, the decision to enter formal politics was not one that suddenly occurred to Williams when he uttered his famous comment about letting his bucket down.

However, the fact of the matter is that especially starting in late 1955, as Williams transitioned from public intellectual to social-movement intellectual, the value of his political currency, much to the dismay of his detractors, had begun to increase significantly. In an interesting observation on Williams's success in creating space in the political arena, U.S. Consul General Jenkins wrote in a dispatch of 18 May 1956 that when he had arrived in Port-of-Spain "five months ago no one to whom I mentioned his name was prepared to admit that Williams could become the leader of a strong political movement." Indeed, Williams had generally been viewed as a "pedantic visionary entirely unacquainted with the rough and tumble of politics, who would be dealt with promptly and finally once he entered the political lists." Albert Gomes, who in Jenkins's mind gave the impression of someone who sensed that he was fighting for his political life, in private conversations with the consul general repeatedly accused Williams of fomenting race hatred and dissension and described him as "the most serious threat to the Colony's political well-being, a megalomaniac seeking to gain power by emphasizing racial enmity and economic inequality."

Jenkins noted that others, such as Pope McLean, the deputy leader of the Butler Party, had sought to belittle Williams on the floor of the Leg Co only to be stopped by a rule of order; and that John Rojas, president of the Oilfield Workers' Trade Union, had castigated Williams in a public lecture. In addition, Roy Joseph, the minister of education and social services, had come out strongly against Williams, and in a private conversation such "widely divergent and antagonistic politicians" as Ashford Sinanan, the deputy speaker of the Trinidad Parliament; Victor Bryan, minister of agriculture and lands; Norman Tang, minister of health and local government; Pat Mathura, mayor of Port-of-Spain and an associate of Bhadase Maraj's; and Gerard Montano, mayor of San Fernando, had all indicated "their awareness of Williams's political strength and their determination to oppose him." In other words, all of the then ministers of government who Williams determined had exemplified the colonial political ethos, against which he was railing, albeit with some trepidation, had recognized Williams's growing political stature.

The above contentions notwithstanding, Jenkins stated that he had failed to discern any propensity on Williams's part to stir up "racial feeling" or any sign that he was "aiming for power for his personal aggrandizement." Moreover, Jenkins felt that Williams's speeches were "well thought out and well organized and rather pedantic with a wealth of historical background information" and that his delivery was "clear and forceful but unspectacular." And, while Jenkins could not explain Williams's power, he suggested that it was perhaps due to a thirst for knowledge on the part of his listeners, to whom Williams paid the compliment of "not talking down to them."[67]

However, whatever Williams's true motives were, his entry and that of the PNM into the political landscape were certainly enhanced by a number of other factors as the election of 24 September 1956 approached. First, the party diligently campaigned throughout Trinidad, outperforming the opposition to an unprecedented degree. For example, in a speech on 29 July, at reportedly the largest political rally ever held on the island, with an estimated attendance of eleven thousand, and in a repeat performance the following evening in San Fernando, with an estimated crowd of forty-five hundred, Williams announced the names of some of the candidates and the districts they would contest. In fact, the presence of the party on the political scene at that moment and Williams's ongoing ability to attract a large audience as a social-movement intellectual moved the consul general to remark that the enthusiasm of PNM adherents in comparison with followers of other parties was impressive. Moreover, "the letters 'PNM' are everywhere; on walls, on automobiles, even on the crates and boxes being delivered through the port. And the drawing power of the party's political meetings continues to grow. During the week ending August 5 it is officially estimated that there was a total attendance of 32,000 at 11 PNM meetings as compared with 4,652 at 26 meetings held by all other parties."[68]

In addition, as in the case of other successful individuals of considerable achievement in various spheres of human endeavor, luck, or more properly the ability to recognize and capitalize on the seeming efficacy of a particular event, also played a part in Williams's successful entry into politics. During a debate in the Leg Co on 15 April 1955, which had degenerated into a stormy session after dinner, when members appear to have drunk rather more than they ate, a motion was passed by a vote of 18 to 5 to ask the British government to postpone the general election, constitutionally scheduled for September 1955 or within 4 months thereafter, until the middle of 1956. As noted above, Bhadase Maraj, in anticipation of the passage of the motion, announced that he would resign his seat and seek vindication in a subsequent by-election. A probably inebriated Ranjit Kumar, another member of the council, reportedly remarked to Maraj, "Do you know who know who will oppose you in that election? The ghosts of Kissoondath and Abid!" Kumar was apparently referring to two unsolved murder cases involving Indians and a rumor that implicated Maraj. Consequent upon the withdrawal of the remark, "Maraj warned Kumar that he would 'deal with him tonight' whereupon the latter countered 'You have threatened to shoot me twice already.'"[69] In a subsequent statement regarding the request for postponement of the election on 5 September, Governor Sir Edward Beetham indicated that the secretary of state for the colonies had decided to "submit to Her Majesty in Council draft of an Order providing that dissolution may be deferred until the normal end of the next session of the Legislature, that is, until 26 May 1956."[70]

The eventual postponement of the elections until September 1956 turned out to be a blessing for Williams and the PNM: "from a modest short term ambition of hoping to return a single member to the new Legislature to watch its interests until the 1961 General Elections, the People's National Movement was, by the sheer force of overwhelming circumstances, pressured into a full scale contest of the 1956 General Elections."[71] Undoubtedly, the PNM saw the incident in the Leg Co as providing another reason to separate itself from this brand of politics and chose to use the extra time to prepare for the election, thereby introducing a new dynamic to the country's political corpus. Lastly, the action of the government, illustrative as it was of intra-elite conflict, constituted another salient facet of the political-opportunity structure[72] and unintentionally provided more space for the PNM in the political landscape. The result was that although the PNM only came into existence in January 1956, it was able to capture thirteen of the twenty-four seats in the Trinidad Parliament in the September 1956 election.

Even though the party won a plurality of the votes and the seats, however, it still was not able to form a government. This was because in addition to the two ex-officio members of the Leg Co (the colonial secretary and the attorney general), five other members could be nominated by the governor, which would bring the total number of members to thirty-one. This meant that the PNM needed a minimum of sixteen members in order to govern in a meaningful way. Two events worked in the PNM's favor. First, the governor announced publicly that the two ex-officio members would vote with a PNM government or any government that was in power. Second, the governor stated that although he had no intention of "nominating party members or men subject to party discipline . . . he would not nominate men who were hostile to the PNM."[73] Following three meetings with Williams and other PNM top brass, and consequent upon instructions from the secretary of state for the colonies, it was announced that the governor had acceded to Williams's request to name two members of the PNM (both of whom were acceptable to the governor) to serve in the Leg Co. These, along with the two ex-officio members, gave the PNM a working majority of seventeen in the Leg Co.[74]

Although the response to the PNM's victory was on the whole favorable, some individuals did have reservations, if not about the process that had culminated in a working majority for the PNM in the Leg Co, then about Williams's appointment as chief minister. A Colonial Office official with whom a U.S. embassy official had discussed the matter, for instance, expressed satisfaction at the PNM's victory, welcoming it as a sign of the "consolidation of political forces and the creation of a political party of practical dimensions." However, he voiced apprehension about Williams's capacity to lead a successful administration, describing him as a "frustrated intellectual" who "heretofore had exhibited no talent for getting along with people [and who] had been a disagreeable and troublesome associate when he was a member of the Caribbean Commission." Nonetheless, he conceded that Williams had "conducted a skillful campaign and might henceforth demonstrate political and administrative talents which many observers thought he lacked."[75] In any event, with Butler outliving his political usefulness, the defeat of Gomes, Joseph, and Tang at the polls, and the obvious supplantation of personality politics by party politics, Williams and the PNM aimed to cross the threshold regarding the politics of "anything goes" on the twin island.

7 The Bachacs Confront the "Hydra-Head" of Colonialism

The American Presence in Trinidad and Tobago

> To talk of independence and in the same breath accept obligations of a nature unknown to us by virtue of a treaty which was not only imposed upon us in the first instance but which is given apparently any interpretation and is used to justify any extension its signatories care to give—that would be to substitute military imperialism of the Americans for the economic imperialism of the British, and the new economic imperialism will probably not be long in following.
>
> —Eric Williams

IN PREVIOUS chapters I examined the manner in which Williams used historical knowledge as a weapon to "curse" the language of oppression exemplified by the various "heads" of colonialism in Trinidad and Tobago. These included imperialism, enslavement, indenture, and the trappings of colonialism in its various forms—political, economic, sociocultural—especially in the sport of cricket. In this chapter I analyze Williams's continuing efforts to use historical knowledge to "curse" another manifestation of Prospero's language, again by nibbling away at the American presence at the Chaguaramas base, which he considered to be the principal, or "Hydra," head of colonialism in Trinidad.[1] In Greek mythology the hydra was a monster that allegedly had nine heads, which were capable of growing back even after they had been cauterized.

The location of an American base at Chaguaramas was the result of a "Ships for Bases" agreement between Her Majesty's government and the U.S. government in 1941. The people of Trinidad and Tobago and the West Indies were not consulted, and the agreement gave the Americans a ninety-nine-year lease for a site on Trinidad's northwestern peninsula. The area, of some thirty thousand acres,[2] was provided in exchange for

"50 over-age destroyers," which in 1930 would have fetched between $263,000 and $340,000, or an average price of $300,000.[3] During World War II the base was an important American naval facility, viewed by the United States as essential to the strategic defense of the Western Hemisphere. For example, in a December 1939 speech Frank Knox, editor of the *Chicago Daily News* and later secretary of the navy, revealed that he had been informed by military friends that "for defense against air raids and to guarantee the safety of the approaches to the Panama Canal, the Caribbean must be made into an American Lake."[4]

The opportunity to satisfy the need for American bases in the British Caribbean was provided by British misfortune. Overburdened by big battleships and cruisers that were of little use in the war against Germany, the British experienced significant shipping losses in 1940. The only potential source of help for Britain was the industrial might of America. It was against this background of interdependence that the British prime minister, Winston Churchill, in May 1940 made a frank and personal appeal to the American president, Franklin Roosevelt, for "a declaration of 'non-belligerency' and the 'loan of thirty or forty of your old destroyers and also whatever airplanes you could spare right now.'"[5]

Sensing, however, that some quid pro quo would be required on the part of the Americans, the British ambassador in Washington, Lord Lothian, suggested on 24 May 1940 that Britain should anticipate U.S. demands and make a "spontaneous offer" of base facilities on the islands of the British Caribbean.[6] The United States also had an economic motive for acquiring bases in the British Caribbean. In order to remain a naval power, the United States needed to control the oil resources of the hemisphere, and by the late 1930s Trinidad had become the eleventh largest oil-producing country in the world, and the most important producer of oil in the British Empire.[7]

The agreement, which stated that the U.S. government would accept "no obligation, no commitment, no alliance [and] was in a position to abandon its undertaking whenever it pleased them to do so with or without consent,"[8] was met with a mixed reaction in the West Indies. While most of the political and upper stratum, which included newspaper editors and influential businessmen, grudgingly approved the agreement, Black West Indian leaders vigorously opposed it on the grounds that *(a)* it was high-handed and had been consummated without the knowledge or approval of any of the legislative councils in the islands; *(b)* any benefits that might accrue to the islands would be offset by the cardinal sin of U.S. racial discrimination; and *(c)* the possibility of insufficient wages being paid by base authorities might create labor problems in the islands.

As EARLY as September 1945, during a conference in Barbados, Vivian Henry, general secretary of the Trinidad Labour Party and secretary of both the West Indies and British Guiana Labour Congress and the Caribbean Labour Conference, opined that some of his comrades might have refrained from voicing their opposition "to the infliction in their colonies of men of the United States Armed Forces" because "a crisis had arisen and they must make allowances for all the happenings to avert that crisis."[9] However, he inveighed against "the practically permanent infliction on the colonies of these alien troops for 99 years . . . made possible by the presence of so many American troops during the War," especially when these leases were contracted and executed "without the peoples whom they concerned ever having been consulted." Therefore, he urged the delegates to put forward the "strongest request that this land-lease agreement, as far as the establishment of U.S. Bases in these colonies was concerned, be revised if not entirely revoked."[10]

For his part, Albert Gomes maintained that the continued presence of the bases was a "threat not only to the prestige and the self-respect of West Indians . . . but it was a threat to their aspirations along the lines of federation and future self-government." Also, Grenada's T. A. Marryshow opined that the bases were a "stumbling block to federation" and that the way should be made "clear for a federated West Indies," with "Self-Government being the object."[11]

For some, the West Indian colonies' lack of involvement in the decision to locate bases within their boundaries was understandable because Britain was engaged in a "hot war" (World War II), with her back to the wall, and a speedy conclusion of the agreement was essential. However, as Trinidad-based U.S. Consul General Douglas Jenkins frankly acknowledged, things had changed by early 1957, and the nonparticipation on the part of the government and the people had become "an irritant and constituted an ever present possible ground for objecting to the existence of the leased areas." According to Jenkins, if the United States wanted to maintain the bases and other military installations, while avoiding friction and recriminations, a concerted effort ought to be made to maintain and foster the closest and friendliest relations possible with the people, the governments, and the nascent federation. This was especially desirable, he felt, in view of the increasing movement toward self-government. However, while the more educated segment of society was aware of America's role in assuming the "responsibility of shielding the area, a burden which the United Kingdom was no longer able to carry, the average man was little impressed by this." Moreover, in view of the extreme insularity of the area, "there is little awareness of what is happening in the rest of the world . . . and no sense of responsibility to take a hand in the struggle between the free and communist worlds."[12]

Thus, there were significant points of friction with the local population, among which was the ninety-nine-year lease to extensive areas of Trinidad without local input, a point the *Trinidad Guardian,* which proclaimed itself to be "pro-American" but "anti-Bases," never failed to mention. In addition, dissatisfaction had arisen over the ongoing presence of "alien armed forces" enjoying immunity from local jurisdiction, which was considered to be a "derogation of sovereignty by both the pro-British element and the local nationalists." While Jenkins's comments obviously spoke to the existence of the bases as a physical space that privileged the Americans and disadvantaged the locals, he noted that the prime source of friction was the acquisition of a space on Trinidad's northern shoreline. This space had been acquired at the expense of the residents, of whom many were small farmers and fisherfolk who had been evicted from places such as Teteron, Tucker Valley, and Macqueripe and others were among the island's more prominent and well-to-do citizens, who had built weekend homes and a hotel close to one of the most attractive and accessible bathing beaches.

These sources of friction, said Jenkins, were aggravated by the requirement that boat owners who had built weekend homes on the small islands off the western tip of the naval station had to obtain passes to moor their boats on the Trinidad side of Staubles Bay, a small enclave within the base. Boat owners were therefore at the mercy of the base's station commander, who was in a position to refuse them a pass and to subject them to the regulations of the U.S. military patrols. This led to frequent petty incidents involving military personnel and Trinidadians, who felt humiliated at having to request passes, to stop at the station entrance to be checked by a marine sentry, and to adhere to a 30-miles-per-hour speed limit on pain of losing the privilege of transiting the base. This was another example of the lifeworld of the dominated—sometimes ephemeral, sometimes palpable, but always present—which might be incorporated into the "self" of the "other."

One instance of friction occurred when a boat owned by a member of the Island Homeowners' Association ran out of gasoline and began drifting toward the shore into "prohibited" waters adjacent to the naval station. The result was that a marine sentry, presumably thinking that the backfiring boat was a gunshot, forced the boat's two occupants ashore at gunpoint and allegedly roughed them up before turning them over to the base commander, who then publicly supported the sentry and revoked the boat owner's pass. The "offenders" were subsequently turned over to the local police, who promptly released them, leading to deep concern on the part of the Homeowners' Association, whose president was the chief justice of the supreme court. The *Guardian,* according to Jenkins, then "had a field day publishing every claim and counter-claim on its front page under banner headlines and devoting its editorial column to caustic comments regarding 'trigger happy' Americans."[13] With this in mind, the consul general recommended, among other things, that special care be taken in selecting officers to command military facilities, whose friendly and sociable manner might go a long way toward smoothing relations with the large number of island homeowners.[14]

This incident is also important because the occupation of the peninsula constituted what Henri Lefebvre refers to as "representation of space," in that the occupation also entailed control of the beach, or "abstract space," that is, natural space. In such a manner, control of a certain physical space, in this case the base, is acquired in order to gain and maintain control over a larger space,[15] in this case the beach and the water. The issue of time assumed relevance because the United States was granted rights to occupation of the peninsula in the first instance for ninety-nine years, and the Chaguaramas Joint Commission Report later recommended that any consideration regarding the question of ongoing occupation would not come up for "ten years or so."

It was against the abovementioned background that the base, annexed for the purpose of U.S. security, continued to be a space for contentious political activity. For example, when the issue of a site for the federal capital of the West Indies came up at a conference in Jamaica, a subcommittee of the Standing Federation Committee (SFC), which was appointed to look into the matter, met in Trinidad in March 1957 and recommended the site of the American naval base at Chaguaramas, "on grounds purely of its location by the sea, scenic beauty and its existing facilities," as "the most suitable site for the Federal Capital." The subcommittee's recommendation was considered by the SFC at a meeting in Trinidad from 6 to 17 May 1957. During the meeting the SFC took note of the assurance "that the foreign power in question [the U.S. government] is anxious to extend the hand of friendship to, and preserve the closest possible links with, our nation in embryo." The SFC agreed with the recommendation of the subcommittee and resolved that the northwestern peninsula should be the site of the federal capital.

Not surprisingly, the SFC's decision led to a number of exchanges between the United States and the government of Trinidad and Tobago (GOTT), as the Americans sought to force the GOTT, now led by Dr. Williams, to abide by the terms of the 1941 agreement. For their part, Williams and the GOTT sought to have the agreement rescinded, or at least renegotiated, and thereby to force the Americans to give up the base or to remain on terms thought to be favorable to Trinidad and Tobago.

SINCE, GIVEN the nature of the dialectical relationship between dominant and dominated, one would expect America, as the putative colonial power, to attempt to defend what it believed to be its space, we will now consider U.S. efforts to do so by using the language of non–decision making. This involves doing what is necessary to ensure that any action involving a shift in what Peter Bachrach and Morton Baratz refer to as the "mobilization of bias" or, simply put, any action that challenges the rules of the game or the rules of engagement, never reaches the point of producing social change that benefits the challengers. Non–decision making, accordingly, may entail *(a)* not responding to requests for change from challengers; *(b)* placing the challenge to the mobilization of bias at a point on a meeting agenda where it never comes up for discussion, much less a vote; *(c)* directing the challenge to a committee or a series of committees populated by individuals who are likely to be transient (e.g., university students, who may give up a challenge to a university administration because preparation for exams takes precedence), as a consequence of which no decision involving change in the rules of the game is made; and/or *(d)* outright annihilation of the challengers.[16] As will be seen, the Americans resorted to the first two strategies, while they appear to have considered the fourth.

Even before the SFC conference in London in July 1957, the United States tried to discourage overtures for change from the Trinidadians. On 8 February 1956 the GOTT expressed an interest in entering into an agreement with the U.S. government for the operation of an idle quarry, then understood to be the Verdant Vale quarry.[17] In March 1957, with Williams in office as chief minister, the GOTT reportedly dispatched a message to the American president, Dwight Eisenhower, and the British prime minister, Harold Macmillan, urging that one of the bases leased by the United States in Trinidad be released for use as the site of the capital of the West Indies Federation. Also, as the date of the conference approached, the American policy of non–decision making regarding the base began to crystallize in the form of semantics.

On 10 May 1957, for example, the American secretary of state, John Foster Dulles, wrote to the American consul general in Port-of-Spain requesting additional information and background on the choice of Chaguaramas as the federal capital and asking that the U.S. ambassador in London be advised that if pressed for a public statement, the consul general should withhold comment on the grounds that the request had not yet been received or considered by the U.S. government.[18] The very next day (11 May), the consul general wrote that the SFC's request for the release of Chaguaramas was apparently motivated by a sincere belief that the base was the best site for the capital. Continuing, he noted that while refusal to accede to the request certainly involved a degree of risk by "providing a basis for virulent and sustained anti-Bases campaign," he believed that "if carefully and sympathetically dealt with vital installations if not the entire area can be retained without serious adverse consequences."[19]

In an effort to effect a degree of consonance between the strategies of the U.S. and U.K. governments, the British Foreign Office expressed the hope that a summary of the American position would be "suitably tailored for Her Majesty's Government to transmit to the SFC delegation." For his part, the U.S. ambassador in London, John Hay Whitney, suggested that in any media coverage of the London conference, the words *facility* and *installation,* rather than *base,* be used in connection with Chaguaramas. He also suggested that *Trinidadians* and *West Indians* be used rather than *Trinidad* in order to put things in a wider perspective.[20]

The 16–23 July 1957 conference, convened by the British Foreign Office in London, laid out the positions of the three parties concerned, the British, the Americans, and the West Indians.[21] In his capacity as chief minister, Williams agreed to serve as a member of the West Indian delegation, but with certain reservations, since the GOTT, desiring to honor its international obligations, could not press for the release of the base. The government would retain an observer status "unless the negotiations reached the stage of working out the conditions of release, i.e. unless the Government of the United States agreed to release the Base without demur." In other words, Williams would only participate if it appeared that the United States would depart from the base. By adopting this posture, he would be in a position to separate himself and his government from any outcome that was inconsistent with U.S. departure.

In any event, during the conference the U.S. government submitted a memorandum setting out reasons why it was not possible to cede Chaguaramas either wholly or partially. However, the government promised to give "sympathetic consideration" to any request for release of part of another base, at Waller Field. The American ambassador to London, while reiterating that it was not feasible for his government to accede to a request to give up the Chaguaramas base, because it was still needed for security purposes, stated that his government would be willing to entertain a future request to relinquish the base. Indeed, he hoped that those present at the conference could "equally appreciate our grave concern to retain the location which best assures the ability to defend the strategically vital Caribbean Area." "The provision of the best defense is important not only to the U.S., but to your Federation, and to the United Kingdom," he concluded.[22]

The British government, though less intransigent, seemed hardly sympathetic to the West Indian cause. For example, David Ormsby-Gore, of the Foreign Office, stated on behalf of his government that the base had originally been established on a quasi-permanent basis and hitherto had been regarded in the United States as "an integral element in the United States defence plans for the Caribbean." And while "all possible regard is paid" to the view expressed by the SFC that Chaguaramas was the most suitable site for the proposed capital, Ormsby-Gore, perhaps remembering the United States' help to Britain during the war, concluded that "we are deeply conscious of the need to collaborate fully with the United States Government in plans for the security of the Caribbean area." Speaking on behalf of the West Indies, Norman Manley, chief minister of Jamaica, stated that after careful investigation he did not believe that "we should have asked for the release of the area had it not been that we were driven by our need and by the fact that we are unable to find any other site suitable for our purposes." It happened that Chaguaramas was not just the "most suitable" site but the "only suitable" site; and while "a Base is a temporary structure; the Capital is intended to last for generations to come."

For his part, Williams noted that a year earlier his party had stated that it accepted the 1941 Leased-Bases Agreement, and at a meeting of the SFC the Trinidad government's representative had abstained from voting on the question of the capital site. Williams, however, stated that he was not now in a position to adhere to his earlier stand in view of the fact that while the Trinidad people had accepted the agreement in good faith, the base was a result of political and defense requirements.

Furthermore, in 1940 the governor of Trinidad and Tobago and the Executive Council had strongly opposed both the choice of the site and its subsequent extension to Tucker Valley in favor of a single combined base in the Caroni Swamp area, as well as the length of the lease, but had been overruled by the war cabinet.[23]

The Chaguaramas issue continued to be of such importance that during a meeting on 5 September 1957 between Secretary Wilson, other top Department of Defense officials, and John Foster Dulles, the U.S. secretary of state was asked about the meaning of a sentence in a letter of 21 July from President Eisenhower to Prime Minister Macmillan concerning the Trinidad base. The letter purportedly suggested that the United States would never force a base where it was not wanted nor remain when it was not welcome. In a carefully worded response designed to belie the impression that a decision favorable to the GOTT's request for release of the base was imminent or even likely, Dulles stated that what the president meant was that if deep-seated opposition to the base were to "develop and persist among responsible elements in the West Indies, he believed that U.S. policy regarding retention of the Base would have to be revised[, which] certainly did not mean isolated demands from politicians that we surrender the Base would cause us to 'grab our hats' and get out."[24]

Dulles's statement did not necessarily mean that the United States would not consider other "solutions" to the Chaguaramas issue. For example, Walter Orebaugh, the American consul general in Trinidad, while noting that Ashford Sinanan, the leader of the opposition in the West Indian legislature, was the target of a suit brought against him by Williams for calling the latter "a degenerate liar," revealed that Sinanan had asked for information on Williams's background to use in his attack against Williams's character. Sinanan has also proposed to write to a Washington lawyer about Williams's marital difficulties.[25] The consul general went on to note that Sinanan, who had been helpful in the past, needed help and that this provided the United States with "the opportunity to put another nail in the political coffin of Eric Williams." In "accepting the policy to erase Williams from political power," Orebaugh continued, "we must speed up the process of cutting him down from his pedestal. The recounting of the marital problems before the federal elections helped, and the Sinanan trial can be even more fruitful."[26]

Orebaugh suggested that since the Williams problem could not be handled piecemeal, it was incumbent upon the United States to deal with Williams: after assessing its position and reviewing its strength, it should devise a plan of action and seek to "disengage with Williams and work for his ultimate demise." In addition, Orebaugh noted in a subsequent missive that the time had come to "get down to cases" and determine what could be done about Williams. He indicated that it was most important to get a policy firmly in place and to carry it through without further procrastination. However, Orebaugh realized that embarking on a course of action to "get" Williams, "without taking the risk of getting into local affairs to a far greater degree than anything we have done heretofore," could be problematic.

Continuing his ominous tone, the consul general expressed his appreciation for "having someone who has access to the full record prepare a dossier on Williams which would contain information that is openly usable in an attack on his character and past associations. The FBI files, CIA records, and most importantly British Intelligence, must have a good deal on him." In recognizing, however, that "how or whether we can use British sources was a touchy subject," Orebaugh nevertheless felt that any available information was needed as soon as possible, as although the court case might not come up for a few months, Williams "could always move to get an early trial to try and damage Sinanan and his party before the up-coming Trinidad Legislative Council by-elections."[27]

Apart from being aware of the positions of the West Indian leaders, the United States sought to appease the third public in the equation, namely, the West Indian masses, especially since the British had made it clear that political independence was a real possibility in the none too distant future. Orebaugh appears to have struck a realistic note when he observed that apart from the "current rumblings of Jamaica's Norman Manley" and the possibility of a "verbal explosion" on the part of Williams,

> now that the die has been cast, and the US-UK rejection of the WI claim is clear, it still remains for the decision to be accepted by the WI. Unless US retention of Chaguaramas is made palatable to the WI, we may only have won a Pyrrhic victory—and in the future, we could reap such fruits as come from offended sensibilities and a sense of frustration on the part of the leading politicians. When this is considered in the light of WI independence within five years, it is not at all unlikely that we will be faced at that time with a demand for US withdrawal from all Bases, in other words, a unilateral abrogation of the 1941 agreement.[28]

Furthermore, Orebaugh observed that whether or not one considered the legality of the treaty, the reality of the matter was that "despite any legal posturing and even given US assurances as to the continuation of the treaty rights, there is little doubt that in the West Indian view it is within the practical power of an independent WI to abrogate the agreement. It boils down to the oft quoted statement that the US will not stay where it is not wanted." On the plus side, however, Orebaugh felt that the United States had the support of the DLP opposition in the Trinidad Leg Co, which might seek to obtain some political mileage from the base issue. Orebaugh supposed that since Williams was facing dissension within his cabinet and more latterly within the PNM, the Chaguaramas issue could be the catalyst for an open break between Williams and three of his ministers, who were troubled by Williams's "dictatorial approach in the present government."[29]

Concluding his assessment, the American consul general noted that in spite of the abovementioned factors and crosscurrents, "the outlook for the successful resolution of the Chaguaramas issue is neither simple nor subject to mere reliance on the legality argument, whether in terms of the 1941 Agreement or in terms of the present constitutional status of the West Indies." Orebaugh suggested that given the continued position of the British government, as well as the support of political allies, the prospects were favorable not only for the retention of the base but also, probably, for laying the groundwork for a longer period of retention. In the long run, however, Orebaugh was less sanguine about U.S. chances for retaining the base unless the Americans could develop and count on West Indian cooperation. Moreover, he continued, U.S. prospects were "likely to be worsened by the degree to which Eric Williams is able to expand his future political role," and it was important to recognize that "we are dealing with forces characteristic of emergent nationalism."[30]

The Chaguaramas issue, Orebaugh conceded, continued to be a cause célèbre in the West Indies and "a source of constant irritation and harassment to the United States."[31] This was because Williams "has kept the issue alive and leaves no stone unturned in pursuing with single-minded purpose the drastic modification of the terms under which the Bases are occupied," which he saw as a nationalist cause. Thus, since "the United States cannot deal reasonably with the man, either now or in the future," it should, "to the maximum extent feasible, and within the means which can be developed, . . . work for the weakening of Williams's political position in Trinidad and his eventual replacement by more rational elements."[32]

Although the consul general did not elaborate on what he meant by "eventual replacement by more rational elements," he did suggest that since Trinidad was still a British colony, the British government should be urged "to use its full influence to contain Williams." He also indicated that the federal government might assert its interest in "developing harmonious U.S.-W.I. relations . . . [and] be prepared to assist in the maintenance of United States Base rights under the 1941 Agreement, until such time as revisions are mutually acceptable and agreed upon."[33]

Finally, the essentiality of retaining the base for strategic purposes, "without at the same time, prejudicing our other present and future military requirements in the area,"[34] was the subject of a State Department position paper. The paper suggested that efforts should be made to foment dissension among the West Indian leadership and the masses, and the best way to do this was to refrain from "public utterances or actions which would appear to make our position regarding the Naval Base 'inflexible.'" Also, attempts should be made to "dissuade the British West Indians from insistence on the Base by judiciously planting doubts in the minds of their leaders as to the reasonableness of their request." Finally, the "strong rivalries which are known to exist among politically vocal groups in the West Indies," the paper suggested, "may help us here, providing we do not irritate the West Indians to the point where they unite against us."[35] This was the language of divide and conquer.

FACED WITH U.S. intransigence characterized by an unwillingness not merely to relinquish the base but even to discuss renegotiation of the 1941 Leased-Bases Agreement, which would involve the GOTT, the United Kingdom, and the United States, Williams and the GOTT sought to make space for their views regarding removal of the Americans by divining a strategy similar to the nibbling activity of the Bachacs. It should be noted that in situations such as this one, involving two territorial entities of vastly different size and strategic resources, a case of David confronting Goliath as it were, the weaker party is forced to choose both its weapons and its tactics, involving choice of opportunities and timing, with great care. This while seizing opportunities not recognized or taken by others.[36] In other words, an effort was being made to make better use of the political-opportunity structure. In this context, the "nibbling away" strategy involved not only attacking different facets of the U.S. presence but also, in some instances, making somewhat doubtful use of the law. Pursuing this line of attack, however, as will be seen, did not mean a divorce from the strategy of moving what Williams perceived to be key elements of the Chaguaramas affair from the periphery to the center of the public sphere.

In keeping with his previously mentioned comments made during the July 1957 London conference and a statement in June 1956 at a meeting at Woodford Square, in his capacity as chief minister of Trinidad and Tobago, Williams launched an attack on the paramount head of colonialism by making an expedient volte-face from the 1956 preelection promise to honor all international obligations.[37] Regarding his change of mind, Williams later noted that the Chaguaramas issue "represented the most important and the most dramatic manifestation of the problem of a Caribbean Economic Community, with particular reference to the question of 'foreignism.'"[38] However, the view of the West Indian governments that Chaguaramas should be surrendered to make way for the federal capital, he went on, raised two problems that placed the PNM on the horns of a dilemma. First, it was in conflict with the PNM election manifesto to honor all international agreements, including the agreement on the American base at Chaguaramas. Second, it was widely alleged, and even more widely believed, that the decision was a deliberately set trap for the PNM in that the unavailability of Chaguaramas as a site for the capital meant reopening the question of where to locate the capital.

However, reading the documents regarding the 1941 agreement, Williams recalled in the PNM party newspaper, the *Nation*, he learned for the first time of

> the tremendous pressures exercised by the Americans on the Government of Trinidad and Tobago . . . the opposition of the then Governor, Sir Hubert Young, and the counter proposal that the Base should be established in the Caroni Swamp which should be reclaimed for that purpose. . . . the opposition from the West Indian territories, Bermuda and Newfoundland at the Anglo-American Conference in London in 1941, of the American refusal to make any payment at all for the areas ceded, of the American insistence on extra-territorial jurisdiction to avoid racial confrontations in the West Indies.[39]

Armed with this new information, he formally proposed *(a)* the evacuation of Chaguaramas by the United States; *(b)* the establishment of a joint commission of the four interested parties—Trinidad and Tobago, the West Indies, the United Kingdom, and the United States—to select a new site for a combined base; and *(c)* the revision of article 28 of the 1941 agreement, involving the transfer of the base to an alternative site and the formal association of the Trinidad and Tobago government as signatories to any such agreement.

With respect to the next "nibble," Williams and the GOTT determined that the sale of citrus fruit from the Tucker Valley plantation at the naval station in Trinidad created "a dollar drain" on the Trinidad economy and should cease. During a press conference on 20 September 1958, for example, Williams referred to the sale as constituting unfair competition for local agriculture. On 24 September, in response to the press conference, the American consul general submitted a memorandum to the acting governor calling attention to "distortions" in the press conference. The consul general also informed him that Williams had ordered the Citrus Growers Association, which marketed the fruit, to deliver the BWI$25,000 due to the navy to his ministry rather than to the Citrus Growers Association.

Undaunted, at his press conference on 27 September Williams was reported as saying that the sale of the fruit was in contravention of article 18 of the 1949 agreement, as a consequence of which Orebaugh recommended that the matter be taken up with the Colonial Office.[40] The *Trinidad Chronicle* noted that the plantation had not been operating at a profit and that what profit had accrued from its activities was unlikely to negatively affect the U.S. treasury. In commenting on what it described as the government's "flimsy justification," the paper concluded that the GOTT would be well advised to reconsider its decision.[41]

Continuing to seek space for its antibases posture, the PNM adopted a resolution at its three-day convention, which concluded on 19 October 1959, declaring that the American base at Chaguaramas, which was part of the 1941 agreement ceding large and valuable areas to the United States and also giving the United States special privileges, was particularly needed as a locale for the federal capital. In the circumstances, "no new nation can be expected to agree to relinquish its right to independence for 85 years by an agreement to which it was never a party; and which is a product of the very colonialism to whose elimination it has dedicated itself." Furthermore, having regard for the commitment and the request of the Trinidad government and the West Indian Federal Labour Party, or WIFLP, for a "Four-Power Conference in Trinidad to discuss this problem and negotiate an amicable settlement," the PNM

> emphatically endorses the stand of the Governments of Trinidad and Tobago and the West Indies for a Four-Power Conference in Trinidad, to consider (a) the presence of American troops and bases in Trinidad; and (b) the terms and conditions consistent with national dignity on which any continued presence of American troops is to be permitted [and to] instruct the General Secretary to forward copies of the resolution, to, among others, the Acting Governor, the Secretary of State for the Colonies, the President of the United States, all

> member parties of the WIFLP, and leading members of Parliament of both parties in the United Kingdom.[42]

Interestingly, the *Guardian* agreed that a review of the Leased-Bases Agreement in about ten years was desirable but added that an "amicable" approach on the part of the Trinidad government might have been more efficacious than "the hectoring of the Americans.[43]

In seeking to regain the upper hand in the battle of wits, Williams, in a move that even the American consul general conceded was "cleverly aimed at making himself appear as the champion of their [i.e., those of the workers facing dismissal] interests," announced that the naval station could not dismiss workers without requesting and receiving the government's approval.[44] Nor did the United States obtain any solace from the British on this matter. Thus, when asked by an official at the U.S. embassy in Great Britain about the legality of the plantation issue, the Colonial Office reportedly replied that it would "rather not have this question put to it formally, because if it were, it would have to say that in their view the selling of citrus fruit from the agricultural plantation was illegal."[45] The British also "implied" that the best way to deal with Williams was to maintain a posture of "restraint and dignity" in the face of his sniping rather than to adopt a posture that might appear as "feuding or public debate."[46]

Williams also used a club at Macqueripe as a reason to rail against the U.S. presence in Trinidad, which he argued was intended for use by U.S. base personnel but was being used by certain members of the island's elite. Williams clearly deemed this practice intolerable, and the club was forced to terminate its courtesy membership to members of the local elite. In a letter to courtesy-card holders, reproduced in an editorial in the *Trinidad Guardian* on 30 June 1959, the commanding officer of the Naval Station made it clear that the closing of the facilities to local residents was a result of the government's attitude, especially a recent public statement by the premier, Williams, questioning the legality of local membership in the club. And while the editorial noted that the premier had denied instructing the Americans to withhold gifts of used clothing or other articles from their household servants, in fact any expression of "certain views" attributed to the premier and/or a Trinidad government spokesmen by their very nature carried much weight.

However, although the editorial referred to the efficacy of the strategy of casting doubt on the legality of payments by Trinidadians for membership in the club that had forced the club's hand, as it were, it nonetheless impugned the creditability of the argument. The editorial also criticized Williams's actions as "pinpricks," or "David"-like attacks on what I refer to as "heads" of colonialism, which were designed to make life difficult for the Americans and which, though petty in themselves, not only were the incurable "symptoms of a deep-rooted disease, but for lack of a shorter name might well be termed 'anti-everything-itis.'"[47]

Although there was no immediate comment from Williams regarding the *Guardian* editorial, during an address on 3 July 1959 at the UWS he reiterated the government's position on the extension of courtesy membership to Trinidadians. He stated that part of the 1942 agreement allowed the U.S. government to operate service clubs like the Macqueripe Club, which was limited to personnel on the base, who were entitled to certain privileges as outlined in the agreement. The club had become, however, one of Trinidad's biggest, most exclusive clubs, with only a privileged few allowed entrance, "except those who hold courtesy cards, representatives of the government and so on . . . [who] pay entrance fees that would be $60.00 a year in the case of bachelors and $120.00 a year in the case of families."[48] This hint at the possible disloyalty of Trinidadians was sufficient to create the desired amount of angst on the part of the local elite. The result was that the club was forced to terminate its policy of extending membership to local Trinidadians.

While the foregoing speaks to Williams's efforts to keep the American presence at Chaguaramas in the public sphere, the questions he raised about the possible existence of radiation constituted another, perhaps less flattering attempt to seek space for his views. In his 3 July 1959 speech at the UWS, Williams, while referring to a range of American misdeeds in Trinidad, reportedly stated that radiation from the tracking station at Chaguaramas was a danger to the Trinidad population and that though he was not qualified to judge the danger posed by the radiation, an expert from the United Kingdom would soon arrive to investigate the issue. As in the past, this statement put the Americans on the defensive and forced the American consul general in Trinidad to issue a statement, which was due to appear in the next day's press. The statement indicated that he had been assured by the officer in charge of the tracking station at Chaguaramas that there was absolutely no danger to the population of Trinidad from radiation connected with this installation, which was subject to constant, rigid testing under complete scientific control. The consul general continued that since the matter had now been raised by the GOTT, he felt sure that "the US government would want to lend all possible assistance to dispel any fears, however unjustified they may be."[49]

According to Winston Mahabir, then the PNM minister of health and social services, as early as April 1957, during a "party speech in public, unratified by ministerial caucus unless [Dr.] Solomon had read it beforehand [Williams] announced in a highly dramatic fashion that he had substantial information of Radiation being used by the Americans at Chaguaramas." Mahabir, who was on the platform and who later described Williams's claims regarding the existence of radiation as "the immaculate deception," stated that "he did not know whether to laugh at him or cry for the gullible crowd which was being ultra-violated."[50] Nonetheless, he decided to postpone judgment until he knew the "facts." However, in a report to the cabinet in mid-July 1959, following a visit to the United Kingdom, Mahabir strongly deprecated the presence of the American base in Trinidad, which he felt "involved our population in hazards over which a Minister of Health has no control." He therefore concluded that "we must oppose the existence of ANY foreign Base on our territory, and offer no alternative accommodation to the Americans, if and when this question arises."[51]

Using the pages of the party's newspaper to convey the PNM's position on the matter, the author of one article suggested that Williams's charge that the tracking station at Chaguaramas was sending out harmful radiation was "sound, following investigations I made with experts on training in health and safety in the United Kingdom." The writer also quoted a spokesman as saying that "if the Trinidad government cannot afford effective safeguards from likely hazards, the island would be faced with formidable dangers." Going further, the writer asserted that on a matter of "such grave consequence, Williams has proved himself to be a man of vivid intelligence and to be courageous and independent, and passionately devoted to the cause."[52]

In another article in the PNM newspaper, dated 18 December 1959 and titled "What About That Radiation Report? Why is it not published. The Doctor Tells Why," Williams stated that the government had disagreed with a Colonial Office suggestion that only summaries of a report dealing with the radiation matter should be published, as there were certain things that it did not want published. As Williams put it, "We replied, Oh no; if we are going to publish, we are going to publish everything. And that is where we are for the time being."[53]

Continuing to keep the Chaguaramas issue viable, Williams, in an article in the *Nation* about two weeks later dealing with the effects of radiation on the human body, outlined various proposals to settle the base issue. These included agreement by the governments of the United

States and Trinidad and Tobago that the United States should evacuate the base by a prescribed date, in a period of less than ten years and that the 1941 agreement should be reviewed clause by clause.[54]

In a move that Mahabir found not merely "offensive" but indeed very much at odds with the letter and spirit of cabinet government, Williams dispatched the ministers Patrick Solomon and John O'Halloran to London "on a secret mission, without the knowledge of three Ministers." When asked to explain this breach of norms requiring prior cabinet consultation by Mahabir, Kamaluddin Mohammed, and Gerard Montano, Williams replied that he had had good reason to distrust them because "many things discussed at ministerial level had found their way back to the American Consul General."[55] Williams's explanation elicited an outburst from Mahabir, who told him for "the first and last time what he could do with my ministry," after which everything was "sweetness for months" on Williams's part.[56]

However, as Williams later observed, "every possible artifice [was used] to keep the Chaguaramas issue alive and before the public."[57] Thus, an article written by the PNM treasurer, A. N. R. Robinson, in the 26 May 1958 issue of the *PNM Weekly* that Orebaugh felt had "the party stamp of approval and was undoubtedly cleared by Williams" stated that the July 1957 appointment of the Chaguaramas Joint Commission "was intended to be merely a stage in the negotiations between the parties." Robinson warned that the words "'Remember Chaguaramas' may well become a fixture in future dealings between the West Indies and the U.K. and the USA."[58]

Unafraid to use the race card, in a speech on 3 July 1959 Williams referred to a recent publication in the United States stating that when the question of taking over the islands had been considered, President Roosevelt had concluded that he would be content merely with "taking certain areas as Bases because he did not want to be involved with two million headaches [as] it would be an economic drag on the USA."[59] In other words, the Americans were interested in place, not people. Such rhetoric, tethered as it was to the Chaguaramas issue, had definite implications for the disjuncture between the U.S. presence and political independence. Moreover, as the consul general recognized, this speech, like Williams's press conferences and other speeches at the UWS, which were later broadcast, provided no opportunity for an immediate response from the United States.[60]

Finally, in referring to what he termed "official information," Williams claimed that over a period of sixteen years, up to 12 February 1958, U.S.

personnel had been involved in "1,127 incidents of offences including accidents, assault, disorderly behaviour, breaches of the Motor Vehicles and Road Traffic Regulations, malicious damage, larceny, found on premises, obscene exposure, discharging firearms, throwing missiles, refusing to pay taxis, wounding and robbery. This did not include incidents of murder or shooting with intent."[61]

As Derek Bickerton maintains, the American presence underpinned "the existence of such direct Trinbagonian creations as the sophisticated prostitute, the 'saga boy,' and the gang leader," all of whom were seen as "working for the Yankee dollar." In addition, the "American capitalist culture, funneled through the filter of the occupying American troops, facilitated the transformation of a small-time hoodlum, Boysie Singh—the 'most famous of Trinidadian criminals'—into the king of the Port-of-Spain underworld, Chicago-style."[62] Lastly, the capitalist culture also helped to create a money basis for local politics and contributed to the new wealth of clever business operators servicing American needs. These operators included Norman Tang in the trucking business and Bhadase Maraj in the sale of land and surplus equipment.[63] The above suggests that like the plantation and the cricket field, Chaguaramas had established a presence beyond the boundary of the base, so to speak, which existed to the detriment of the dominated. No doubt, these activities also helped Williams and the PNM distance themselves from the politics of "anything goes."

In the final Bachacs-like nibble, John O'Halloran, the PNM minister of industry and commerce, told the Leg Co that the GOTT had flatly rejected a proposal by the U.S. government for the use of Piarco International Airport by its military aircraft, which he said would have resulted in substantial financial savings to the U.S. government.[64] This included the cost of maintaining its own airfields and involved a substantial subsidy by the Trinidad government in terms of the additional costs brought about by the heavy use of the airport by American service planes.

The U.S. consul general was informed that in correspondence between the secretary of state for the colonies (SSFC) and the British ambassador in Washington, the SSFC had agreed to waive fees with respect to technical landings by U.S. aircraft at Piarco, which O'Halloran noted was a repetition of the fundamental action of the 1941 agreement, which had excluded input from the Trinidad government. He also contended that the government "cannot accept any arrangement in 1960 representing the outcome of protracted negotiations from which it was excluded and designed to regularize a long standing practice on which it was never consulted."[65] The result was that the Trinidad government imposed a ban on the landing of American airplanes at the Piarco airport that took effect after 30 April 1960.

It might be noted in passing that a series of top-secret messages involving the commander of the Caribbean area, the SSFC, Trinidad and Tobago Governor Sir Edward Beetham, and Lord Hailes, governor general of the West Indies, indicated that the British had first entertained, then dismissed, the idea of sending troops to the twin island in the period 24–29 June 1959.[66] This had been owing to a message from Lord Hailes to the SSFC stating that "the arrival of a warship at this stage would at least raise strong feelings throughout the Federation." Echoing Lord Hailes's sentiments, Governor Beetham observed that "I can think of nothing (repeat nothing) more calculated to provoke the highly explosive situation and make possible settlement with Amery [a visiting British government official] out of the question than the arrival of warships or troops at this stage" and that "if naval or military assistance should be required I will let you know immediately."[67] It is not supposed that the Americans knew about these plans, as if they did, it is more than likely that they would have used the uneasiness of the local and Colonial Office authorities to further attempt to undermine Williams's position. It is also not known whether Williams was aware of these plans.

THE OPPOSITION Democratic Labour Party also sought to make its presence felt, albeit at the expense of Williams and his anti-Chaguaramas rhetoric. For instance, during a conversation on 10 July 1959 between the American consul and Ashford Sinanan, leader of the opposition in the federal government, and Simboonath Capildeo, a member of the opposition in the Leg Co, the 2 DLP leaders expressed concern that Williams was being appeased by the Colonial Office and the United States. Sinanan felt that Julian Amery, the parliamentary undersecretary to the SSFC, who was visiting Trinbago, had come prepared to accede to Williams's demand for local control of the police and that the DLP leaders were convinced that Williams was out to impose his complete will first on Trinidad and eventually on the West Indies as a whole.

However, having unsuccessfully opposed Williams on the question of constitutional change and ministerial control of the police, the DLP leaders were said to be "wary about sticking their necks out," though they remained wedded to the necessity of U.S.–West Indian cooperation. Consequently, they were unwilling to challenge Williams's "anti-Americanism."[68]

It appears that the opposition seriously considered resigning from the Leg Co and the county councils but decided that nothing would be gained from such a move. Raising the "race question" once again, both Sinanan and Capildeo expressed fears that the Indian and White communities would increasingly be treated as minorities, without any real say in the island's political affairs, and that Williams and his advisers were "negro racists" who had brought race warfare to Trinidad.[69]

This probably explains the actions during the 1961 election of Capildeo's younger brother, Rudranath, who had replaced an ailing Bhadase Maraj as DLP leader at the party's convention on 27 March 1960. Born on Carnival Tuesday in 1920, Rudranath Capildeo learned to speak "pidgin English" in his Hindu home and viewed "the English language as a difficult foreign tongue."[70] Nonetheless, he attended Queen's Royal College, where he distinguished himself by winning the island scholarship in 1938, after which he departed for England to further his education. While in England he earned a first-class-honors bachelor of science degree in mathematics and physics, a master's degree with distinction in mathematics, and a doctorate, all from London University, and qualified as a barrister. Capildeo taught for some time at London University and, like Williams, realized that as a colonial subject he could only go so far in the academic world in England and that a permanent university post was unlikely.

As Ivar Oxaal put it, at forty years old "he can rightly be called Trinidad's Most Educated Man,"[71] a suitable candidate to match Williams's knowledgeism and another exceptional mind with whom Williams would come in contact. But while Williams the "mystery man" could give "licks like fire" when it came to political activity, Capildeo, who was dubbed "the mad scientist," was both emotionally and temperamentally unsuited for the rough-and-tumble of Trinbagonian politics, especially the *fatigue* (pronounced *fateeg*) that was part of heckling during political meetings.[72] The U.S. consul general reported that following Capildeo's election as DLP leader there was "considerable and open hostility toward Rudranath on the part of Simboonath Capildeo and Mitra Sinanan, and the semblance of party organization is deteriorating rather than improving." The consul general also noted that Rudranath's "conduct of affairs since the election has been marked by singular political ineptitude which must be overcome if the DLP is to be successful in the next election."[73] Heckled by Negro attendees at meetings, an exasperated Capildeo called on his Indian supporters to take up arms against his tormentors during the 1961 election. In the end, however, the PNM won the election with

190,003 votes, or 56.97 percent of the popular vote, compared with the DLP's 138,901, or 41.66 percent.

WILLIAMS CONTINUED his resolute approach throughout the twin island to make the case for revisiting the base issue. A speech at Arima on 17 July 1959, which came to be titled "From Slavery to Chaguaramas" and was one of Williams's more important on the subject of the American presence, "set the tone for my public campaign," as he put it.[74] In that speech, with its clear implications regarding the connection between one form of servitude (enslavement) that had beset Trinbago, on the one hand, and the American presence in Chaguaramas, on the other hand, Williams reiterated the argument that the British governor had opposed the agreement that ceded Chaguaramas without any input from the Trinidad government. He warned that "the population of Trinidad and Tobago can no longer be traded and bartered as if they were still chattel slaves." He also repeated his contention that the American base constituted a space of privilege for American service personnel. There was wholesale smuggling that robbed the island of much-needed revenue, along with the loss of fees from landing rights of U.S. aircraft at the Piarco airport. Moreover, there was race discrimination in the form of an unwillingness to have White servicemen who contravened Trinidadian law tried in courts over which Black magistrates presided.

Lastly, Williams attacked the tendency of the dominant to seek legal means to justify its hegemony of the dominated by arguing that the law, unjust or not, had to be obeyed by the disadvantaged. Thus, Williams sought to impugn the validity of America's efforts to justify its occupation of Chaguaramas on legal as well as moral grounds with the comment, "I, too would like to know the clause in Adam's will which denies the West Indian people a share of the world especially a share of the world that rightly belongs to them." This was in keeping with Henri Thoreau's and Martin Luther King's efforts to frame antihegemonic conduct in terms of a moral obligation to disobey an unjust law. In this instance, the frame-transformation process involved the application of an injustice frame to *(a)* portray the occupation of Chaguaramas in terms of a lifeworld characterized by dispossession and colonialist exploitation and subjugation; *(b)* ascribe responsibility for the problem to American and British imperialism; and *(c)* postulate a possible solution to the problem, namely, renegotiation of the lease and the subsequent departure of the Americans. Finally, like leaders of other movements of the aggrieved, by assuring his followers that time was on their side and not on that of the Americans and the injustice associated with colonial exploitation, Williams sought to enjoin his followers to have faith that relief and redemption would soon be theirs.

This, however, was not all. In his ongoing efforts to align the Chaguaramas issue with that of political independence, Williams used as a setting for his ongoing "cursing" the fourth annual convention of the PNM in March 1960. Responding to his question "What does independence mean?," Williams thundered that "it means first and foremost a strong Federal Government with some capacity, however small, for the self-defence and independence in its external relations. In other words it means Chaguaramas." Making use of the notion of binary opposites, juxtaposing indices of hegemony and antihegemony for effect, he noted:

> We are not independent if we accept that Agreement imposed on us when we were colonials. We are not independent if we allow Anglo-American policy to ram down our throat an interpretation of an official report of the Joint Commission which we do not share or a unilateral undertaking to consider review of the Agreement after, "say ten years." Independence, unless it is a sham and an imposture, means a clean slate, the throwing off of the burdens imposed on us by the imperialist power. If there is to be any agreement at all, if there is to be any recognition of agreements made before independence, those agreements must be reached freely, with us as active and equal participants. Especially an agreement, like Chaguaramas, involving the stationing of troops for 80 years more on our soil.[75]

THE FINAL effort in the anti-Chaguaramas struggle occurred during a meeting at the "University of Woodford Square" on 22 April 1960, a day that Williams "predicted" would be Independence Day. During that meeting, a rain-drenched Williams hoisted the Trinidad flag and led a peaceful march through the streets of Port-of-Spain, after which the demonstrators returned to the UWS to listen to a memorial address by the premier demanding independence for the West Indies. However, even before the march occurred, speculation was rife as to what should happen. Some writers of letters to the editor in the newspapers, for example, whimsically but unsuccessfully "called for the establishment of refreshment and games' stands along the route of the march . . . and the landing of the fishing fleet at Stauble's Bay with the Premier dressed in the uniform of an Admiral."[76] It appeared that there would be no *Bacchanal,* to use the Trinbagonian term for noisy revelry with particular sexual overtones. Such calls therefore went unheeded. This is all the more interesting in view of Williams's later admission that he had no intention of marching on Chaguaramas, though he saw no reason to divulge that information long before the appointed day, and his insistence that the march would be peaceful as the island was law abiding.[77]

The demands of the memorial were full internal self-government for Trinidad and Tobago; an independent federation; revision of the 1941 U.K.-U.S. base agreement at a conference in which Trinidad and Tobago enjoyed direct, separate, equal, and independent representation; the return of Chaguaramas by the United States; and the inalienable and imprescriptible right of Trinbagonians to decide their destiny. Copies of the memorial, which described the 1941 Leased-Bases Agreement as "the most deadly menace that has yet appeared to Trinidad's material interests," were presented to Edwin Moline, the U.S. consul general, by Mrs. Isabel Teshea, the "Lady Vice-Chairman" of the PNM, as well as to the governor general, with a request that it be forwarded to Her Majesty's Government.

Not one to dismiss the value of theater or, evidently, the religious significance of the number seven and the revolutionary impact of fire, Williams then burned, or "consigned to the flames," what he called the seven deadly sins of colonialism in Trinidad, each act of conflagration accompanied by the words, "I consign it to the flames. . . . To hell with it." During the performance Williams made an unambiguous connection between the existence of the American base and the dynamics of colonialism. Beyond that, he praised former Port-of-Spain mayor and labor leader Captain Cipriani, labor leader Uriah Butler, and former governor Sir Hubert Young. The documents that constituted the seven deadly sins were the constitution of Trinidad and Tobago; the constitution of the West Indies; the U.S.-Chaguaramas agreement; the Mudie Report on the siting of the federal capital; the Telephone Ordinance of 1939; the "Racial Statements of the DLP" in the Leg Co two weeks earlier; and, perhaps not surprisingly, an issue of the *Trinidad Guardian*.

Doubtless, the alignment of the documents with the term *sins* also resonated with the audience, as did the Catholic injunction that sins must be expiated by penance on the part of the sinner, which in this case involved the final solution, destruction by fire. Some marchers unfurled banners emblazoned with the words "Dignity is incompatible with colonialism" and "Road to independence passes through Chaguaramas." Whether they realized it or not, the participants in the march were making and participating in history; the whole 22 April 1960 event was a powerful demonstration of the social construction of the public sphere.

This was because the event involved *(a)* the use of a physical space—the "University of Woodford Square"—as the setting and *(b)* the ongoing use of collective-action frames in the service of consensus building and mobilization for social change.

For its part, the *Guardian* said that it was difficult not to see in the Trinidad government's ban on the use of the Piarco airport by American military aircraft the unfolding of a pattern with which the country had become increasingly familiar: Williams unilaterally repudiated the bases agreement his party had sworn to honor. Concluding, the paper stated that it "stood for a just and fair settlement of outstanding differences with the Americans, and if the Premier were to act in a decent and civilised manner the entire question could no doubt have been settled to everyone's satisfaction long ago."[78]

The *Guardian* did not say how such a settlement might have been effected, but in criticizing Williams personally, it also noted, in the context of the seven deadly sins, that if in Williams's mind these were holding the country back, then "there was one sin more deadly and one sinner whose name it is needless to mention, who sits in high places and whose deeds unfortunately belie his lofty station." That sinner worked on emblems, rituals, and other devices to bewitch and befuddle the masses and embodied all the frustrations and resentments of a small mind. The paper warned that the day of reckoning would come for "men whose image of reality is distorted and who consciously and of set purpose play upon the emotions of the masses [and] may for a time delude the gullible into full acceptance of their fantasies."[79]

The number of participants in the march, according to the *Guardian,* ranged from 10,000 to as high as 35,000; and according to the *Nation,* it was as high as 35,000. Regardless, therefore, of Williams's motives and of what one thought of him and his efforts to reclaim and to seek space for his views regarding Chaguaramas, the event also showed the world that as a movement intellectual the *doctah* continued to capture the imagination of many of the citizens of the twin island. His most effective public, the masses, whose numbers had increased numerically from the time he was essentially a public intellectual, had spoken, and in a dramatic fashion. This was possibly also proof that he had dealt with the free-rider issue. In any event, both the Americans and the British were forced to sit up and take notice.

Like his speech on the night in June 1955 when he let his bucket down in politics, the 22 April 1960 performance demonstrated the extent to which all of the negative experiences related to the U.S. presence were not simply portrayed as those of Williams but indeed were *articulated* as those of *all* Trinbagonians. However, since the moment when the dissent embedded in the hidden transcript crosses the threshold into the realm of public discourse is always a politically charged occasion, that day in April 1960, with its saturnalia and drama, was of critical importance to the wider nationalist struggle. As James Scott put it, "It is only when this hidden transcript is openly declared that subordinates can fully recognize the full extent to which their claims, their dreams, their anger is shared by other subordinates with whom they have not been in direct touch."[80] This is not to suggest that the efforts of Williams and his cohorts were being placed on a tabula rasa, as much prior *learning* had already taken place, for example, Behind the Bridge, and in the deliberations of the Bachacs and the Teachers' Economic and Cultural Association, among organized groups of females, and in previous performances by Williams. The events of 22 April 1960, therefore, were more a recognition of the existence of the "great public" who, if only for that moment, had become close relatives of the hidden transcript, rather than merely being essentially empty vessels to be filled with novel ideas.

Ironically, even before the 22 April event there was, if not a softening, then perhaps a more realistic appraisal of the Chaguaramas situation on the part of the Americans. This realignment in policy was probably influenced by the previously mentioned comments by Colonial Office officials working on Caribbean affairs. During those talks in October 1959 the head of the American Department at the Foreign Office had advanced the idea that the United States should state that it was prepared to close the Tucker Valley plantation if demanded to do so by the Trinidad government.

In addition, Colonial Office representatives began to say that although their views were tentative and might never congeal, basically three kinds of meetings were envisaged. With respect to a U.S.-Trinidad meeting, the British concluded that Williams was a politician who had staked his political future on such a meeting. Therefore, some in the Colonial Office suggested that it would be wise to agree to such a meeting but to limit it to matters not related to the United States' right to be in Chaguaramas. Others felt that, in any case, the coming of independence to the federation in perhaps five years was likely to force some revision of the 1941 agreement. In the circumstances, it was felt that "leisurely negotiations with the Federal government sometime before the independence date might well achieve a harmonious revision of the agreement." The local people would have participated in the revision, and their obligations could be more readily assumed upon independence. Finally, with respect to a private U.S.-U.K. meeting, it was suggested that the United States might want to consider holding talks on a whole range of issues connected with its use of bases in the British Caribbean.[81]

The new American consul general, Edwin Moline—whom Williams would later describe as "a personable young man" with whom "one could talk as an equal" and with whom "we could do business"[82]—in a lengthy assessment noted, among other things, that what had begun as a specific request for a "particular piece of ground" had devolved into "a wider desire among the responsible leaders of the West Indies for a review and readjustment of US Base rights."[83] Williams's nemesis, Walter Orebaugh, had left by then. Judging by a comment made by Ashford Sinanan in a previously mentioned conversation with American consul Philip Habib on 10 July 1959, the United States' accession to Williams's request that Orebaugh be removed was a mistake and "a victory for Williams."[84] Getting to the heart of the matter, Moline observed that nationalism in the West Indies

> wishes its recognition. West Indian awareness of United States Base policies in other parts of the world is informed and discerning. The West Indian nationalist, and all politicians are nationalists in the West Indies, cannot accept that standards applicable in other parts of the world are less than acceptable in his bailiwick. . . . The oft-expressed desire for "modernization" of the 1941 agreement has a solid foundation and cannot be shaken. Even those most sympathetic to the United States concede such a need and they hope for its achievement through the maximum of statesmanship on both sides.[85]

Thus, he continued, "in place of an agreement with which they were constitutionally prevented from being directly identified, we should seek, and indeed they will demand, to be a party to any agreement that will have practical effect in the future." Turning to the problems that he considered basic and of overriding significance, Moline stated that there was no question in the minds of West Indians that "the 99 year lease, with 81 years to go is unacceptable." And although it might be argued that this included "elements of fetishism or elements of pride or elements contrary to past commitments," the United States would likely face a reiterated desire for the West Indies capital to be located at Chaguaramas. Regarding reparations, Moline noted that the West Indies clearly expected to be compensated financially for the ongoing use of the base by the United States.

In order to protect the essential rights of the United States, Moline, while conceding that negotiations were inevitable, noted that however one looked at it, the United States was about to enter into a series of negotiations with the West Indians and the United Kingdom in order to modify base rights held since 1941. Moreover, while the question of compensation remained of "sweeping significance," Moline acknowledged that "in brutal terms what is involved would be buying the right to stay," which might conceivably entail an offer of substantial financial compensation coupled with a "judicious combination of technical assistance, economic aid and maximum goodwill."

Finally, although he recognized that the "hard nut to crack" was going to be the West Indians' demand for Chaguaramas so that they could locate their capital there, "the sooner the problem was approached, the less costly and most beneficial in terms of the continuity of a U.S. presence in the area." Moline therefore concluded, quite pithily, that "passing time, rigid initial positions and undue reliance on seemingly impregnable legal positions or prior assurances do not of themselves resolve the problem in the negotiating situation we face." Furthermore, he warned that it would be "a grave negotiating mistake to expect an imposed solution or to believe that the problem in all its dimensions can be solved by exclusion of contentious subjects."[86]

Moline's statement was a recognition of the linking of Chaguaramas with West Indian nationalism as part of the legitimate aspirations of the region, as well as the need to negotiate with the West Indians and, of course, the United States. While it is not known whether Williams was aware of the consul general's thinking, Williams later stated that the 22 April event "demonstrated to us and the world how extensive these resources were, [and] made it impossible to deny the PNM claim for renegotiation of the Treaty and laid the foundation for West Indian independent nationhood, in theory if not in practice."[87]

THERE THEN followed a series of events that included an unprecedented visit from the colonial secretary, Iain McLeod, who proposed three-stage talks, comprising a London stage; a Trinidad stage, between the United States, the United Kingdom, and federal observers; and a second Trinidad stage for signing a new agreement. The third stage took place in Tobago between 28 November and 9 December 1960, when the United States agreed to a phased withdrawal from the base, to be completed by the end of 1977, and to participation in certain high-priority projects, including a developmental project involving the construction of a college of arts and sciences, with a suitably endowed library, at the University College of the West Indies.[88] With the emergence of the St. Augustine campus of the University of the West Indies, which replaced the Imperial College of Tropical Agriculture, in 1961, a long-held dream of Williams's was realized.

In sum, as a social-movement intellectual Williams was able to center the base issue in the public sphere, in political as well as moral terms, and to effectively use historical knowledge, in particular, to educate and mobilize his "public" regarding the "truth" of the matter and the *relevance* of political independence. As the first public, Williams and the GOTT were better able than the second public, the local press and the American consulate, to get their side of the story out to the critical third public, the masses. Both the local press and the consulate turned out to be "weak publics," especially when it came to opinion formation involving the masses, or what Nancy Fraser refers to as a "strong public."[89] Lastly, by utilizing the analogy of spatial differentials, Williams was able to frame the base as a space involving "two Trinidads," one that disadvantaged the Trinbagonians and the other as a space appropriated by the Americans, which, as Scott might put it, became a "domain of public mastery and subordination [involving] rituals of hierarchy, deference, speech, punishment and humiliation," fed by an "ideological justification for these inequalities."[90]

8 Caliban and the Anticolonial Tradition

History . . . is not merely something to be read. And it does not refer merely, or even principally, to the past. On the contrary, the great force of history comes from the fact that we carry it within us, are unconsciously controlled by it in many ways, and history is literally present in all that we do.

—James Baldwin

IN THIS CHAPTER I seek to provide a summary of Williams's intellectualism and to situate it within the wider context of the diasporan intellectual. In spelling out the parameters of intellectualism, I noted that intellectuals never seem to be satisfied with the way things are and that they provide settings for their antiestablishment railing as they create an audience and a space for the "new" knowledge that is produced. Williams's early experiences with the language of oppression involved his exposure to the habitus, or "rules of the game," regarding social differentiation, which was based on race, marriage, and the acquisition of what was considered to be relevant knowledge. These early experiences took the form of immersion in the classics and colonial history and inculcation of the values of the dominant through sport and public humiliation of the "other." Especially pertinent were various experiences as a member of his family household and at Queen's Royal College, where West Indian history was not taught, which accounted for Williams's decision to study history instead of medicine and, most important, to be a teacher, which influenced his entire career as an intellectual.

At Oxford, Williams learned the rules of the game consistent with being a professional historian. Learning the rules of the game involved the productive use of time, writing, and travel to various places in Europe, such as the Netherlands, Copenhagen in Denmark, Spain, and French cities such as Paris, Bordeaux, and Nantes, where he did research on the slave trade and the West Indies and on colonial history. In addition to his teachers, Williams was in contact with other intellectuals while at

Oxford, where as an outsider within he was also exposed to the subtleties of discrimination based on race as well as nation. These experiences help to explain his subsequent political behavior.

The Howard University experience allowed Williams to continue to acquire cultural capital through his teaching, research, and published work, especially *Capitalism and Slavery,* through his association with a number of exceptional minds, and through a deeper immersion in the "rules of the game" regarding knowledge accumulation and marketing. These written efforts in various ways "cursed" the language of colonialism with respect to imperialism, enslavement, and indenture; pointed to their negative impact on the existence of the colonized; and addressed efforts by subalterns to end their oppression as stigmatized racialized "others."

Toward the end of his sojourn at Howard, Williams used his *cultural capital* as a professional historian to acquire *symbolic capital.* This, in turn, permitted him to acquire *symbolic power,* which he used to seek space as a public intellectual and, later, as a social-movement intellectual. He cosponsored a very important conference on economic relations in the Caribbean, and two fellowships, along with part-time employment with the Anglo-American Caribbean Commission, enabled him to travel extensively throughout the Caribbean and thereby become acquainted with the colonial experience in various territories. Lastly, Williams was involved in a number of off-campus activities that brought him into contact with other West Indians and individuals from various British colonies in Africa, who were also involved in "cursing" colonialism. The result was that by the time he returned to Trinbago as deputy chair of the Research Council of what had become the Caribbean Commission, he had already made a name for himself as a historian and scholar (academic and public intellectual), with a profound knowledge of the Caribbean and its peoples.

Back on the twin island, as we have seen, Williams continued to travel and to do research, gave a number of lectures dealing with colonialism, and was involved in a well-publicized debate with another individual with a doctorate. These experiences enabled him to further construct an audience for his knowledge and to use his *symbolic capital* and the concomitant *symbolic power* to seek space in the political spectrum. I have argued that also during this period, having decided that the cake was not worth the candle, as it were, Williams began the process of changing the habitus concerning knowledge production and his activities as a teacher of history. Words, always the chosen means for knowledge communication by *Homo academicus,* were no longer utilized primarily in the academy, but in the public library and other publicly accessible spaces. Also, his written work was no longer being published primarily in books by recognized publishers and in articles in refereed journals, but as pamphlets in Trinbago, which were made available to his increasing public in nontechnical language, and at a modest cost. It was becoming clear, however, that his antihegemonic renderings were beginning to ruffle the feathers of powerful others, especially in the Caribbean Commission, and that a political career was a distinct possibility. As he put it in a 1954 letter to the Jamaican premier, Norman Manley, since he is being persecuted because of his writing, he proposed to write some more, and if, as it seemed, "they" did not want him as a public servant, perhaps they would prefer to deal with him as a politician.

WILLIAMS'S TRANSITION from public intellectual to social-movement intellectual, I suggested, began in June 1955, when he gave a speech at Woodford Square announcing his departure from the Caribbean Commission and his intention to let his bucket down in Trinidad. Therefore, as the leader of the political-independence movement and a teacher with considerable knowledge of West Indian history, he set about changing further the habitus regarding the production of knowledge in Trinbago. This took the form, we saw, of promulgating the idea of the "University of Woodford Square" and the institutionalization both of a public space in the twin island's capital of Port-of-Spain and of the newspaper of the twin island's first mass-based party, the People's National Movement, as settings for, respectively, the spoken and written knowledge regarding political independence. Speaking, writing, editing, and the acquisition of a printing machine, which eventually led to the emergence of the PNM publishing company opened up opportunities for the ongoing performance of intellectual labor by Williams and other movement intellectuals.

Also, as a social-movement intellectual Williams used various resources to educate and mobilize his growing public and to forge a collective identity with respect to political independence. Resources included time, historical knowledge, and a number of previously organized entities, such as schoolteachers and political activists concerned with the political education of the masses, which led to the emergence of the PNM, the activities of females, and those of a loosely knit aggregation of subalterns from an area in downtown Port-of-Spain. In addition, Williams used various frames in order to interpret the ways in which the language of oppression manifested itself. These included a bridging frame, to interpret the link between race and education and colonial oppression in Trinbago; an amplification frame, to refer to the relationship between oppression in Trinbago and oppression in other parts of the world; and an injustice frame, to portray the Anglo-American agreement that led to the U.S. presence at the Chaguaramas base in Trinidad as being inherently amoral.

Additionally, I noted that the political-opportunity structure of the twin island's politics enabled Williams and other movement intellectuals to create space for the emergence of the PNM both as an innovative social-movement organization and as the first mass-based party to be elected to office in Trinbago, dedicated to the decimation of the colonial politics of "anything goes" and personalized political activity. His renderings on the question of party politics inevitably led to pronouncements regarding the role of the party newspaper and that of its editor with regard to knowledge production in its written form. Williams also referred to the manner in which the party press might be instrumental in the publication of the work of Trinbagonian and West Indian writers who were based locally. The circulation of their work within the region would constitute another form of education for the masses. This was especially crucial because, although these writers drew their inspiration from the region, more often than not they had to go abroad to be published and recognized.

It can also be argued that, apart from the Greek tradition, three intellectual streams undergirded Williams's intellectualism. These are the Enlightenment, historical materialism, and Max Weber's views regarding the Protestant ethic. Enlightenment thinkers stressed the idea of rational thought as a basis for explaining and analyzing human conduct. Conceivably, this approach to intellectualism was evident in Williams's thinking with respect to the imperialist variant of capitalism and in his abiding faith in the power of the intellect, especially as far as the masses were concerned. This was why, C. L. R. James concluded, "so few have ever created a University of Woodford Square."[1] The historical-materialist approach speaks to the extent to which the economy influenced, in myriad negative ways, the life chances of the plantation laborer during enslavement and indenture and, as we saw, the role played by education, religion, the polity, and race relations in the service of colonial economic exploitation. Finally, the Protestant ethic emphasized hard work and planful action as preconditions for what Weber referred to as the "spirit of capitalism." These habits, I suggested, were apparent in what I referred to as Williams's "purposiveness," or his commitment to hard work and his indefatigability when it came to his knowledge-production activities.

Perhaps most important, Williams's effort to ally colonial history with West Indian history in his antihegemonic intellectual endeavors was an instance of what Silvio Torres-Saillant refers to as the use of the cultural synecdoche. This was evident in Williams's deliberations on Crown Colony politics and on the colonial economy and in his "Massa Day Done" speech. Noticeably also, Williams used history to evoke the collective memory of West Indians, Trinbagonians, and the non-White population of the twin island.[2] As Barry Schwartz notes, the collective memory is a metaphor that "formulates society's retention and loss of information about its past in the familiar terms of individual remembering and forgetting."[3]

However, only a small part of the collective memory of a society's past is experienced in this manner. Indeed, what individuals learn of their past comes from, among other things, "oral chronicles preserved by tradition, written chronicles stored in archives, and commemorative activities [such as observance of holidays and anniversaries] that enable institutions to distinguish significant events and people from the mundane, and so infuse the past with moral meaning."[4] This Williams sought to do also by his various references especially to the putative role of education in the service of oppression, on the one hand, and the collective resistance by the members of these groups to their oppression, on the other hand.

As a diasporan intellectual, Williams understood what Patricia Hill Collins refers to as the importance of the articulation of a specific body of knowledge emanating from a group's shared experiences associated with their location in the hierarchical power relations, which conduces to equally specific political action.[5] The relevance of lived experiences is of twofold significance. First, as Collins suggests, in the context of Black American females as the "other" these experiences constitute a framework for the provision of "new" knowledge.[6] Second, as Anthony Bogues observes, they allow for an assessment of "observation" as a different methodology, as occurred in the manner in which, while growing up, "the window" in C. L. R. James's house allowed him to observe and thus understand the game of cricket, especially beyond a boundary.[7] In Williams's case, this form of standpoint theorizing can be traced back to a plethora of lived experiences, especially transformative ones, as a Black person growing up in Trinidad, at Oxford University, and in the United States and during his employment with the Caribbean Commission. These experiences no doubt shaped his orientation regarding the connection between race and class and colonialist oppression, on the one hand, and his intellectualism, on the other hand.

This special insight into the minds and thinking of the dominant that is acquired by the lived experiences of the oppressed, the African American scholar-activist W. E. B. Du Bois maintains, enables the oppressed to be "singularly clairvoyant" with respect to the language of the oppressor and to see the latter from "unusual points of vantage."[8] This was especially evident in Williams's iteration of the efforts of the enslaved to contribute to their emancipation, torching the plantations on occasion and responding to the "coercion and punishment" of the planters with "indolence, sabotage, and revolt. Most of the time [the enslaved person] was as idle as possible. That was the usual form of resistance—passive." This suggests that once Caliban became aware of his humanity and that he was not a "monster," an inanimate object, or, as Williams put it earlier, that he had a mind, which was the "greatest danger," then "cursing" Prospero's language was inevitable.[9]

It was clear that in pointing to the manner in which Caliban used the language of oppression to "curse" the oppressor, Williams noted in conclusion, "the Negroes had been stimulated to freedom by the development of the very wealth which their labor had created."[10] In other words, capitalism, as Karl Marx had argued, contains within it the seeds of its own destruction. This view of history from the bottom up was also apparent in Williams's efforts to "select out" certain indicators of colonialism, as he sought to make his knowledge both credible and relevant to political independence for the public he constructed. As he noted in a 30 May 1960 oration, while the "political relationship of the West Indies with the metropolitan country inevitably determined the social relations of production in the West Indies . . . the system of exploitation necessarily carried the seeds of its own destruction."[11] This was the impact of Williams's "personality, the historical accident. And yet in the Hegelian dialectic the organic movement proceeds by way of accidents and the sum of accidents constitutes the organic movement."[12] As a form of oppression, therefore, colonialism would morph into nationalism by way of thesis, antithesis, and synthesis.

In addition, mindful of the expectation that knowledge was meant for the edification and mobilization of the masses, Williams used the "popular" approach to the production of knowledge as a public and social-movement intellectual, rather than what Daniel Bell refers to as the "vernacular" approach of the academic intellectual–cum–professional historian. The latter operates within a bounded field of knowledge, a tradition; seeks to find his or her place in it by adding to the accumulated and tested knowledge of the past; and is less involved with the self. The public intellectual and/or movement intellectual, by contrast, begins "with *his experience, his* individual perceptions of the world, *his* privileges and deprivations, and judges the world by these sensibilities, [so that] his judgments of the society reflect the treatment accorded him."[13] Williams's speeches, therefore, were teachable moments and, as George Lamming notes, exemplified the idea "of the teacher, in the noblest sense of teacher, turned politician, and of the politician, in the truly moral sense of politician, turned teacher."[14]

As the historian Hilary Beckles suggests, Williams's use of the "popular" approach to intellectual activity paved the way for a whole gamut of West Indian radicalized academic intellectuals, who, in addition to adopting the "vernacular" model (consistent with their specific discipline requirements), also embraced the "popular" model of knowledge transmission.[15] In sum, Williams was an engaged intellectual, and his formulation and exchange of ideas exemplified Antonio Gramsci's contention that "the mode of being a new intellectual can no longer consist in eloquence, which is an exterior and momentary mover of feelings and passions, but in active participation in practical life, as constructor, organizer, 'permanent persuader' not just simple orator."[16]

As previously noted, intellectuals, in addition to being socially constructed types, are influenced by "historical" circumstances, in the sense that their knowledge tends to reflect the spirit of the age in which they live. In his letter to Norman Manley of 17 June 1954, for example, Williams indicated his familiarity with the work of Martinique's Aimé Césaire, as well as André Breton's observations that Césaire handled the French language better than any Frenchman and that the same might be said of Barbados's George Lamming with respect to the English language. Indeed, James points out that Williams, in addition to contributing a massive essay entitled "Race Relations in the West Indies" to a three-volume study commemorating the work of the Cuban scholar Fernando Ortiz, had met with Césaire in Paris while Williams was in Brussels working with the International Confederation of Free Trade Unions as a consultant on plantation workers.[17] It should also be remembered that Williams had considered including in an earlier version of his autobiography a chapter titled "The Intellectual in the Caribbean, 1948–1954," with the "astonishing" work of Sam Selvon, Vic Reid, Edgar Mittelholzer, Roger Mais, and, of course, Lamming in mind. One can only imagine the impact such a chapter might have had on Caribbean epistemology.

In situating Williams's intellectualism within the wider anticolonial tradition, it should be noted that Césaire, for example, was born two years after Williams, on 25 June 1913, to a mother who was a dressmaker and a father who was a local tax inspector. And although his father was a well-educated historian, as Robin Kelley observes, the family, though sharing the cultural sensibilities of the petite bourgeoisie, lived on the edge of rural poverty.[18] Young Aimé, however, was a precocious student who at the age of eleven won a scholarship to the Lycée Schoelcher, a secondary school named after Victor Schoelcher, the principal proponent of abolition in 1848 and defender of the interests of non-White Martinicans, that helped prepare students from Martinique, Guadeloupe, and French Guiana to enter the academy in France.[19]

After graduation in 1931, Césaire moved to Paris and enrolled in the Lycée Louis Le Grand to prepare for the grueling entrance exams to the École Normale Supérieure, a high-level teacher-training college in Paris, where he studied history and culture. While at the École Normale Supérieure, Césaire collaborated with his high-school classmate Léon Damas and the future Senegalese intellectual Leopold Senghor to launch a journal titled *L'Étudiant Noir* (The Black student). In the March 1935 issue of the journal, Césaire wrote a tract in which, possibly for the first time, he "cursed" the language of the colonizer and used the term *Négritude* in opposition to the idea of assimilation.

Césaire's intellectualism as a poet was influenced by three major concepts, namely, poetry as a weapon in the anticolonialist struggle; surrealism; and Negritude, all of which were reflections of his lived experiences and webbed relationships with various biographical others. As he put it in his 1944 essay *Poetry and Cognition,* "Poetic knowledge is born in the great silence of scientific knowledge." In other words, poetry is the only means for achieving the kind of knowledge needed to go "beyond the world's crises."[20] As Kelley suggests, Césaire maintained that "what presides over the poem is not the most lucid intelligence, the sharpest sensibility or the subtlest feelings, but experience as a whole." All of these points, which underscore in particular Césaire's reference to nature as the fount of human existence, are to be found in his poetic renderings, especially his nostalgic references to the fauna and flora of Martinique. This viewpoint is evident in his *Notebook of a Return to the Native Land,* which was first published in 1939.

Césaire's views regarding surrealism suggest that "everything, every history, every future, every dream, every life form, from plant to animal, every creative impulse is plumbed from the depths of the unconscious,"[21] which invites us to view the obvious from the perspective of the unobvious. Finally, Césaire's notion of Negritude, which is linked with his views on assimilation in the culture of the dominant, is rooted in the history of caste and class in Martinique. Until the middle of the nineteenth century, as long as the labor power of the enslaved was used, it was not uncommon for the mulatto offspring of White slave masters and Black enslaved females to be given their freedom and often a parcel of land.[22]

Césaire's views regarding Negritude crystallized during a transformative seven-month visit to Haiti after reading about the efforts of Toussaint L'Ouverture to get rid of the French. As he put it during an interview with the Haitian poet and militant René Depestre in 1967, *Notebook of a Return to the Native Land* was not only an autobiographical book but one in which he tried to gain an understanding of the self. "These were my first contacts with my country after an absence of ten years," Césaire observed, "so I really found myself assaulted by a sea of impressions and images. At the same time I felt deep anguish over the prospects for Martinique."[23]

In *Notebook of a Return,* using his prose/poetic style, Césaire writes from a historical perspective of Caliban's lifeworld as an enslaved person, with Martinique in mind. He notes, for example, that for centuries the land screamed that humans "were bestial brutes, and that the human pulse stops at the gates of the barracoon: that we are walking compost hideously promising tender cane and silky cotton and they would brand us with red-hot irons and we would sleep in our excrement and they would sell us on the town square and an ell of English cloth and salted meat from Ireland cost less than we did, and this land was calm, tranquil, repeating that the spirit of the Lord was in its acts."[24] However, while Césaire is not blind to the technical mastery of the colonizer, much as Williams does in his statement of the triangular trade, Césaire, also "curses" and rejects the colonial system when he writes:

> Hear the white world
> horribly weary from its immense efforts
> its stiff joints crack under the hard stars
> its blue steel rigidities pierce the mystic flesh
> hear its deceptive victories tout its defeats
> hear the grandiose alibis of its pitiful stumbling
> Pity for our omniscient and naive conquerors![25]

In his *Discourse on Colonialism,* first published in 1950, Césaire also uses history not only to deal with the minds of both the colonizer and the colonized within the context of surrealism and Negritude but to continue to shed light on Caliban's assimilation dilemma, in this instance being both French and of African heritage. In dealing with the mind of the colonizer, for example, Césaire portrays colonialism as working, variously, to *decivilize* and *brutalize* the colonized and to "awaken him to buried instincts, to covetousness, violence, race hatred, and moral relativism."[26] However, the *savagery* in colonialism, Césaire contends further, was tolerated when it was applied to non-European peoples, such as the Arabs of Algeria, the "coolies" of India, and the "niggers" of Africa. It was only when, by way of Hitler's fascism, the victims became European Jews that there was a negative reaction to this form of oppression.[27] There is nothing inadvertent about the appropriation of the resources of the colonized by the colonizer, Césaire continues. This is because "no one colonizes "innocently" or "with impunity either." Indeed, a nation that colonizes and a "civilization which justifies colonization—and therefore force—is already a sick civilization, a civilization which is morally diseased."[28]

Moreover, the colonial enterprise, which is based on dehumanization and contempt for the native and justified by that contempt, is prefigured by seeing the "other" as *an animal,* which enables the colonizer to ease his conscience. He feels compelled to reason that the colonized belong to "a different *category* of being." Therefore, as Charles Lyons maintains, the colonizer feels the need not merely to put some distance between himself and the colonized but to persuade himself that that distance is natural and inevitable. Hence, it is quite common, as was noted regarding the encounter between Prospero and Caliban, for the oppressor to describe the oppressed as savage, heathen, and backward and to develop elaborate theories explaining why this is so.[29] Hence for Césaire, "colonization = 'thingification.'"[30]

THE QUESTION of assimilation is a very important one for the diasporan intellectual, but it is one upon which Williams did not dwell openly, possibly because enslavement and indenture led to the differential assimilation of the two majority populations in Trinbago, African and Indian. Such was the nature of the colonial experience in Trinbago (and in British Guiana) that while enslavement sought to obliterate the culture of the enslaved African, the same did not apply to the indentured Indian, who was permitted to retain much of his culture—names, marriage customs, dress, language. This despite the expectation that Trinbagonian pedantry in the nineteenth century required familiarity not only with proper English but also with proper French and Spanish. In addition to decrying "a culture and a set of values and tastes largely imported from outside" or the tendency to look outward for direction, Williams seemed to favor a policy of cultural integration and creolization. This was stoutly resisted by the Indians, who feared a loss of their cultural identity, which in turn reinforced the notion of Indians as a recalcitrant minority.[31]

Martinique was always viewed as a *départemente* of France—Césaire himself had served as a "French deputy" representing Martinique in the French Assembly—so that assimilation had a different meaning for Martinicans. Thus, Césaire notes that he does not deny the influence of French literature, that whether he wants to or not, as a poet he expresses himself in French. At the same time, however, he concedes that "I have always striven to create a new language, one capable of communicating the African heritage. In other words, for me French was a tool, qua language, that I wanted to use in developing a new means of expression. I wanted to create an Antillean French, a black French that, while still being French, had a black character."[32]

In reference to his sensitivity to the concept of liberation and his view that surrealism lends itself to the calling forth of "deep and unconscious forces," Césaire suggests that the surrealist approach enabled him to "summon up" unconscious forces. This for him was "a call to Africa. I said to myself: it's true that *superficially* we are French, we bear the marks of French customs; we have been branded by Cartesian philosophy, by French rhetoric, but if we break with all that, if we plumb the depths, then what we will find is fundamentally black."[33] Apart from being surrealist, some of these views were also a reflection of Césaire's orientation toward Negritude, which was influenced by his disenchantment with Marxism's emphasis on the White working class as a true revolutionary force and his own belief that the history of the Negro had to be present in any construction of an Antillean revolutionary ideology. Césaire's views regarding Negritude, as Paget Henry suggests in his discussion of Frantz Fanon's views on the oppressed "self," meant that the oppressed became the *subject* rather than the *object,* or as Williams put it, that the colonized had a mind.[34]

In *A Tempest,* Césaire's version of Shakespeare's *The Tempest,* first published in 1968, Caliban's exchanges with Prospero are much more pointed. During one exchange Ariel reminds Prospero of his promise to free him, to which Prospero retorts, "As for your freedom, you'll have it when I'm good and ready. In the meantime see to the ship."[35] The exchange between Ariel and Prospero contrasts sharply with the exchange between Caliban and Prospero when Caliban responds to Prospero's summons. During this exchange, Caliban reveals that the fact that he has learned the language of the oppressor does not mean that he retains none of his own language, which in Césaire's mind represents the Antillean culture and the African ideology.

Thus, Caliban responds to Prospero by using the word *uhuru* (the Swahili word meaning "freedom," used especially in connection with the Freedom Movement in Africa), to which Prospero replies, "Mumbling your native language again! I've already told you. I don't like it. You could be polite, at least: a simple 'hello' wouldn't kill you." Prospero's concern is understandable because Caliban's use of "his" language suggests a weakening in Prospero's ability to use his own language to continue to oppress Caliban. Still defiant, Caliban replies, "May today hasten by a decade the day when all the birds of the sky and beasts of the earth will feast upon your corpse!" Reflecting his view of Caliban as "nonhuman," Prospero refers to Caliban as an "ugly ape!" and asks, "How can anyone be so ugly?" Caliban responds, bitingly: "You think I am ugly . . . well I don't think you're so handsome yourself. With that big hooked nose." And in a reference to the fact that vultures feast on unwanted carcasses, Caliban continues laughingly, "You look just like some old vulture. An old vulture with a scrawny neck!"[36]

Continuing to dwell on the language question, Prospero informs Caliban that the least he can do is thank him for "having taught you to speak at all. You savage . . . dumb animal, a beast I educated, trained, dragged up from the bestiality that still clings to you." Countering, Caliban informs Prospero that he really did not teach him anything, "except to jabber in your own language so that I could understand your orders." In other words, Prospero's imparting of his language was hardly altruistic; it was intended to facilitate Caliban's oppression. In any case, Caliban tells Prospero that he took care not to provide him with access to any of his "learning," as "all your science you keep for yourself alone, shut up in those big books."[37] This distinction between knowledge and learning suggests that Prospero was careful not to provide Caliban with information that would help him to gain his freedom.

Césaire alludes to the cultural underbelly of oppression and the mind of the oppressor as Caliban informs Prospero that for years he has bowed his head to Prospero's insults, his ingratitude, and, worst of all, his degrading condescension. And although he concedes that Prospero is still stronger than he is, Caliban now states that he does not "give a damn about Prospero's power or for his police, his dogs or his inventions," because in the end he will get Prospero. By expressing himself in this manner, Caliban lifts the halo of Prospero's dominance, thereby liberating himself from the mystique of his domination. Exultantly, he informs Prospero that as an old hand at deception who lied to him about himself, Prospero had ended up by imposing on Caliban an image of himself as being "underdeveloped" and "undercompetent." But it is over, Caliban informs Prospero, referring to the demise of colonialism, as "the old order is crumbling and since although you can, I am sure you will not pick up and leave and return to Europe."[38]

Césaire's description of the mind of the colonizer in this context echoes not only Williams's reference to the manner in which the language of imperialism benefitted everyone except those whose labor power made it possible and profitable but also his insights into the mind of the colonizer. In his "Massa Day Done" oration, for example, Williams argued that Massa was not only an uncultured man with an illiberal outlook but a frequently absent owner of a West Indian sugar plantation who dominated his defenseless workers with threats of punishment or imprisonment and used his political power for the most selfish ends. In addition, according to Williams, Massa stood for colonialism, believed in racial inequality, was determined not to educate the oppressed as he felt that to educate was to emancipate, and, after deliberately stunting the economic potential of the society, he returned to England leaving the West Indian island of Nevis as poverty-stricken as he had found it.[39]

While both Williams and Césaire were primarily concerned with colonialist oppression, Juan Emilio Bosch's main concern was "cursing" the postcolonial system, a dilemma of another sort for the diasporan intellectual. In a prefatory comment to his book *The Unfinished Experiment: Democracy in the Dominican Republic,* which was first published in 1964, while he was in exile in Puerto Rico, Bosch writes that a democratic government is sustained by the will of all social strata and of all the individuals who have responsibilities to it as citizens. If that will is lacking, a democratic government cannot survive.

Like Williams and Césaire, Bosch was born in the early twentieth century, on 30 June 1909, in Santo Domingo, Dominican Republic, where he was educated and where he died on 1 November 2001. Williams, Césaire, and Bosch, therefore, were born within four years of one another. Like Williams and Césaire, Bosch was a historian, educator, and politician, in addition to being a short-story writer. When Rafael Trujillo came to power in the Dominican Republic as a result of a military coup in 1937, Bosch opposed Trujillo's dictatorial regime; after a period of imprisonment, in 1938 he fled to Puerto Rico. There, he formed the Dominican Revolutionary Party (PRD) in 1939 and functioned as the leader of the opposition to Trujillo's regime outside of the Dominican Republic, that is, in exile. Bosch subsequently migrated to Cuba, where his literary career blossomed. He won the Hernandez Cata Prize in Havana for short stories written by a Latin American author and was regarded as among the most prominent writers from the Dominican Republic.

Upon Trujillo's death in May 1961, Bosch returned to the Dominican Republic and headed a campaign designed to teach democracy to the masses. As president of the Dominican Republic, he set about restructuring the country's social institutions. Thus, he promulgated a new constitution that granted unprecedented freedoms to the people, such as the right to form labor unions, safeguards for the homeless, and the rights of children and farmers. He also moved to break up the latifundia, which enabled large landowners to control much of the land in the country.

Bosch also noted that in looking at the social-historical context, it was important to understand that his short-lived administration had come on the heels of twenty-four years of dictatorship by Trujillo. An entire generation had grown up under the leadership of Trujillo and consequently knew no other form of government. The country had been isolated, and students had not understood the social-class structure. This isolation had been exacerbated by the fact that Trujillo maintained tight control over the media, so that only information favorable to him tended to emerge. As Hermannus Hoetink put it, the Trujillo regime was able to "popularize its ideas because of its control of the more effective vehicles of communication and indoctrinating institutions such as schools, armed forces and the political party."[40]

Bosch maintained that in the absence of one of the major facets of a democracy, that is, a free press, gossip—who told what to whom—which had become an important means of receiving and transmitting information during the Trujillo regime, became intensified and deceitful and held the seed of slander. In the Dominican form of personalized politics, everything political manifested itself in terms of persons. Emphasis was therefore placed not on national problems and the generation of solutions to those problems but on one man's virtues and another's vices. The Dominican situation mirrored that of Trinbago, where, as we have seen, because information was transmitted by way of "ole talk," the colonial government, the church, and the sugar plantocracy influenced the educational diet of the masses. Also, the press was not always sympathetic to Williams's and the PNM's anticolonialist railings, which emphasized mass political education as a precondition for nationalism. Because of this situation, as Williams had done in Trinidad and Tobago, Bosch was able to seize an opportunity, in this case Trujillo's death, to educate the masses and to create space for his and the PRD's democratic agenda of ameliorative social change.

Such was the nature of the social-stratification system, however, that prestige was associated with membership in the first families, that is, the Trujillo family structure. Thus, despite having both integrity and intelligence, one stood to lose caste if one did not belong to this social stratum. Additionally, while there was a degree of affinity between the rural peasant and the urban poor, as well as between the rural peasant and the lower stratum of the middle class, there was no such affinity among those entering, or involved with the concerns of, the middle stratum. Furthermore, the middle and upper strata had practically no relationship with the peasants, the workers, and the unemployed. For Bosch, therefore, a way of speaking (language) had to be developed that all, namely, the masses and the middle stratum, would understand, especially since while these two groups heard the same language, they interpreted it differently.[41]

This meant that Bosch and the PRD had to "curse" the language of the Trujilloists and replace it with a new "language," that of the masses. As an intellectual in the role of educator, and in an effort to focus on knowledge that was *relevant,* much as Williams did, Bosch spoke to the masses about *(a)* what democracy was and how it functioned; *(b)* what the country's economic problems were; and *(c)* how the society was organized. Regarding democracy, Bosch explained what a constitution was and what laws were, how the separate powers of government functioned and were interrelated, how and why people voted, and what a political party was. He also explained such abstruse concepts regarding the economy as balance of payments and foreign exchange, what a bank was, why the society must produce more and how to go about doing so, and finally, the difference between foreign and domestic markets. Additionally, in an attempt to account for why the masses were subjugated by a minority, Bosch indicated that he qualified the term *minority* with the adjective *tutumpote,* a Dominican colloquialism meaning "big shot."

The invention of a term, Bosch explained, was autochthonous and in contradistinction to the Trujillo political ideology, because in Bosch's mind there was no bourgeoisie in the Marxist sense, only a "creole bourgeoisie" in the sense that there was "an upper middle class engaged in trade, landholding, and even industry to some extent."[42] Consequently, he had to invent a word that would encompass the concept of elite. The word, however, had to sound attractive and be catchy and sufficiently self-explanatory that it did not have to be explained on a daily basis to the masses who their traditional exploiters were.[43] Like the PNM in Trinidad and Tobago, the PRD was not merely a political party: it would assume office on the vote of the people, and it sought to offer an unprecedented opportunity to educate the masses with respect to democracy, an opportunity that clearly had not existed during Trujillo's regime.

However, Bosch's policies, which some viewed as betraying communist leanings, drew the ire of powerful others such as the Catholic Church, which felt that he was trying to oversecularize the country; the military, which felt that he was trying to weaken their influence; and above all a skittish America, already covertly involved in what was then British Guiana and oversensitive to any perceived leftist leanings after the establishment of Cuba, seemingly, as part of the Soviet bloc. In pointing to the role of the Catholic Church, Bosch noted that the older Dominican clergy had comprised foreigners and long-time residents. This included higher-ups in the church, who acted like members of the first families or of the upper-middle class. As Bosch states,

> Apparently without being aware of it, they were obeying a powerful impulse that, although not very clearly defined had placed many priests in opposition to the masses in the PRD's following. Probably without realizing it they were behaving like members of the Dominican upper-middle class. The Catholic hierarchy in the country lived in the same atmosphere as the elite and the upper-middle class, and had no contact with or knowledge of the masses. It had no notion that they constituted a social class that aspired to something beyond what it then represented. The clergy knew this social group only as poor people, who were given alms from time to time and who should be conquered in the name of the faith.[44]

Therefore, when the new constitution—there had been many during Trujillo's regime—was promulgated on 29 April 1963, the church declined to send a representative to the official ceremony. High church officials acted like those in the White elite and the upper stratum of the middle class, who said that the constitution was "invalid because it was drafted by 'unimportant' and 'ignorant' people."[45]

In addition to class-based policies, successive Dominican governments have introduced race-based policies by showing a preference for European over all other immigrants. As Hoetink put it, "To govern is to populate."[46] As a result, despite nationalist activities during the Trujillo era, which included the purchase of U.S.-owned factories and other enterprises, thousands of Haitians living in the Dominican border areas were massacred in 1937. Also, Haitian labor power continued to be exploited, compared with that of other Dominicans, and Black Dominican roots tended to be absent from the national dialogue.[47] After seven months in office, on 25 September 1963, the Bosch government was overthrown in a military coup, after which Bosch immediately went into exile, this time in Puerto Rico. He would later reappear on the political scene in the Dominican Republic as the leader of a new political party and would unsuccessfully run for the office of president.

THE WORK of George Lamming also seems to be pertinent to an assessment of the anticolonial tradition, although he was born on 8 June 1927, almost two decades after Césaire, Williams, and Bosch. Lamming's autobiographical novel *In the Castle of My Skin* was first published in 1953. In the 1970 Collier edition, Richard Wright, with whom Williams was in contact, observes that with "poetic prose, Lamming tells the story of millions of simple folk who . . . are today being catapulted out of their peaceful, indigenously earthy lives and into the turbulence and anxiety of the twentieth century."[48]

In the book, Lamming introduces the reader to life in a Barbadian village, which he viewed as a microcosm of the colonialist lifeworld of Barbadians. He writes, for example, that in the village there was the landlord, who lived in a "large brick house hoisted on the hill" and whose friends were "mainly planters whose estates in the country had remained agricultural; or otherwise there were English visitors who were absentee landowners of estates which they had come to see."[49] Then there were the overseers, who constituted a social stratum between the landlord and the "ordinary" villagers and who, although they were themselves villagers, were granted special privileges, such as "attending on the landlady or owning after twenty years' tenure the spot of land on which their house was built." The overseers patrolled the land at all hours of the day and were "fierce, aggressive, and strict," and since theft was not unusual, the landlords depended entirely on the overseers to scare away the more dangerous villagers. "The overseers also carried bunches of keys strung on wire which they chimed continually, partly to warn the villagers of their approach, and partly to satisfy themselves with the level of their authority." Since the landlord was prone to accuse the overseers of conniving with the villagers, the overseers found it necessary to vent their feelings on the villagers, who they thought were "envious, jealous, and mean."[50]

As a stratum at the bottom of the social system, the villagers were a socially constructed stigmatized "other," buttressed by custom and image. "Low down nigger people was a special phrase the overseers had coined" to describe the villagers, who, according to the overseers, "couldn't bear to see one of their kind get along without feeling envy and hate."[51] Lamming contends that the divide-and-rule strategy

> had created a tense relationship between the overseer and the ordinary villager. Each represented for the other an image of the enemy. And the enemy was to be destroyed or placated. The overseer was either authoritarian or shrewd. The villager hostile or obsequious. The landlord's complaint heightened the image, gave it an edge that cut sharp and deep through every layer of the land. And this image by continual assertion had become a myth which like a rumour drifted far beyond the village. Even the better educated who had one way or another gone to the island's best schools and later held responsible posts in the Government service . . . were affected by this image of the enemy . . . and the enemy was my People. My people are low-down nigger people. My people don't like to see their people get on.[52]

This was the language of the overseer, the language of the civil servant, and later the language of the "lawyers and doctors who had returned stamped like an envelope with what they called the culture of the Mother Country," which was employed to describe and define the other villagers, "my people." And this myth had eaten through their consciousness, Lamming continues, like "moths through the pages of ageing documents." By way of innuendo and character attribution, therefore, the "ordinary villager" had become the enemy, and there had thus emerged an attitude that the overseer "wore like a uniform and which became his substitute for duty." The motto was "Take no chances. Be on the look-out always, everywhere. Be fierce. Be strict. Be aggressive. That was duty."[53]

According to Lamming, the system of surveillance that was part of the lifeworld of the colonized was such that the overseer was a "shadow of the police constable who patrolled the village at night." In Lamming's words, he "always arrived alert, ready, prepared." When he came, it was not "to explain, inform, interpret or share experience like other men in the ordinary run of social intercourse. He came to arrest. Something had to be wrong." Moreover, whenever the constable appeared "there was apprehension," and people who were normally "relaxed and composed became fidgety [and] began to suspect themselves."[54] Conceivably, then, the keys of the overseer, like the whip used by the slaver on the enslaved and by the principal of Queen's Royal College in Williams's time, functioned as a fetish for the dominated and reflected Prospero's language of fear.

The aura of control and oversight of the people manifested itself also in the person of the supervisor of the public bath, who "sat behind the narrow table, looking strict, important and aggressive."[55] His job was not only to ensure that all went well with those who took baths but also, as Lamming pointed out, to maintain certain standards of public decency and decorum. For example, when one bather was showing his upright penis, to the amusement of other boys, the supervisor, with "appropriate discreetness," ordered all the boys: "Get your clothes on and go. And don't come back."[56]

The parade celebrating the Queen's birthday further demonstrated the symbiotic relationship between the colonized, Barbados (Little England), and the colonial power, England (the mother country). As James Scott has shown, parades are intended to be public displays of the power of the dominant and, by extension, the lack of power of the dominated. Parades, as authorized assemblies, exemplify the dominant's power to determine when, where, and for what purposes the dominated may assemble.[57] In Barbados, celebrations of that ilk took place, for example, in a school compound—the school was managed by a White minister, who oversaw the curriculum—and required a visit from the inspector of schools, who was "white and smooth and cool like a pebble," and various preparations by the male head teacher, with a "face richer and stronger, burnt black in the sun."[58]

During one such visit from the inspector of schools, following the rendition of "God save our gracious King, Long live our noble King, God save the King," a speech by the inspector, and the distribution of prizes for the best class, the inspector departed, but not before there was a giggle during a speech by the head teacher. The head teacher's countenance immediately changed from one grinning with the inspector to one that was "coarse and savage and sad . . . his voice was low and choked with a kind of terror."[59] After demanding that the offending student own up to "grinning like jackasses when respectable people are around" and giggling "like buffoons in the presence of respectable people, people of power and authority," the head teacher threatened to "beat every blasted one of you from top to bottom," if no one confessed.[60]

One boy stood up and started to speak. No one knew whether he was the guilty one or was merely trying to inform on someone. It did not matter, however, as he was not allowed to continue. In a public display of humiliation, "with the aid of four boys who bound him hands and feet and stretched him flat over a bench," the boy was beaten by the head teacher. The first blow "rent the pants and left the black buttocks exposed," eliciting from the boy "a brief howl like an animal that had had its throat cut." "No one," Lamming continues, "could say how long he was beaten or how many strokes he received. But when he stood supported by the four boys who had held him down he was weak. The knees tottered and the filth slithered down his legs. The boys lifted him out of the school and carried him under the pipe in the school yard."[61]

Unlike for Williams, who viewed the public whipping of two boys at QRC as a holdover from enslavement and part of the system of colonial oppression, for Lamming whipping had a deeper meaning in that it

> produced an extraordinary reaction in the slaves. It seemed that they had come to identify all movement with whipping; and sometimes they would not move until they were whipped almost to the point of death. In a sense they were giving a lesson in pain to the agents of their torture. This attitude of deliberate fatalism undermined the effects of the owners' bestiality. Whatever the owner pretended, the slave's choice had set up a reciprocity between them in this total contract of master and slave. The master could not withdraw; for he was the embodiment of his orders, and the orders had to proceed if his régime were to survive according to his will.[62]

As Supriya Nair observes, for Lamming, "Louis Althusser's theory of the ideological state apparatuses, including educational systems, as disciplinary sites that reproduce existing forces and conditions of production is particularly pertinent to the colonial situation."[63] This was clear not only from Lamming's view of colonial oppression but also from the manner in which middle-rung members of the colonized, such as the overseer, the policeman, the bath attendant, and the head teacher, functioned on behalf of the "system" to keep members of the stratum below them "in their place." For Lamming, it was also clear that, in addition to the village, the school and the bath functioned as spaces of domination.

FINALLY, THE work of Frantz Fanon is of contextual relevance to the discussion of Caliban's anticolonial posturing. Fanon was born in Martinique on 20 July 1925 and died 6 December 1961. Irene L. Gendzier notes that in answer to the question "Who am I?" Fanon responded, "It is the duty of every man to pose that question, and to refine it further by asking, "Have I been all that I am capable of being? Am I who I am?"[64] Fanon grew up in a Martinique in which skin color was of much importance—as opposed to race, which was a critical factor, for example, in Williams's Trinbago—in a layered society that was predominantly white, mulatto, and dark-skinned. Fanon came from a family of eight children, which, it appears, belonged to the upper middle class. Fanon's father was of mixed Indian-Martinican origin, while his mother was of Alsatian origin and was the illegitimate daughter of parents of mixed race. Thus, as Gendzier notes, to know the meaning of whiteness "in the Antilles among non-Whites is to understand the full range of identity-confusion that was in store for Fanon—the darkest in the family—and for others like him."[65]

In the early years of his life, between 1939 and 1945, like his brothers and sisters, Fanon went to school at the local private lycée, in the capital, Fort-de-France, where Aimé Césaire would later teach. However, the Second World War and the occupation in Martinique of French troops between 1940 and 1945 were to influence Fanon's views, especially regarding white-nonwhite race relations. In April 1943, Fanon went to Dominica to join the Free French Movement, and by the end of that year he had joined the French army, later seeing service in Europe, where he learned that the French army and the French troops in Martinique were no freer of color consciousness. After more than two years of military service, Fanon returned to Martinique in 1946, where he and a brother worked in Césaire's election campaign.

In 1947, Fanon left for France to further his education, and by the end of 1951, he had completed and defended his medical thesis and had started his practice of psychotherapy. In the summer of 1952, he began work as a resident under the direction of Professor François Tosquelles, which turned out to be a transformative experience for Fanon. Tosquelles greatly influenced Fanon's work not only in terms of methodology but also with respect to the problems that Fanon chose to study. As Gendzier notes, Fanon and the other young doctors "listened to the organic conceptions of psychiatry and medicine that Tosquelles espoused. The conception of sociotherapy, with its emphasis on the importance of the social role and the social context of patients in hospitals, was part of a more extensive critique of existing psychiatric methods and hospital care."[66] After 1956, Fanon moved to Algeria and became involved in, and was politically molded by, the independence struggle of that country (1954–1962). Sociocultural context would remain a feature of Fanon's analysis of the colonial experience.

FANON'S INTELLECTUALISM is grounded in an acute sense of "what it is to be wronged, of what it is to be misunderstood, misinterpreted, rejected. . . .

The dream of a just world, of recognition, of order, stood parallel to the realization of injustice, the lack of recognition, and disorder."[67]

Because, as previously discussed, writing is an important factor in knowledge communication, it is apposite to note that very early in his life Fanon concluded that "he needed to understand himself as he was, as he believed himself to be, and as the world saw him. For this, he chose to write. Not as a way of describing the world or himself, but as a way of understanding it, its absurdities, and the possibilities of its rationalization. To write was a form of action; it was in its origins self-centered and reflexive. But by its very nature it was also a method of communicating, of reaching out to tell and to teach others."[68]

In 1952, at the age of twenty-seven, Fanon published his first book, entitled *Black Skin White Masks: The Experiences of a Black Man in a White World.* In that book, in a comment that could well serve as an epigraph for this study, Fanon wrote, "But society, unlike biochemical processes, cannot escape human influences. Man is what brings society into being."[69] Indeed, the whole history of Trinidad and Tobago—beginning with the arrival of the colonists, and how through their efforts plantations, schools, and public parks, to name some examples, were transformed into physical spaces—spoke to the social condition of the colonized as the "other" and the Object and, as Fanon put it, in a "zone of nonbeing."[70]

Although Fanon's anticolonial renderings were informed by a methodology involving observation, especially as a psychiatrist in Algeria, he remained mindful of historical and sociocultural context in his assessments of the Manichaean experiences involving colonizer and colonized. Thus, in a comment about the system of apartheid in South Africa, he writes that "the non-white populations of South Africa are at an impasse. All the modern modes of slavery make it impossible for them to flee from this scourge. In the case of the African especially, white society has smashed his old world without giving him a new one. It has destroyed the traditional tribal foundations of his existence and it blocks the road of the future after having closed the road of the past."[71]

Additionally, Fanon considered aspects of personal biography to be important, and in particular, relationships during one's early life. Thus, he contends that childhood issues must be addressed to combat the Manichaean implications of narcissism—the white man is sealed in his whiteness and the black man in his blackness: to "lay bare the anomalies of affect that are responsible for the structure of the complex . . . it is imperative to eliminate a whole set of defects left over from childhood. Man's tragedy, Nietzsche said, is that he was once a child."[72]

As we look at the anticolonial tradition and portrayals of oppressive conduct emanating from the pens of Williams, Césaire, Bosch, Lamming, and Fanon, it is appropriate to note certain commonalities. These involved treatment of the social-stratification system, the role of religion as a component of oppression, the cultural underbelly of oppression, the exploitation of the economic resources of the oppressed, the importance of education both in the service of oppression and against it, the utilization of history as a weapon in expatiating upon the language and the mind of Prospero, the anticolonial railings used to "curse" that language by Caliban, and the use of different spaces for the purpose of hegemonic activity. Also, Williams, Bosch, and Lamming all mentioned the power of the priest, and Williams and Bosch, the sometimes backward position taken by the Catholic church when it came to the oppression of the masses.

Again, like Césaire, Bosch, and, obviously, Williams, both Lamming and Fanon adverted to the manner in which Prospero's language of oppression provided fodder for Caliban's antihegemonic language. Referring to the incendiary actions of the enslaved in Haiti on that fateful night in July 1791 when they planned to massacre the Whites and destroy their estates, Lamming writes, "Language had changed its name. A new word had been spoken. . . . The ploughs had spoken. The human spirit had been redeemed, inscribed in fire by one act of freedom."[73] Here, Lamming's use of the term *language* suggests that by teaching Caliban his language, Prospero risked the likelihood of Caliban's resistance because of "an unstated history of consequences, an unknown history of future intentions" inhering in language. Thus, the "gift of Language meant not English, in particular, but speech and concept as a way, a method, a necessary avenue towards areas of the self which could not be reached in any other way. It is this way . . . which makes Caliban aware of possibilities."[74]

Also, like Césaire, Fanon addressed the implications of Caliban's immersion in the language of Prospero for the Being of the colonized. He states, for example, that there is a "retaining-wall relationship between language and group" and that "to speak a language is to take on a world, a culture." He notes, in addition, that the word "black" is associated with negative connotations and the word "white" with goodness and "light." Thus, in Europe in the collective unconscious of *homo occidentalis,* the "Negro" and the color black symbolize evil, sin, wretchedness, death, war, famine, or, as in Martinique, are associated with "bad luck," all of which conduces to "aberrations of affect" for the colonized that are at the core of the colonial universe.[75] But contrary to Jungian psychology, which views the collective unconscious as "an archetype: an expression of the bad instincts, of the darkness inherent in every ego, of the uncivilized savage, the Negro who slumbers in every man," the collective unconscious is "simply the sum of prejudices, myths, collective attitudes of a given group."[76] It is therefore "not dependent on cerebral heredity; it is the result of what I call the unreflected imposition of a culture."[77]

In his reference to Hegel's discussion of *Lordship and Bondage,* Fanon stresses three elements—recognition, reciprocity, and struggle—in relation to the social construction of self and the Other. As he puts it, "It is on that other being, on recognition by that other being, that his own human worth and reality depend." But in the Hegelian dialectic, for the former slave (the colonized) to be recognized, there must be "an absolute reciprocity." If this does not occur, the latter is deprived of his "being-for-itself." Then, "he who is reluctant to recognize me opposes me," and a "savage struggle" is likely to ensue during which "I am willing to accept convulsions of death, invincible dissolution, but also the possibility of the impossible."[78] In this manner the dialectic plays out and ameliorative social change for the colonized is realized.

Finally, all of these intellectuals spent extended periods of time in the country of the colonizer, which further enhanced their knowledge and understanding of the language of the colonizer. While all five refer to travel as an important underlying factor with respect to intellectualism and "cursed" the language of oppression, Lamming, in particular, privileges the exilic factor with respect to the novel "as an imaginative interpretation of West Indian society by West Indians." All of those writers who took their inspiration from their native habitat, such as Edgar Mittelholzer, Vic Reid, Roger Mais, Sam Selvon, John Hearne, Jan Carew, V. S. Naipaul, Andrew Salkey, and Neville Dawes, Lamming muses, had felt the need "to get out."[79]

Yet, in responding to this exilic tendency, Lamming writes that, like any other writer, the West Indian writer would like to function in his own country and be recognized just as any other professional worker is. Moreover, "he would like to be supported, through that recognition, by the readers native to that country." His knowledge could then be viewed "as his country's cultural exports to the world beyond the West Indies. That is how Europe and America would come to know them."[80]

However, the matter is not as straightforward as that. As Lamming also notes, the exile is a "universal figure," and the proximity of our lives to the major issues of our time has demanded of us all some kind of involvement. And although we may not always have the right kind of information, eventually we are impelled to act, by speaking and/or writing. "To be an exile," Lamming concluded, "is to be alive."[81]

Contextualizing further and with respect to the manner in which time spent in learned reflection is converted into the production of knowledge, Williams noted that, with the pressures from individual citizens and sectional interests and the consequent paucity of time for private reflection, he found it necessary

> to make do with my private study upstairs, turning off the lights downstairs, taking the telephone off the hook and read and write as a private citizen, maintaining his sanity and seeing the daily chores, stresses and strains in clearer perspective, determined to prove that, like Dante's Ulysses, I
>
> Could conquer the inward hunger that I had
> To master earth's experience, and to attain
> Knowledge of man's mind, both good and bad.[82]

Clearly, then, for Williams intellectualism was to be associated in particular with the satisfaction of the "metaphysical needs of the human mind, as it is driven to reflect on ethical and religious questions, driven not by material need but by an inner compulsion to understand the world as a meaningful cosmos and to take position toward it."[83] This drive to understand the world and to take a position in it, as seen, was manifest in the intellectual-as-stranger status occupied by Williams, who in England was an outsider within and who also was *in* but not necessarily *of* Trinidad and Tobago and, for that matter, the Caribbean.

To sum up preliminarily regarding Caliban's dilemma, for Williams the dilemma seems to have been how to deal with the deeply rooted manifestations of the Trinbagonian self, expressed in the politics of "anything goes," *mauvaise langue,* the free rider, ole talk, as well as other behaviors and thinking, which he clearly considered to be inimical to the goal of political independence. For Césaire, it was the need to reconcile being a black Martinican and being French, while being fully cognizant of the apparent paradox that in order to curse in the language of Prospero, Caliban was forced to immerse himself in that language, while reverting to his roots, that is, the African being. More generally, as Richard Burton put it, "To master 'le français français' . . . was also, potentially, to be able to turn it, Caliban-like, against the white or coloured Prosperos that taught it and the colonialist values they embodied."[84]

However, if, as some note, Negritude was merely a disguised or inverted form of assimilationism, then Martinican epistemology would be destined to look outward—rather than inward—to France and Africa. This is why the more autochthonous concept of *creolité,* which is the totality of an inner-directed discourse or linguistic pattern that seeks to incorporate the multicultural diversity of Martinique, which includes in its population Blacks, Whites, Indians, Chinese, Lebanese, and all their different interpermutations, remains promising.[85] In other words, the outward thrust should be toward similarly situated Caribbean societies with diverse populations, such as Jamaica, Trinidad and Tobago, Surinam, and Guyana.

As we have seen, however, the effort to build a national consensus bereft of racial considerations remained a challenge for Williams. One reason for this is that whether in the case of caste or religion as in India, tribe as in Africa, or race as in Guyana and Trinbago, an integral facet of colonialism has been the utilization of these differences for hegemonic purposes. This explains, as we saw, Consul General Orebaugh's suggestion that efforts be made to pit West Indian leaders against the masses in the Chaguaramas discourse. These divisions, Frantz Fanon maintains, conduce to Manichaean tendencies (indwelling of love and hate) on the part of the native.

In an observation, that continues to have all sorts of implications for internecine and other conflict among former colonized subjects all over the world, Fanon notes that "whereas the colonist or police officer can beat the colonized subject day in and day out, insult him and shove him to his knees," it is not unusual "to see the colonized subject draw his knife at the slightest hostile or aggressive look from another colonized subject."[86]

The propensity for oppressed individuals and formerly colonized peoples to fight among themselves arguably is somewhat akin to W. E. B. Du Bois's notion of the double consciousness of the oppressed. Some of the implications associated with the tendency of the oppressed to view themselves in terms of their experiences as the "other," as well as in terms of the oppressor, are to be found in Fanon's work dealing with the African "self," expressed in the desire of the colonized subject to be European and thus continue to be in the "zone of nonbeing." This model of "self" of the colonized individual, to be found especially in the chapter titled

"The Fact of Blackness" in Fanon's *Black Skin, White Masks,* for Paget Henry provided Caribbean philosophy with a new model of the "self" that combined colonial and anticolonial dimensions.[87] Williams's intellectualism, then, like that of Césaire, James, and Frantz Fanon is part of the philosophical poeticist/historical tradition that was an outgrowth of what Henry refers to as the late period, that is, the third quarter of the twentieth century, and the postcolonial period.[88]

But as Silvio Torres-Saillant has shown, Caliban has not always behaved honorably, as the Caribbean has a long history of leaders who have committed atrocities against the people. In addition to Trujillo, these leaders include François "Papa Doc" Duvalier of Haiti and Joaquin Balaguer of the Dominican Republic, who after the death of Trujillo in 1961 never appeared to be discomfited by the corruption or by his complicity in the genocide of Haitians at the border when he served as a henchman in the dictatorship of Trujillo in 1937.[89]

These leaders' exploitation of their own people probably prompted Bosch to attribute "serious congenital disadvantages" to his compatriots and to suggest that "at the outset the social breakdown of the Dominican people began at birth, with the society's coming into being as if from a 'poisoned womb.'"[90] These disadvantages also might have predisposed Barbados's Kamau Brathwaite to speculate that if, instead of learning to "curse" Prospero in his own language, Caliban "had listened to his mother's voice; if he could speak to her [*sic*] in their language/He might have had a better chance when the chance for revolt came his way."[91]

It is likely that the eponymous Eric Williams Memorial Collection, the brainchild of Erica Williams-Connell, which came into existence in 1998, will continue to play a role in the production of knowledge by researchers in Trinbago and beyond. This could occur if more scholars make use of the EWMC to study Williams's multifaceted legacy of scholarship. Such individuals would likely spend money on the twin island, which would benefit the economy, particularly if they come from abroad. And more than likely, they would make the fruits of their labors, in the form of published books, book chapters, articles, and so on, available in Trinidad and Tobago.

This activity can lead to what John McCarthy and Mayer Zald refer to as a social-movement industry, as business opportunities for booksellers and further economic benefits to Trinidad and Tobago occur. The same might be said for the existence of the EWMC newsletter, which Williams-Connell edits, permitting her to act as a gatekeeper regarding the production of knowledge with respect to her father's intellectualism. Lastly, the existence of the EWMC suggests that as a diasporan intellectual, Williams understood the importance of leaving a body of knowledge for later generations to peruse and critique, and in the process, one hopes, to generate more knowledge of a relevant nature.

This is possible, as Richard Posner points out, because the lineal intellectual descendants of Caliban are more likely to have overcome adversity in the face of oppression. In Williams's case, it appears that he was deeply in love with Soy Moyou, his second wife and the mother of his daughter Erica Williams-Connell, who died when Williams-Connell was an infant. Errol Mahabir, a former Trinidad and Tobago cabinet minister, recalls being shocked when, on a trip to Japan, at dinner one night Williams asked him to get the strolling violinists "to play Limelight for me, I'll be loving you eternally. . . . So they played this thing and I saw for the first time a moment of weakness and I saw tears fill Dr. Williams' eyes." When Mahabir later asked the significance of the song, Williams replied that it was the song playing the first time he danced with Soy Moyou on their first date.[92] Williams-Connell recalled that her father told her on numerous occasions that had her mother lived, he would never have entered politics. Her mother was against it, and he would have respected her wishes. However, Williams-Connell also noted that the fact that her father made that promise to her mother does not necessarily mean that he would not later have entered politics, as changing circumstances might have led to a mutual decision that would have freed him from that promise. Apparently, after Soy Moyou's death Williams made a conscious decision to enter the political arena.[93] Williams was also an attentive and concerned father who sought to shield his daughter from the harm that could come to the daughter of the political leader of Trinidad and Tobago.[94] Indeed, one of her father's favorite sayings was, "A prime minister should never have a wife; he should never have a daughter; and under no circumstances should he ever have both." The political man must devote his entire being to politics and to his country.

Williams-Connell also noted that her father did not suffer fools gladly and that the older he grew, the more disillusioned he became. Moreover, intellectual that he was, Williams probably would never have been fully satisfied with the way things were. He was disappointed with "the mentality of our countrymen [whom] He thought were much too frivolous, insular, and not interested in a team effort . . . inefficiency annoyed him . . . and incompetence was a constant thorn in his side."[95] Williams could be rude and abrasive, tended to put people in "cold storage" (not talking to them or acknowledging them for extended periods of time if they incurred his wrath), and had to have his own way. As we have seen, he sometimes violated the mandate given to him by the mandator, or fellow movement intellectuals, that he speak on their behalf only after checking with them. C. L. R. James described Williams as "fundamentally dishonest," but he also noted that, far from displaying the hubris that some have claimed, Williams was willing to listen and to consider points of view other than his own but was intolerant of those who would waste his time, which was very "precious to him."[96] Finally, despite possible protestations on Williams's part to the contrary, according to Elton Richardson,

> Eric was never a democrat though in the West Indian sense he knew that he lived in a world in which democracy was all pervading. He himself was a great scholar and would know of Greek democracy and how it came into being. He knew more than enough about it so that he could confute and confuse others. But he himself was like the king above the law. In the early days of the party he was most willing to listen to what all had to say. But as the bandwagon started to take shape he began to think about who alone was going to drive it? . . . In hindsight these things were uppermost in Eric's mind and he had all the instincts that a feudal monarch needed to keep his throne.[97]

In the final analysis, whatever his shortcomings, it is fair to say that Williams came, he saw, he stayed, and he conquered. Clearly too, he succeeded not only in describing and analyzing the colonial system of Trinidad and Tobago of which he was a product but also in changing it. And, although he may not have achieved all he would have liked to achieve, Williams the teacher and intellectual forced his country's people to view politics and themselves differently, as his emphasis on political education percolated throughout the twin island. He was the quintessential Caribbean man, the driving force behind the movement for political independence, and an intellectual in no less than three senses of the word.

Williams was a creature of, and his intellectualism was influenced by, a generation preoccupied with the warps and wefts of colonial oppression. However, as an organic intellectual above all else, Williams exemplified, in Gordon Lewis's words, "Burke's definition of the politician, the philosopher in action, bred out of the radical intellectual's conviction that the cloistered virtue of academic life becomes sterile save as it seeks to translate its knowledge into social purpose, bred, too, out of his professional historian's conviction that, as Lord Acton put it, the historian must be judge as well as witness."[98]

Indeed, Williams's application of history from the bottom up as an intellectual suggests that he understood the manner in which different spaces—a school, a university, a plantation, a ship, public parks, a foreign base, Kent House, the headquarters of the Caribbean Commission, and so on—are converted into arenas that involve patterned relationships between the dominated and the dominant. However, since, as Georg Simmel observed, the dominated play an important part in the domination process, if only momentarily, as in the case of rebellions or "laziness" on the part of the enslaved, "all leaders are also led; in innumerable cases, the master is the slave of his slaves. Said one of the greatest German party leaders referring to his followers: 'I am their leader, therefore I must follow them.'"[99] Additionally, Williams used the symbolic capital of the highly qualified academic and professional historian to provide a consensus regarding the meaning of political independence. History, for him, was not merely a recitation and analysis of events, dates, places, and people but a weapon to be used to interpret the *past* in order to inform the *present* so as to procure *future* ameliorative social change. Also, while he would probably have agreed with Paulo Freire's view that "to teach is not [simply] to transfer knowledge but to create the possibilities for the production or construction of knowledge,"[100] as Barbara Ransby might argue, Williams would have failed to "tame the ego" in the process.[101]

Perhaps Williams's most significant intellectual legacy, however, was his contribution to the development of the "great public" in Trinbago. In the Western world, for example, the discovery of the printing press and the existence of clubs, universities, salons, newspapers, magazines, novels, the television, and so on, were instrumental in spawning a reading and discussing public. In Trinbago, by contrast, this was accomplished via, in addition to the *Beacon* magazine, the main library, public spaces like the "University of Woodford Square," barber and rum shops, the streets, and areas like Behind the Bridge, and by the Bachacs, teachers, females, and limers and others who listened to and read Williams's speeches. One can therefore conclude that what Williams's father did not achieve with his brains, he certainly did with his loins.

Afterword

The Head That Wears the Crown Lies Uneasy

THERE ARE instances when, according to Frantz Fanon, a member of the oppressed stratum who has acquired power may be perceived as a betrayer of the oppressed masses. This occurs when native political leaders of former colonies occupy the positions left vacant by former colonists and transform themselves into the new bourgeoisie by enriching themselves and exploiting the masses for their own benefit. The peasantry, then, is systematically left out of most of the propaganda of the nationalist parties.[1]

Roughly a decade after the 22 April 1960 march to the "University of Woodford Square" demanding that the Americans vacate the Chaguaramas base, and nearly eight years after the euphoria of attaining political independence, a so-called revolution that lasted from 26 February to 21 May 1970 occurred on the twin island. The disturbances are contextualized as an intergenerational conflict of ideas regarding political independence, mobilization for collective action using various resources, reconstruction of physical spaces like streets and the "University of Woodford Square" as protest sites, and seeking space in the sociopolitical fabric for these ideas by a post-political-independence generation. According to a U.S. intelligence report, the unrest appeared to have its roots in

> the shattered dream that political independence and political power in the hands of black men would bring a quick solution to economic problems and an end to discrimination against and exploitation of the black man. Unemployment remains high and most of the nation's finances and much of the its commerce is in the hands of whites, Orientals, or foreigners. . . . The lower class workers, farmers, and the unemployed are almost EXCLUSIVELY people of unmixed Negro or Indian blood. It is from the Negro sector of this latter group that the demonstrators have drawn their principal strength.[2]

The precursors to the disturbances were a thematic protest by three bands during Carnival Monday on 9 February 1970; the reaction to the banning of Trinidad-born, U.S.-based Black Power activist Stokely Carmichael; and the reaction to the arrest and trial of Trinbagonian students in Canada, allegedly for the destruction of a computer at Sir George Williams University. These activities morphed into a protest led by the University of the West Indies students Geddes Granger and Dave Darbeau and the Oilfield Workers' Trade Union leader George Weekes, among others, that was initially directed at the Canadian High Commission and the Royal Bank of Canada in Port-of-Spain. There was also a demonstration by some two hundred individuals who entered the Roman Catholic Cathedral of the Immaculate Conception in downtown Port-of-Spain. Nine members of an organization known as the National Joint Action Committee (NJAC), formed in 1969, were then arrested for "unlawful assembling in the vicinity and within" the cathedral.

This was followed by a mammoth Black Power protest involving about ten thousand people against unemployment and poverty in Port-of-Spain and foreign control of the economy, led by Geddes Granger, who was president of the UWI Guild of Undergraduates.[3] Granger, who was educated at St. Mary's College and who later changed his name to Makandal Daaga, founded what was described as an "inspiration, a movement, a spirit," rather than an organization, called Pegasus. In Greek mythology, Pegasus was the name of a horse from which the Greeks drew their courage, their inspiration, and their strength.[4] Pegasus soon began creating space for its ideas, especially those of Granger, regarding independence (as opposed to political independence) in the social system.

Seeking to obtain space in the political spectrum, the movement introduced a system of national awards to honor not only the nation's "artistes, but also our national heroes."[5] Another idea Pegasus introduced was Project Independence—"The way to Independence"—which organized national debating competitions throughout the country to "give young people a greater appreciation of themselves as a free and independent people in the family of nations." In addition, Pegasus staged a project called the Model United Nations, in which students from secondary schools throughout the country were brought together to engage in discussions in a manner similar to that of the U.N. General Assembly. Later, Pegasus also embarked on a project involving the construction of a national stadium.

Faced with what appeared to be governmental intransigence regarding the national-stadium project and a PNM meeting at the very time and place that the project was to be launched, Granger swore to Ray

Mitchell, one of Pegasus's leaders, that he would "bring Williams to his knees for this."[6] Granger may have seen Williams, as Alistair Hennessy put it, as an organic intellectual, part of the new class of intellectuals who used their status as intellectuals to further their own selfish interests and were "betrayers" of the people.[7]

During a 26 February demonstration of support for West Indian students on trial for arson in Canada, Granger frequently used the term *white bastards*. On 4 March, members of Black Power organizations from throughout the twin island came together to express their solidarity with the NJAC individuals who had been arrested. Then, on 5 March, a crowd chanting "Power, Power," gathered outside the magistrates' court where the cases of the young men who had been arrested were to be heard. Following a confrontation with baton-wielding policemen, the crowd smashed the display windows of nine business houses, stores throughout the city closed their doors, and schoolchildren were sent home. After nightfall a lighted flambeau was thrown into the home of the minister of education and culture, a priest was beaten, and a garment factory located in San Juan was destroyed by fire, leaving sixty employees jobless.[8] On 6 March an estimated twenty thousand demonstrators walked from Woodford Square to San Juan.

On 12 March, Granger led an estimated twenty thousand individuals on a long march in the hot sun from Port-of-Spain to the sugar belt in Caroni, an area populated mostly by Indians, a distance of twenty-six to twenty-eight miles. The march was seen as an effort to forge a sense of solidarity with the Indian sugar workers, who were viewed as also being oppressed in Trinbago. The support of the Indo-Trinbagonians did not materialize, however; a few comments in the local newspapers capturing the sentiments of the group revealed that most of its members did not consider themselves to be black. Indeed, previously, during the 1968–69 academic year, the Society for the Preservation of Indian Culture (SPIC) had been formed by Indian students at the University of the West Indies "largely in reaction to the formation of NJAC."[9]

On Friday, 3 April, during a visit by Granger to Tobago, a group of individuals numbering "hundreds or so" reportedly entered a white enclave just outside Scarborough screaming, "Whites, get out of Tobago. We don't want you here. If you don't get out we'll throw you out." The next day "about two hundred marchers, and riders in trucks and cars, entered the Tobago Golf Club, where they smashed tableware, large stone flower pots; destroyed a counter in the vestibule, tore up the guest book on the counter; and tore down the British flag, and demolished it."[10]

Then, on 21 April, a small section of the country's Defense Force at the Teteron base, including a few officers, mutinied. As Raffique Shah, a young lieutenant in the Defense Force later put it, he and other members had to decide whether to obey orders "and proceed to quell the revolution in a way that only the military could—by brute force"—or to "follow the dictates of our consciences, our political convictions, and refuse to be used against our Black Power brothers." They chose the latter course of action.[11] Ironically, many of the demonstrators came from Behind the Bridge and had previously supported Williams. In addition, some individuals complained of a general insensitivity to the needs of the people, including the Indian community, especially the Hindu population, none of whose members appear to have been included in a Williams cabinet. Shah also claimed that the Defense Force was poorly administered, lacked discipline, and was characterized by a great degree of malaise.

Also on 21 April, coincidentally the day that Indian sugar workers had planned a march, the GOTT declared a state of emergency, fifteen Black Power leaders were arrested, and a dawn-to-dusk curfew was imposed. That same day, a U.S. intelligence report revealed that Williams had requested military assistance from a number of countries, including the United States and Britain. Finally, on 3 May, during a television address to the nation titled "I Identify Myself Fully With Constructive Black Power," Williams referred to the disturbances. He stated that he identified fully with the constructive aspect of the Black Power movement and that Black economic aid would be intensified, but he could not countenance the breakdown in law and order that had taken place. He also announced the relaxation of the curfew.

Making use of resources such as time (always available to university students, who would not have classes all day, and, of course, to the unemployed) and energy, the protesters were led by the charismatic Geddes Granger, always an individual of ideas and "new" knowledge. The protest was nourished somewhat by an ideology of Black Power, which, although not well articulated, permitted the protesters to present a formidable challenge to the government. The action of the protesters was aided by the culture of dissident discourse previously put in place, ironically, by the efforts of political-independence leaders like Eric Williams.

However, while Granger would proclaim, somewhat disingenuously, that "I never marched because I was black, I marched because I saw people hungry,"[12] the fact of the matter was that his "inviting" the Indian dispossessed to join the protest was an afterthought, and was seen as such. While the government of Eric Williams committed the "heresy" of locking the gates of the UWS so as to deny the protesters a physical space where they could meet, the latter simply reconstructed the streets and the university campus as physical spaces for their antigovernment collective action and transformed the streets in particular into dangerous spaces.

As the protests petered out, Granger and a number of his followers were arrested and jailed, and officers found guilty of mutiny—not treason—were dismissed from the army and received terms of imprisonment. "Knees" intact, Williams was able to walk away. The Americans in particular and the British, while providing military equipment for which the GOTT was required to pay, declined to provide boots on the ground unless the lives of their citizens were in danger. Several of the university students who were detained during the emergency were permitted to take their final exams while in jail, and a number went on to lead productive lives.[13] Fortunately, when the challengers demanded bread, they were not offered cake by the GOTT. Doubtless, the university leaders of the disturbances learned about the varied, often contradictory functions of the university, which often has "to conserve and at the same time innovate."[14]

Knowledge is a commodity that is socially produced and rendered historically relevant by product entrepreneurs. As with other products, however, because of market conditions obsolescence is a cultural inevitability. The ideas promulgated by Makandal Daaga and others during the 1970 disturbances must therefore be seen as a manifestation of the tendency toward obsolescence, in this instance, regarding Williams's intellectualism.

Notes

Introduction

1. Bourdieu, *Language and Symbolic Power.*

2. C. Mills, *Sociological Imagination.*

3. Camp, "Mexican Intellectuals and Collective Biography."

4. Le Bon, *Crowd.*

5. Hoffer, *True Believer.*

6. Smelser, "Theoretical Issues of Scope and Problems"; Smelser, *Theory of Collective Behavior.*

7. Cohen, "Strategy or Identity"; McAdam, *Political Process;* McCarthy and Zald, "Resource Mobilization and Social Movements"; Morris, "Reflections on Social Movement Theory."

8. Morris, *Origins of the Civil Rights Movement;* Melucci, *Nomads of the Present.*

9. Robnett, *How Long? How Long?*

10. Snow and Benford, "Master Frames and Cycles of Protest"; Snow et al., "Frame Alignment Processes."

11. Tarrow, *Power in Movement;* Tarrow, "States and Opportunities"; Tilly, *From Mobilization to Revolution.*

12. Eyerman and Jamison, *Social Movements;* Eyerman, *Between Culture and Politics.*

13. Mueller, "Building Social Movement Theory," 7.

14. Other helpful statements on intellectuals include Lewis Feuer's "What Is an Intellectual?"; Aleksander Gella's *Intelligentsia and Intellectuals;* Jeffrey Goldfarb's *Civility and Subversion;* Christopher Lasch's *New Radicalism in America;* Karl Mannheim's *Essays on the Sociology of Knowledge* and *Ideology and Utopia;* and Edward Shils's "Intellectuals and the Powers."

15. Coser, *Men of Ideas,* viii.

16. Lipset and Dobson, "Intellectual as Critic and Rebel."

17. Eisenstadt, "Intellectuals and Tradition," 1.

18. Goulbourne, "Institutional Contribution of the University of the West Indies," 21.

19. Foucault, *Power/Knowledge,* 132.

20. Ibid., 133.

21. Habermas, *Theory of Communicative Action.*

22. Lipset and Basu, "Roles of the Intellectual and Political Roles."

23. Flacks, "Making History and Making Theory."

24. Habermas, *Structural Transformation of the Public Sphere.* For a similar approach but with respect to the role of ideologies, see Bell, *End of Ideology.*

25. Flacks, "Making History and Making Theory," 3.

26. Hennessy, "Intellectuals: The General and the Particular."

1. Colonialism in Early Twentieth-Century Trinidad and Tobago

1. Brereton, *Modern History of Trinidad,* 13.

2. Ibid., 32–33.

3. Williams, *Inward Hunger.* For an unpublished version that contains various handwritten and typewritten notes and observations about Williams's early life and the nature of the society, see "Inward Hunger: No. 1, Early Drafts," Eric Williams Memorial Collection, West India Section, University of the West Indies Library, St. Augustine, Trinidad (hereafter EWMC), folder 139.

4. Boodhoo, *Elusive Eric Williams;* C. Palmer, *Eric Williams and the Making of the Modern Caribbean;* Ryan, *Eric Williams: The Myth and the Man.*

5. Eric Williams to Norman Manley, 17 June 1954, EWMC, folder 39.

6. Ibid.

7. Goffman, *Stigma,* 1.

8. Ibid., 4.

9. Quoted in Frisby, *Georg Simmel,* 126ff.

10. Urry, "Sociology of Space and Place," 11–12.

11. McCall and Simmons, *Identities and Interactions.*

12. Gilroy, *There Ain't No Black in the Union Jack,* 43. For a perceptive treatment of the family as a metaphor for the nation-state and its policies, see also Collins, *Black Feminist Thought,* 56ff.

13. Smith, *Creole Recitations,* chap. 1.

14. Feagin, *Systemic Racism,* 37.

15. Williams, "Inward Hunger: No. 1, Early Drafts," EWMC, folder 139.

16. Pocock, *Out of the Shadows of the Past.*

17. Boodhoo, "Eric Williams: The Myth and the Man," 6.

18. Williams, "Chap. II, 1911–1922," EWMC, folder 139.

19. Williams, "Inward Hunger: No. 1. Early drafts, Chap. 2, Life with Father 1911–1932," ibid.

20. "Williams, "Chap. 2, Life with Father," ibid.

21. Ibid.

22. Williams, "Chap. 2, Life with Father 1911–1932," EWMC, folder 139.

23. Ibid.

24. Smith, *Creole Recitations,* 51.

25. Williams, "Chap. 2, Life with Father 1911–1932," EWMC, folder 139.

26. Williams, "Life with Father, chap. 3," ibid.

27. Williams, "Inward Hunger: No. 1, Early drafts, Chap. 2, Life with Father 1911–1932," ibid. The notes are handwritten in pen, and a line is drawn across this entry.

28. Williams, "Chap. 2, Life with Father," ibid.

29. Williams, "Chap. III, 1922–1932," typewritten, ibid.

30. Williams, "Chap. 2, Life with Father 1911–1932," ibid.; Boodhoo, *Elusive Eric Williams.*

31. "Chap. II, 1911–1922," typewritten, EWMC, folder 139.

32. Gilroy is discussing Frederick Douglass's narrative about a turning point in his life when, providentially, at the age of seven or eight he was sent by his master to live, one presumes, with a White family in Baltimore. Gilroy, *Black Atlantic,* 69. Both Gilroy and Kenneth Mostern advert to the importance of these self-emancipating and independent acts as a key dimension of the autobiography, which Mostern, in particular, views as having implications for identity politics. Mostern, *Autobiography and Black Identity Politics,* 11.

33. Williams, "Chap. 2, Life with Father," EWMC, folder 139.

34. Ibid.

35. Ibid.

36. Williams, "Chap. 2, 1911–1922," typewritten, EWMC, folder 139.

37. Williams, "Chap. II, 1911–1922," ibid.

38. After cajoling and remonstrating, Williams's father eventually gave in, but "with poor grace." *Inward Hunger,* 39.

39. Campbell, "Education and Black Consciousness," 36.

40. Ibid., 45.

41. Quoted in Ibid., 47.

42. Williams, *Inward Hunger,* 69.

43. Campbell, *Young Colonials,* chap. 1.

44. Ibid., 71.

45. Ibid., 72.

46. Smith, *Creole Recitations,* 40.

47. According to Campbell, resistance to education of non-Whites by Whites was also exemplified by the comment of an inspector of schools that the purpose of education for the common people was to make them "industrious, contented and happy" and also by the comments of the Roman Catholic archbishop of Port-of-Spain, who in his Lenten pastoral letter of 1883 opined that the class structure of the colony was "God-given, and that the aspirations of lower class children in primary schools was unchristian." Campbell, *Young Colonials,* 69.

48. For a fuller statement of this process, see St. Pierre, "School Experience of the W.I. Elite."

49. It should be pointed out that Williams was not opposed to the existence of these subjects as such. He later commented that his knowledge of Latin was very useful to him during his first year at Oxford University, as was a working knowledge of French and Spanish in his historical research.

50. Smith, *Creole Recitations,* 41.

51. Williams, *Inward Hunger,* 35.

52. Seecharan, *Muscular Learning,* 5.

53. Ibid., chap. 2.

54. Sandiford, *Cricket Nurseries of Colonial Barbados,* 72.

55. St. Pierre, "Old School Tie," 419.

56. James, *Beyond a Boundary,* 49.

57. Ibid., 71.

58. Boodhoo, "Eric Williams: The Myth and the Man," 5.

59. W. Mahabir, *In and Out of Politics,* 7.

60. Williams, *Inward Hunger,* 30.

61. Lawrence, "QRC 100."

62. Alleyne, *QRC 2004.*

63. Williams, "Chap. II, 1911–1922," EWMC, folder 139. It should be noted that public whipping and its unhappy companion, public humiliation, were also practiced at other leading secondary schools in the West Indies. For an example of the British Guiana experience at Queen's College, see St. Pierre, "Old School Tie"; and for the Jamaican experience at Jamaica College, see G. Mills, *Grist for the Mills.*

64. Williams, "Chap. 2, 1911–1922," EWMC, folder 139.

2. Life Abroad

1. V. J. K. Brock to Williams, 29 March 1932, EWMC, folder 002, "Oxford University: No. 1, Undergraduate Years."

2. Brock to Williams, 16 May 1932, ibid.

3. For an insightful treatment of impression management and the presentation of the self in the context of biography and biographical others, see Goffman, *Presentation of Self in Everyday Life.*

4. Williams, *Inward Hunger,* 42.

5. Brock to Williams, 3 August 1935, EWMC, folder 002, "Oxford University: No. 1, Undergraduate Years."

6. Brock to Williams, 7 August 1935, ibid.

7. Williams, *Inward Hunger,* 46–47, Williams's interpolation.

8. Ibid., 52.

9. Brock to Williams, 20 April 1936, EWMC, folder 002, "Oxford University: No. 1, Undergraduate Years."

10. Williams, *Inward Hunger,* 52.

11. George Sutton to Williams, 3 July 1936, EWMC, folder 002, "Oxford University: No. 1, Undergraduate Years."

12. Green, "Race and Slavery," 26.

13. Williams, *Inward Hunger,* 50.

14. Martin, "Introduction," xi. This introduction contains a very informative description of William's efforts to get a job at the Anglo-American Caribbean Commission and is therefore germane to our argument regarding the emergence of Williams as an academic and a public intellectual.

15. Cutteridge to Williams, 6 July 1936, EWMC, folder 002.

16. Quoted in Howat, *Learie Constantine,* 162.

17. N to Williams, n.d., EWMC, folder 002, "Oxford University: No. 1, Undergraduate Years."

18. Munro and Sander, *KAS-KAS,* 36.

19. Ibid.

20. Ibid., 36–37.

21. James, *Special Delivery.*

22. Ibid., 180.

23. Ibid., 324.

24. Williams, *Inward Hunger,* 57.

25. Tony Martin, feature address, book launch of the republished *Economic Future of the Caribbean,* The Forum, Blackburn Center, Howard University, 30 March 2005.

26. Heywood, "Eric Williams: The Howard Years."

27. Ibid., 19.

28. Franklin, "Eric Williams and Howard University," 23, my emphasis.

29. Ibid., 25.

30. Williams to M. B. Schnapper, 18 October 1941, EWMC, folder 124.

31. Williams to John A. Krout, 26 January 1942, ibid.

32. Krout to Williams, 6 April 1942, ibid.

33. The dedication read, "To Professor Lowell Joseph Ragatz, Whose monumental labors in this field may be amplified and developed but can never be superseded."

34. Williams to Krout, 1 June 1942, EWMC, folder 124.

35. For another example of Williams taking a very proactive role in correspondence with a publisher, in this case regarding the length of his autobiography, *Inward Hunger,* and another book, *From Columbus to Castro,* see ibid., folder 084.

36. Bourdieu, "Social Space and Symbolic Power," 19.

37. Franklin, "Eric Williams and Howard University," 27.

38. Martin, "Introduction."

39. Williams to D. W. Brogan, 12 May 1942, EWMC, folder 028.

40. Brogan to Williams, 31 May 1942, ibid.

41. Tawney taught economic history at London University and was sometime fellow of Balliol College at Oxford.

42. Brogan to Williams, 30 July 1942, EWMC, folder 028.

43. Williams to R. H. Tawney, 3 September 1942, ibid.

44. Williams to Harlow, 7 September 1942, ibid.

45. Williams to John Huggins, 28 October 1932, ibid.

46. Williams to Brogan, 3 November 1942, ibid.

47. See, e.g., "Dr. Williams Takes Post on Research Body," *Trinidad Guardian,* 26 March 1944.

48. See, e.g., "Dr. Williams on Visit to Colony," *Sunday Chronicle,* 16 April 1944. The article also mentioned the considerable research Williams had done in the social sciences and on British West Indians.

49. Heywood, "Eric Williams: The Howard Years," 21.

50. Martin, "Eric Williams, ca. 1943."

51. Martin, "Introduction."

52. Frazier and Williams, *Economic Future of the Caribbean,* 80.

53. Williams, *Negro in the Caribbean,* 92ff.

54. Martin, feature address, book launch.

55. Martin, "Eric Williams: His Radical Side," 112.

56. Ibid., 116.

57. Martin, feature address, book launch.

58. For a complete statement, see Eric Williams, "The British West Indian University," memorandum prepared for the Committee on Higher Education in the West Indies, March 1945, CO 318/459/5, National Archives, London. For a truncated version, see Williams, "Idea of a British West Indian University," in which he addresses three main considerations for such a university: (1) a university is not a mere collection of colleges faculties and students, but an expression of the social order in which it functions; (2) the British West Indian university should create an intellectual climate in which the methods, aims, and purposes of the modern world are adapted to the British West Indies; and (3) the university should be independent of internal political pressures and, externally, of those of other universities.

59. Williams, "Idea of a British West Indian University," 147.

60. Ibid., 154.

61. Williams, *Education in the British West Indies,* xi.

62. Ibid., 41.

63. Goffman, *Frame Analysis,* 21.

3. The Native Son Returns

1. Szacki, "Intellectuals between Politics and Culture," 231–32.

2. Williams, *Inward Hunger,* 92.

3. Ibid., 93.

4. Carlton Comma to Williams, 18 May 1944, Trinidad Public Lectures, EWMC, folder 172.

5. Williams to Comma, 29 May 1944, ibid.

6. Richardson, *Revolution or Evolution,* 24–25.

7. Williams, *Eric E. Williams Speaks,* 49.

8. Oxaal, *Black Intellectuals Come to Power,* 104–5.

9. See Williams, *Case for Party Politics in Trinidad and Tobago.*

10. Escoffier, "Community and Academic Intellectuals," 27. For a very helpful statement on the role of the intellectual in the generation of accredited knowledge that rises to the level of truth and ultimately speaks to the university as a space for knowledge qua power, see Foucault, *Power/Knowledge,* chap. 6.

11. Gouldner, *Future of Intellectuals.*

12. Oxaal, *Black Intellectuals Come to Power,* 104.

13. Rogers, *Rise of the People's National Movement.*

14. For a very informative discussion of the concept of the performance defined as "all the activity of an individual which occurs during a period marked by his continuous presence before a particular set of observers and which has some influence on the observers," see Goffman, *Presentation of Self in Everyday Life,* chap. 1. Since Williams was a master at performance, it will be necessary to return to this question.

15. Rogers, *Rise of the People's National Movement,* 38–39.

16. "Crowds Ask More and More Aristotle," *Trinidad Guardian,* 11 November 1954, 2.

17. "'Religion The Essence of Civilised Living, Aristotle Aimed at Producing a Good Man' Says Dom Basil," ibid., 12.

18. Ibid.

19. Richardson, *Revolution or Evolution,* 25.

20. Williams to Dom Basil Matthews, EWMC, folder 172.

21. Norman H. Booth, "People Interested in Aristotle Invited to Extra-Mural Classes," letter to the editor, *Trinidad Guardian,* 17 November 1954, 6.

22. See "Aristotle Drew 837 Pennies," ibid., 19 November 1954, 7.

23. "Dom Basil Concealed Slavery In Aristotle's Ideal State, Dr. Williams Replies to Monk's Eulogy," ibid., 18 November 1954, 10.

24. Rohlehr, "Culture of Williams," 851.

25. At that time Williams and Gomes were on good terms, and Gomes helped Williams in his career. This, however, would change.

26. "Dom Basil Called on To Make Choice Publicly, 'Either Catholicism, or Aristotelianism' Says Dr. Williams," *Trinidad Guardian,* 20 November 1954. According to Bridget Brereton, the word *jamette* refers to a "lower-class person whose life centres around fighting, singing, dancing, drumming and Carnival. The word is derived from the French *diamêtre* which means or underworld type." Brereton, *Race Relations in Colonial Trinidad,* ix.

27. Williams, *Capitalism and Slavery,* 18.

28. Fraser, "Rethinking the Public Sphere," 123.

29. For an interesting statement of these points, especially in the context of marketing knowledge and the public intellectual, see Posner, *Public Intellectuals,* esp. chap. 2.

30. Mr. Mackay, "Background Information on the Caribbean Commission," attachment to office memo, 24 October 1949, confidential, file 844.00/10/2449, RG 59, National Archives and Records Administration, College Park, MD (hereafter NARA).

31. Ibid.

32. A. Palmer, "United States and the Commonwealth Caribbean," 61.

33. A. D. Emmart, "Caribbean Cooperation—1, Background For An Experiment," *Baltimore Evening Sun,* 4 May 1943. This was the first of four articles on the AACC written by Emmart from 4 to 11 May 1943.

34. Quoted in A. D. Emmart, "Caribbean Cooperation—4: What It Points To," ibid., 11 May 1943.

35. For a discussion of these problems, see A. Palmer, "United States and the Commonwealth Caribbean," chap. 4.

36. Ibid.

37. Eric Williams, *My Relations with the Caribbean Commission, 1943–1955, By Eric Williams: A Public Lecture given under the auspices of The People's Educational Movement of the Teachers Economic and Cultural Association in Woodford Square—Port-of-Spain Trinidad, June 21st, 1955,* 23, University of the West Indies Library, St. Augustine, Trinidad.

38. *Monthly Bulletin of the Caribbean Commission* 1, no. 11 (June 1948), NARA, RG 59, file 844.00/9-1748.

39. Corkran, *Patterns of International Cooperation,* 39. This book contains very helpful information about both the AACC and the Caribbean Commission and Williams's relationship with these two organizations.

40. For a statement regarding Williams's tenure at the commission, see his *My Relations with the Caribbean Commission.*

41. Snow et al., "Frame Alignment Processes," 238.

42. Williams, *Negro in the Caribbean,* 72–73. Williams is quoting here from "Report of Select Committee of the Legislative Council on Restriction of Hours of Labour" (1926), 30–31.

43. Ibid., quoting "Report of Select Committee . . . ," 32.

44. James Frederick Green (acting chief, Division of Dependent Affairs) to Ward M. Canaday, 24 November 1948, personal and confidential, NARA, RG 59, file 844.00/11-2448.

45. Green to Canaday, 14 April 1949, confidential, ibid.

46. Williams to Norman Manley, 17 June 1954, EWMC, folder 39.

47. Ibid.

48. Corkran, *Patterns of International Cooperation,* 95.

49. K. Mohammed, "Dr. Williams' Political Education Campaign—1955," 7.

50. Williams, *My Relations with the Caribbean Commission.*

51. Ibid.

52. Bourdieu, *Language and Symbolic Power,* 58.

53. Corkran, *Patterns of International Cooperation,* 97.

4. In Search of Relevance

1. Fraser, "Rethinking the Public Sphere."
2. Habermas, *Theory of Communicative Action,* 27.
3. Ibid., 43.
4. Ibid., 160.
5. Habermas, *Structural Transformation of the Public Sphere.*
6. Harvey, "Political Economy of Public Space," 17.
7. Moore, *Cultural Power, Resistance and Pluralism,* 78.
8. Scott, *Domination and the Arts of Resistance.*
9. Trotman, "Public History."
10. De Barros, *Order and Place,* 144–45.
11. Brereton, *Modern History of Trinidad,* 21.
12. Williams, *Perspectives for the West Indies,* 10.
13. Fergus, "Centring the City," 117.
14. Williams, *Perspectives for the West Indies,* 9.
15. Williams, *Constitution Reform in Trinidad and Tobago.*
16. Williams, *Inward Hunger,* 158.
17. Eric Williams, *Our Fourth Anniversary . . . The Last Lap, By Dr. Eric Williams: Political Leader's Address on September 24, 1960 at the University of Woodford Square, marking the Fourth Year of P.N.M.'s First Term of Office* (P.N.M. Publishing, 1960), 4, University of the West Indies Library, St. Augustine, Trinidad.
18. Ibid.
19. Ibid.
20. Kelley, "Poetics of Anticolonialism," 8.
21. Williams, *Our Fourth Anniversary . . . The Last Lap,* 4.
22. Erica Williams-Connell, interview by author, 31 May 2005, Dominican Republic.
23. "A Jamaican's Impression of the University of Woodford Square," *PNM Weekly,* 10 February 1958.
24. Habermas, *Structural Transformation of the Public Sphere,* 100.
25. Fraser, "Rethinking the Public Sphere," 110.
26. Goffman, *Presentation of Self in Everyday Life,* 24.
27. Oxaal, *Black Intellectuals Come to Power,* 112.
28. Williams, *Perspectives for the West Indies,* 11.
29. L. Beckles, "PNM Weekly Newspaper."
30. Ibid., my emphasis.
31. Williams, *Inward Hunger,* 152.
32. Williams, *Our Fourth Anniversary . . . The Last Lap,* 6.
33. Ibid.
34. Eric Williams, "The Approach to Independence" (address, fourth annual convention of the PNM, March 1960), 19.
35. Ibid.

36. Ibid., 20.
37. Ibid.
38. Ibid., 21.
39. For a discussion of James's influence on Williams and his activities with respect to the party, see Ryan, *Race and Nationalism in Trinidad and Tobago.*
40. The letter, reprinted in C. L. R. James, *Party Politics in the West Indies,* 73–74, was addressed to "My Dear Bill" and signed "N." See postscript on p. 74.
41. Ibid., 75, addressed to "Dr. Williams" and signed "C. L. R. James." Apparently, James did not actually resign until 14 July 1960. Ibid., 96.
42. James, *Party Politics in the West Indies,* 82.
43. Ibid., 5.
44. Ibid., 17.
45. Ibid., 77.
46. Williams, *Eric E. Williams Speaks,* 71.
47. Quoted in Worcester, *C. L. R. James,* 155.
48. Constantine, *Cricket in the Sun,* 62–65.
49. Williams, *Our Fourth Anniversary . . . The Last Lap,* 6.
50. W. Mahabir, *In and Out of Politics,* 70.
51. Ibid.

5. Exploiting the Political-Opportunity Structure

1. McCarthy and Zald, "Resource Mobilization and Social Movements."
2. Ibid., 1218.
3. Melucci, *Nomads of the Present.*
4. Morris, *Origins of the Civil Rights Movement.* Morris refers to the Black Church and various other groups that provided a useful foundation for the emergence of the Southern Christian Leadership Conference and other civil rights organizations.
5. Robnett, *How Long? How Long?,* 25.
6. W. Mahabir, *In and Out of Politics,* 17.
7. Allsopp, *Dictionary of Caribbean English Usage,* 57.
8. Boodhoo, "Eric Williams: The Myth and the Man," 5.
9. W. Mahabir, *In and Out of Politics,* 17.
10. Donald Granado, "An Autobiography," 1987, University of the West Indies Library, St. Augustine.
11. Ibid.
12. Alexander, "Birth of the PNM."
13. For a very helpful treatment of this argument and the writer's objection to the resource-mobilization stress on mobilizing elites rather than the socially marginal and a mass base, see McAdam, *Political Process.*
14. Alexander, "Birth of the PNM," 5.
15. Ibid., 6, my emphasis.

16. Resocialization is the process by which individuals unlearn behavior considered to be socially inappropriate, while learning or relearning behavior deemed inappropriate. In the context of Trinidad and Tobago, politically this was clearly an important facet of the PNM's formation, seeking as it did to make a clean break with the politics of the past.

17. Alexander, "Birth of the PNM," 37.

18. John B. Thompson, "Editor's Introduction," in Bourdieu, *Language and Symbolic Power,* 26–27.

19. Ibid.

20. Granado, "Autobiography."

21. Ibid., 10.

22. Ibid.

23. Ibid., 11.

24. Richardson, *Revolution or Evolution,* esp. 23ff.

25. Amcongen [American consul general], Port-of-Spain, to Department of State, Washington, No. 395, 10 August 1955, NARA, RG 59, file 741M.03/8-1055, box 3209.

26. American Consul A. John Pope Jr., dispatch titled "Announcement of Formation of New Political Party by Dr. Eric Williams," Amcongen, Port-of-Spain, to Department of State, No. 75, 14 September 1955, NARA, RG 59, file 741M.00/9-1456, box 3209.

27. "Officers of Dr. Williams' Newly Organized Party," Amcongen, Port-of-Spain, to Department of State, No. 222, 19 January 1956, NARA, RG 59, file 741M.00/1-1956, box 3209.

28. For more on James's helping Constantine, see James, *Beyond a Boundary.*

29. See "Officers of Dr. Williams' Newly Organized Party."

30. Birbalsingh, *Rise of Westindian Cricket,* 156.

31. Ibid., 158.

32. Stollmeyer's decision to join the PNM, apart from creating the impression that there was room for Whites in the party and the movement, had a "tremendous effect." According to a prominent businessman who was a former member of the Party of Political Progress Groups and also a former classmate of both Stollmeyer and Williams, the decision shook him and others as well. The POPPG was led by Albert Gomes and according to the historian Fitzroy Baptiste was the party of "the status quo 'French Creoles' of French, Spanish, English and Portuguese descent into which were being incorporated descendants of the newer Chinese and Syrian-Lebanese immigrants and also of the 'older' and staid black and coloured middle classes[. It] was hailed by the US Consulate in 1952 as 'the only party in the Colony which has firmly rejected socialist and welfare state doctrines.' However, POPPG translated to the 'little people' as 'Press on Poor People Guts.'" Baptiste, "Emergence of Eric Williams," 2. In fact, Williams himself concluded that so popular was Stollmeyer "that he could beat Minister Gomes in his own constituency, if the cricketer would run for office." Williams

made this statement in a conversation with the U.S. vice consul, Stanley Schiff. See "Memorandum of Conversation with Dr. Williams," attachment to Amcongen, Port-of-Spain, to Department of State, No. 403, 26 June 1956, NARA, RG 59, file 741M.00/6-2656, box 3209.

33. "Time Marches on—Backwards," *PNM Weekly,* 1 November 1956.

34. Granado, "Autobiography," 13.

35. Rogers, *Rise of the People's National Movement,* 29.

36. Ibid., 2.

37. Ibid., 14–15.

38. Ibid., 25.

39. Williams, *Inward Hunger,* 146.

40. Rogers, *Rise of the People's National Movement,* 25.

41. Rogers, "Out of This Womb Came PNM," 8.

42. Reddock, *Women, Labour and Politics.*

43. Williams, *Education in the British West Indies,* 90. It is noteworthy that the introduction to the book was written by De Wilton Rogers, director general of the TECA.

44. Gordon, "Oral Reminiscences," 151.

45. Reddock, *Women, Labour and Politics,* 306.

46. Ibid., 307.

47. Allsopp, *Dictionary of Caribbean English Usage,* 399.

48. Annette Palmer, interview by author, 20 October 2003.

49. Rogers, *Rise of the People's National Movement,* 71.

50. Ibid., 33.

51. Ibid., 38.

52. According to Max Weber, pariah intellectuals are very often self-taught subalterns "at the lower end of or altogether outside of the social hierarchy [who] are capable of an original attitude toward the meaning of the cosmos." Weber, *Sociology of Religion,* 126.

53. Rogers, *Rise of the People's National Movement,* 43.

54. Scott, *Domination and the Arts of Resistance,* 120ff.

55. Ibid., 120.

56. J. Henry, *Under the Mas',* xi.

57. Jenson, "What's in a Name?"

58. Ibid., 107.

59. Alexander, "Birth of the PNM," 35.

60. Durkheim, *Elementary Forms.*

61. "Balisier," 6.

62. Durkheim, *Elementary Forms,* 250.

63. "Balisier," 35.

64. Ibid., 36.

65. Douglas Jenkins to Department of State, No. 234, 27 January 1956, NARA, RG 59, file 741M.00/1-2756, box 3209.

66. “Balisier,” 35.

67. Tarrow, *Power in Movement,* 86.

68. Constitution Committee on Local Government Reform Draft Trinidad and Tobago (Constitution) Order, June 1949, CO 295/640/4, National Archives, London.

69. Hubert Rance (Governor Trinidad and Tobago) to Secretary of State for the Colonies, incoming telegram, No. 533, 19 September 1950, CO 295/649, ibid.

70. For a further statement of these circumstances, see Solomon, *Autobiography,* 53ff.

71. Eric Williams, “The PNM Restates Its Fundamental Principles. A Lecture Delivered at the University of Woodford Square by Eric Williams: Political Leader of the P.N.M.,” 14 June 1956, EWMC, folder 757.

72. Solomon, *Autobiography,* 61.

73. “Note on Mr. Albert Gomes, Trinidad Minister of Labour, Industry and Commerce,” 15 January 1952, confidential, CO 1031/962, National Archives, London.

74. Ibid. For a similar view regarding Gomes’s inconsistency, see Solomon, *Autobiography,* 61.

75. Gomes, *Through a Maze of Colour,* 7.

76. Ibid., 9.

77. Ibid., 12.

78. Quoted in Ramchand, introduction, 7.

79. G. Lewis, *Growth of the Modern West Indies,* 222.

80. Ibid.

81. “Widening Influence of Bhadase Sagan Maraj (Maharaj),” Amcongen, Port-of-Spain, to Department of State, No. 269, 2 March 1956, NARA, RG 59, file 741M.00/3-256, box 3209.

82. Ibid.

83. Baptiste points out that part of the U.S. disenchantment was the result of Maraj’s purchase of surplus equipment from the local Office of the Foreign Liquidation Commissioner (OFLC). Following subsequent U.S. efforts to have the sale rescinded and allegations that an office boy at the OFLC was in the pay of Maraj, it appears that Maraj prevailed in the end and used his financial good fortune to launch himself in politics. For more on this, see Baptiste, “Emergence of Eric Williams”; and various dispatches in Collady to Department of State, No. 38, 19 October 1948, NARA, RG 59, file 844C.24/10-1948, box 1.

84. “The Political Campaign,” Amcongen, Port-of-Spain, to Department of State, No. 20, 24 July 1956, NARA, RG 59, file 741M.00/7-2456, box 3209.

85. For more on the feeling among some Indians that they would not benefit from a Trinidad and Tobago presence in a West Indian Federation, see Baptiste, “Emergence of Eric Williams.”

86. Ryan, *Race and Nationalism in Trinidad and Tobago,* 147.

87. Ibid., 148.

88. Bolland, *Politics of Labour,* 259. This book contains a very helpful account of the unrest that occurred in Trinidad during the 1930s.

89. Brereton, *Modern History of Trinidad,* 180.

90. Reddock, *Women, Labour and Politics,* 139.

91. "Notes on the Political Campaign," Amcongen, Port-of-Spain, to Department of State, No. 40, 15 August 1956, NARA, RG 59, file 741M.00/8-1556, box 3209.

92. Reddock, *Women, Labour and Politics,* 271.

93. "The Political Campaign."

94. McAdam, *Political Process,* chap. 3.

6. From Pedantic Visionary to Elected Politician

1. For a discussion of this aspect of organizational analysis, which has implications for the emergence of political parties as social-movement organizations, see Aldrich, *Organizations Evolving.*

2. A good example is the ideology of nonviolence, espoused by Martin Luther King Jr. and the Southern Christian Leadership Conference, which, as King put it, sought to reconcile the truths of two opposites, namely, acquiescence and violence, while avoiding the extremes and immoralities of both. Thus, nonviolence eschewed acquiescence to oppression, which must be resisted, by avoiding recourse to the evil of violence. See esp. King, "Non Violence."

3. Marx and Engels, *German Ideology,* 64ff.

4. For more on Bell's view of the origins and conceptualization of the term *ideology*, see his *End of Ideology,* 394ff.

5. Eric Williams, "The PNM Restates Its Fundamental Principles. A Lecture delivered at the University of Woodford Square by Eric Williams: Political Leader of the P.N.M.," 14 June 1956, EWMC, folder 757, 2.

6. Ibid., 6.

7. Ibid., 7.

8. "Memorandum of Conversation with Dr. Williams," attachment to Amcongen, Port-of-Spain, to Department of State, No. 403, 26, June 1956, NARA, RG 59, file 741M.00/6-2656, box 3209.

9. Williams, *Capitalism and Slavery,* 19.

10. Lamming, *Pleasures of Exile,* 97–98.

11. Williams, *Capitalism and Slavery,* 37–38.

12. Ibid., 52.

13. Ibid., 20.

14. "Labour and the Sugar Industry" (address, mass meeting of sugar workers, Couva Recreation Ground, 25 September 1955), EWMC, folder 757.

15. "Notes on the Political Campaign," Amcongen, Port-of-Spain, to Department of State, No. 40, 15 August 1956, NARA, RG 59, file 741M.00/8-1556, box 3209.

16. Eric Williams, "The Danger Facing Trinidad and Tobago and the West Indian Nation. Speech by Eric Williams Political Leader, P.N.M.," 1 April 1958, CO 1031/2490, National Archives, London.

17. Ibid.

18. Ryan, *Eric Williams: The Myth and the Man,* 180; C. Palmer, *Eric Williams and the Making of the Modern Caribbean,* 267.

19. W. Mahabir, *In and Out of Politics,* 80.

20. Ibid.

21. Quoted in C. Palmer, *Eric Williams and the Making of the Modern Caribbean,* 270.

22. Baptiste, "Emergence of Eric Williams."

23. "Cross-Currents in East Indian Racial Tension," Amcongen, Port-of-Spain, to Department of State, No. 68, 4 March 1955, confidential, NARA, RG 59, file 741M.00/3-455, box 3209.

24. St. Pierre, *Anatomy of Resistance,* 138.

25. K. Mohammed, "Oral Reminiscences," 158.

26. Parmasad, "Among a Recalcitrant People," 79.

27. Samaroo, "Race Factor."

28. P. Mohammed, "Very Public Private Man," 176.

29. Lamming, "Legacy of Eric Williams," 35.

30. Ibid.

31. Williams, *Perspectives for Our Party,* 13.

32. Eric Williams, "Massa Day Done" (address, Woodford Square, 22 March 1961).

33. See Williams, *Case for Party Politics in Trinidad and Tobago.*

34. Eric Williams to Norman Manley, 18 January 1955, personal and confidential, EWMC, folder 39.

35. Williams, *Case for Party Politics in Trinidad and Tobago,* 8.

36. Ibid., 11.

37. Ibid., 13.

38. Richardson, *Revolution or Evolution,* 55.

39. Williams, *Perspectives for Our Party,* 13.

40. Williams, *Case for Party Politics in Trinidad and Tobago,* 13.

41. Ibid., 17.

42. Ibid., 20.

43. Ibid., 23.

44. Eric Williams, "The State of the Nation by Eric Williams Political Leader, PNM. An Address delivered to the Second Annual Convention of the PNM 28 September 1957," 9, EWMC, folder 757, typewritten.

45. Ibid.

46. Eric Williams, *RESPONSIBILITIES OF THE PARTY MEMBER by Dr. Eric Williams Premier of Trinidad and Tobago, Full Text of the Political Leader's*

Address to the Fifth Annual Convention on Friday 30 September 1960 (Port-of-Spain: P.N.M. Publishing, 1960), University of the West Indies Library, St. Augustine, Trinidad.

47. Ibid., 2.

48. Ibid., 3.

49. The main proponent of this concept is Mancur Olson, in *Logic of Collective Action,* who deals with the "free rider" using an economics model that speaks to the question of rational choice, a theoretical perspective that is also employed by sociologists.

50. Williams, *Perspectives for Our Party.*

51. See Oxaal, *Black Intellectuals Come to Power,* chap. 8; and Rogers, *Rise of the People's National Movement,* chap. 7, which begins with the statement by Napoleon that "vanity made the revolution, liberty was only a pretext" (166), and where he deals with the bypassing of ministers (127).

52. Ferree, "Political Context of Rationality," 38.

53. Williams, *Perspectives for Our Party,* 16.

54. Ibid., 9.

55. Ibid., 11–13.

56. James, *Party Politics in the West Indies,* 4–5.

57. Ibid., 13.

58. Williams to Manley, 17 June 1954, EWMC, folder 39.

59. Williams to Manley, 18 January 1955, ibid.

60. "First Admittedly Political Speech by Dr. Eric Williams in Trinidad," Amcongen, Port-of-Spain, to Department of State, No. 52, 30 December 1955, NARA, RG 59, file 741M.00/12-3055, box 3209.

61. Solomon, *Autobiography,* 9.

62. Ibid., 136.

63. Ibid.

64. Donald Granado, "An Autobiography," 11, 1987, University of the West Indies Library, St. Augustine.

65. Rogers, "Out of This Womb Came PNM," 8.

66. Alexander, "Birth of the PNM," 35.

67. "Estimate of the Strength of Eric Williams and the People's National Movement," Amcongen, Port-of-Spain, to Department of State, No. 365, 18 May 1956, confidential, NARA, RG 59, file 741M.00/5-1856, box 3209.

68. "Notes on the Political Campaign."

69. "Trinidad Legislature Votes to Request Election Delay," Amcongen, Port-of-Spain, to Department of State, No. 311, 20 April 1955, confidential, NARA, RG 59, file 741M.00/4-2055, box 3209.

70. "Statement by the Governor," attachment to "Postponement of Elections in Trinidad and Tobago," Amcongen, Port-of-Spain, No. 72, 9 September 1955, NARA, RG 59, file 741M.00/9-955, box 3209.

71. Alexander, "Birth of the PNM," 37.

72. For more on this facet of the political-opportunity structure, see Tarrow, *Power in Movement;* and Tarrow, "States and Opportunities."

73. See "Possible Constitutional Crisis," Amcongen, Port-of-Spain, to Department of State, No. 80, 1 October 1956, NARA, RG 59, file 741M.00/10-156, box 3209. According to the U.S. consul general's dispatch, the press was in full agreement with the governor in his unwillingness to appoint individuals who were subject to party discipline, as this would have been tantamount to "usurping the function of the electorate and creating an artificial majority."

74. "Governor Announces the Names of the Nominated Members of the Legislative Council," Amcongen, Port-of-Spain, to Department of State, No. 93, 17 October 1956, NARA, RG 59, file 741M.00/10-1756, box 3209.

75. "Colonial Office Comment on Trinidad Leader," American Embassy, London, to Department of State, No. 965, 19 October 1956, confidential, NARA, RG 59, file 741M.00/10-1956, box 3209.

7. The Bachacs Confront the "Hydra-Head" of Colonialism

1. Eric Williams, "The Approach to Independence" (address, fourth annual convention of the PNM, March 1960).

2. Louis V. Riggio (assistant officer in charge, Trinidad and Tobago) to Stephen C. Sunderland, 15 March 1963, NARA, RG 59, box 1.

3. "The US Leased Areas in Trinidad and Tobago," statement by the chief minister in the Leg Co, 20 June 1958, EWMC, folder 740.

4. *New York Times,* 5 October 1939.

5. "US Leased Areas in Trinidad and Tobago," 71.

6. Ibid.

7. A. Palmer, "United States and the Commonwealth Caribbean," 31.

8. Chaguaramas Joint Commission Report, EWMC, folder 740.

9. "Caribbean Labor Conference at Barbados, September 1945, Full Conference—United States Naval and Air Bases, Proceedings as reported in *The Barbados Advocate,* 20 September 1945. American Consulate, Barbados, Report No. 62, from S. Reid Thompson, U.S. Consul to Department of State, 28 September 1945," restricted, NARA, RG 59, file 844C.5043/9-2845.

10. Ibid.

11. Ibid.

12. Amcongen to Department of State, No. 196, 29 January 1957, secret, NARA, RG 59, file 711.56341B/1-457, box 2891.

13. Ibid.

14. Ibid.

15. Lefebvre, *Production of Space,* chap. 4.

16. Bachrach and Baratz, *Power and Poverty.*

17. Solomon Hochoy (acting colonial secretary) to American Consul General, Port-of-Spain, No. 238, 7 February 1956, NARA, RG 59, file 711.56341BB/2-756, box 2891.

18. Dulles to Am Consul, Port-of-Spain, Priority 206, 10 May 1957, confidential, ibid., file 711.56341B/5-857, box 2891.

19. Port-of-Spain to Secretary of State, No. 204, 11 May 1957, confidential, ibid., file 711.56341B/5-1157, box 2891.

20. John Hay Whitney to Secretary of State, No. 68, 2 July 1957, confidential, ibid., file 711.56341B/7-257, box 2891.

21. The West Indian delegation was made up of Grantley Adams of Barbados; Norman Manley of Jamaica; Eric Williams of Trinidad and Tobago; Robert Bradshaw, minister of trade and production of St. Kitts, Nevis and Anguilla; and F. A. Baron, minister of trade and production of Dominica.

22. "London Conference on West Indies Federal Capital Site, 19 July through 23 July 1957," American Embassy, London, to Department of State, No. 619, 9 September 1957, confidential, NARA, RG 59, lots 64D 38 and 66D 43, box 1.

23. Ibid.

24. Memorandum, "Secretary Dulles Statement on Release of Chaguaramas Naval Base," 9 September 1957, top secret, ibid., file 711.56341G/1-356, box 2895.

25. It appears that Williams had been held in contempt of court for failing to pay child support following his divorce from his first wife, whom he had allegedly abandoned when he left America. No doubt, it was in the interest of not only Williams but also the United States to settle the matter, since it would have been an embarrassment to the United States if Williams traveled to the America on official business only to be arrested for contempt of court. See esp. "Marital Difficulties of Eric Williams, Prime Minister of Trinidad," memorandum for the files, 12 September 1962, confidential, and James J. Laughlin to Dean Rusk, 14 November 1961, ibid., Bureau of Inter-American Affairs, Records Relating to Trinidad and Tobago, 1955–63, box 1.

26. Walter Orebaugh to William N. Dale, Office of British Commonwealth and Northern European Affairs, Department of State, 14 May 1958, secret, ibid., box 1.

27. Orebaugh to Willoughby, Dale, and Swihart, office memorandum, July 1959, confidential, ibid., file 711.56341B, box 2894.

28. "The Chaguaramas Issue—Current Perspective and Outlook," Orebaugh to Department of State, No. 328, 29 May 1958, confidential, NARA, RG 59, file 711.56341B/5-2958, box 2893.

29. Ibid.

30. Ibid.

31. "The Chaguaramas Issue—Current Situation and Outlook," Orebaugh to Department of State, No. 98, 17 October 1958, confidential, NARA, RG 59, file 711.56341B/7-358, box 2893.

32. Ibid.

33. Ibid.

34. See "Talking Points to be Raised at Joint Chiefs of Staff Meeting Regarding Chaguaramas Naval Station," circa early 1958, confidential, Bureau of Inter-American Affairs, Records Relating to Trinidad and Tobago, 1955–63, NARA, RG 59, box 1.

35. Ibid.

36. For a very suggestive statement on how weaker opponents sometimes prevail over much stronger adversaries, see Ganz, "Why David Sometimes Wins."

37. During a lecture delivered at the University of Woodford Square on 14 June 1956, seeking to allay suspicions that the PNM either was "subversive" or sought to "threaten political stability" in Trinidad and Tobago, Williams stated "categorically that it [the PNM] will honour all international obligations, both economic and military, and especially the defence arrangements with the United States of America." See Eric Williams, "The PNM Restates Its Fundamental Principles." A Lecture Delivered at the University of Woodford Square by Eric Williams: Political Leader of the P.N.M., 14 June 1956, EWMC, folder 757.

38. "Reflections on the Caribbean Economic Community," 9.

39. Ibid.

40. Orebaugh to Secretary of State, No. 69, 2 October 1958, confidential, NARA, RG 59, file 711.56341B, box 2893.

41. "Folly," editorial, *Trinidad Chronicle,* 16 October 1958.

42. "New Deal Urged In US Bases Agreement," enclosure to Orebaugh to Department of State, No. 100, 22 October 1958, NARA, RG 59, file 711.56341B/7-358, box 2893.

43. "Do It The Friendly Way," editorial, *Trinidad Guardian,* 23 October 1958.

44. Orebaugh to Secretary of State, No. 90, 27 October 1958, confidential, NARA, RG 59, file 711.56341B/7-358, box 2893.

45. "U.K. Attitude Regarding Chaguaramas Plantation Citrus Problem," memorandum of telephone conversation, Department of State, 23 October 1958, ibid.

46. Whitney to Secretary of State, No. 2249, 24 October 1958, secret, ibid.

47. "An Incurable Malady," editorial, *Trinidad Guardian,* 30 June 1959.

48. Orebaugh to Secretary of State, No. 12, 5 July 1959, NARA, RG 59, file 711.56341B/7-259, box 2894.

49. McGregor to Secretary of State, No. 9, 4 July 1959, ibid.

50. W. Mahabir, *In and Out of Politics,* 83.

51. Quoted in C. Palmer, *Eric Williams and the Making of the Modern Caribbean,* 122.

52. "Radiation: From a Correspondent in Britain."

53. *Nation,* 4 December 1959, 10.

54. "Radiation: What It Is And How It Affects You," 1.

55. W. Mahabir, *In and Out of Politics,* 84.

56. Ibid., 85.

57. Williams, *Inward Hunger,* 213.

58. Orebaugh to Department of State, No. 331, 29 May 1958, NARA, RG 59, file 711.56341B/5-2958, box 2893.

59. Ibid., sec. 2.

60. "Chaguaramas Issue—Current Perspective and Outlook."

61. Williams, *Inward Hunger,* 220.

62. Quoted in G. Lewis, *Growth of the Modern West Indies,* 211.

63. Ibid., 212.

64. "Trinidad Turns Down US Deal on Piarco, House Told of Loss in Airport Revenue," Legislative Council Debates (Hansard), 9th legislature, 4th sess. (Port-of-Spain: Trinidad and Tobago Government Printing Office, 14 April 1960), cols. 2146-52.

65. Ibid.

66. The details of these messages are to be found in CO 1031/2595, WIS 185/12/02, National Archives, London.

67. Sir E. Beetham to Secretary of State for the Colonies, Personal No. 50 (repeated to Governor General, The West Indies No. 17), 27 June 1959, emergency, top secret, and personal, ibid.

68. "DLP Views on the Scene in Trinidad," memorandum of conversation between Ashford Sinanan, Simboonath Capildeo, and Philip Habib, No. 18, 10 July 1959, confidential, NARA, RG 59, file 711.56341B/1059, box 2894.

69. "Views on Chaguaramas and Other Current Issues in Trinidad," Habib to Department of State, No. 18, 14 July 1959, ibid., file 711.56341B/7-259, box 2894.

70. Oxaal, *Black Intellectuals Come to Power,* 161.

71. Ibid., 168.

72. In Trinidad *fatigue* refers to "continuous teasing, banter, or joking at somebody else's expense." Allsopp, *Dictionary of Caribbean Usage,* 226.

73. "Bi-Weekly Summary of Trinidad Press Highlights," sec. 3, "April 22 'Flag March' Excites Comment," Amcongen, Port-of-Spain, to Department of State, No. 359, 12 April 1960, file 741J.004-1260, box 1674.

74. Williams, *Inward Hunger,* 220.

75. Williams, "Approach of Independence," 5.

76. "Bi-Weekly Summary of Trinidad Press Highlights."

77. Williams, *Inward Hunger,* 227.

78. "Sins And The Sinner," editorial, *Trinidad Guardian,* 23 April 1960, 8.

79. Ibid.

80. Scott, *Domination and the Arts of Resistance,* 223.

81. Whitney to Secretary of State, No. 2249, 24 October 1959.

82. Williams, *Inward Hunger,* 225–26.

83. "The West Indies and Revision of the 1941 Leased-Bases Agreement," Amcongen, Port-of-Spain, to Department of State, No. 225, 23 December 1959, secret, NARA, RG 59, file 711.56341B/12-1159, box 2985.

84. "Views of DLP Leaders on Chaguaramas and Other Current Issues in Trinidad," Amconsulate, Port-of-Spain, to Department of State, No. 18, 14 July 1959, confidential, ibid., file 711.56341B/7-259, box 2894.

85. "The West Indies and Revision of the 1941 Leased-Bases Agreement."

86. Ibid. The new American Consul General, Edwin Moline was evidently recommending the advisability of a more flexible approach, including negotiations, especially against the backdrop of nationalism and impending independence.

87. "Reflections on the Caribbean Economic Community," 10.

88. Williams would later reveal that the Tobago Conference nearly broke down over this provision, which had led to a serious split between the Head of the American delegation who was in agreement with the proposal and the State Department delegate who demurred, but who was overruled from Washington. Ibid., 10–11.

89. Fraser, "Rethinking the Public Sphere."

90. Scott, *Domination and the Arts of Resistance,* 111.

8. Caliban and the Anticolonial Tradition

1. James, *Convention Appraisal.*

2. For a very interesting treatment of this term using the experience of African Americans in the America as a point of departure, see Berry and Blassingame, *Long Memory,* and with reference to the use of sorrow songs by African Americans, see Du Bois, *Souls of Black Folk,* chap. xiv.

3. Schwartz, "Iconography and Collective Memory," 302.

4. Collins, *Fighting Words.*

5. Collins, *Black Feminist Thought.*

6. Ibid.

7. Bogues, *Caliban's Freedom,* 14.

8. Du Bois, *Darkwater,* 17.

9. Williams, *Capitalism and Slavery,* 202; Eric Williams, *Our Fourth Anniversary . . . The Last Lap, By Dr. Eric Williams: Political Leader's Address on 24 September 1960 at the University of Woodford Square, marking the Fourth Year of P.N.M.'s First Term of Office* (P.N.M. Publishing, 1960), 4, University of the West Indies Library, St. Augustine, Trinidad.

10. *Capitalism and Slavery,* 208.

11. Williams, *Perspectives for the West Indies,* 4.

12. James, *Convention Appraisal.*

13. Bell, *End of Ideology,* 402.

14. Lamming, "Legacy of Eric Williams," 29.

15. H. Beckles, "Williams Effect."

16. Gramsci, *Selections from the Prison Notebooks,* 9, 10.

17. James, *Convention Appraisal.*

18. Kelley, "Poetry and the Political Imagination," viii.

19. A. James Arnold, "Prologue: Being Black and Being French," in Arnold, *Modernism and Negritude,* 4.

20. Kelley, "Poetics of Anticolonialism," 17.
21. Ibid., 18.
22. Arnold, "Prologue," 6.
23. "Interview with René Depestre," in Césaire, *Discourse on Colonialism,* 81.
24. Césaire, *Notebook of a Return to the Native Land,* 28.
25. Ibid., 36.
26. Césaire, *Discourse on Colonialism,* 35.
27. Ibid., 36–37.
28. Ibid., 39.
29. Lyons, "Colonial Mentality," 182.
30. Césaire, *Discourse on Colonialism,* 42.
31. Parmasad, "Among a Recalcitrant People," 79, 81.
32. "Interview with René Depestre," in Césaire, *Discourse on Colonialism,* 83.
33. Ibid., 84.
34. P. Henry, *Caliban's Reason,* 82–84.
35. Césaire, *Tempest,* 16.
36. Ibid., 17.
37. Ibid.
38. Ibid., 62.
39. Eric Williams, "Massa Day Done" (address, Woodford Square, 22 March 1961).
40. Hoetink, "Ideology, Intellectuals and Identity," 139.
41. Bosch, *Unfinished Experiment,* 83.
42. Ibid., 86.
43. Ibid.
44. Ibid., 129.
45. Ibid., 130.
46. Hoetink, "Ideology, Intellectuals and Identity," 138.
47. Ibid., 140.
48. Richard Wright, introduction to Lamming, *In the Castle of My Skin,* v.
49. Lamming, *In the Castle of My Skin,* 17.
50. Ibid., 18.
51. Ibid.
52. Ibid., 18–19.
53. Ibid., 19.
54. Ibid.
55. Ibid., 21.
56. Ibid., 22.
57. For a discussion of unauthorized gatherings with regard to antihegemonic activity see Scott, *Domination and Arts of Resistance,* 58–66.
58. Lamming, *In the Castle of My Skin,* 31.
59. Ibid., 34.

60. Ibid., 34–35.
61. Ibid., 35.
62. Lamming, *Pleasures of Exile,* 122.
63. Nair, *Caliban's Curse,* 89.
64. Gendzier, *Frantz Fanon,* 3.
65. Ibid., 11.
66. Ibid., 19.
67. Ibid., 4.
68. Ibid.
69. *Black Skin White Masks,* 13.
70. Ibid., 10.
71. Ibid., 185.
72. Ibid., 12.
73. Lamming, *Pleasures of Exile,* 125.
74. Ibid., 109.
75. *Black Skin White Masks,* 190–91.
76. Ibid., 188.
77. Ibid., 191.
78. Ibid., 217–18.
79. Lamming, *Pleasures of Exile,* 41.
80. Ibid., 42.
81. Ibid., 24.
82. Williams, *Inward Hunger,* 343.
83. Weber, *Sociology of Religion,* 117.
84. Burton, "Between the Particular and the Universal," 196.
85. Ibid., 207.
86. Fanon, *Wretched of the Earth,* 17.
87. P. Henry, *Caliban's Reason,* 83.
88. Ibid., 5ff.
89. Torres-Saillant, *Intellectual History of the Caribbean,* 239.
90. Quoted in ibid., 213.
91. Ibid., 240.
92. E. Mahabir, "Eric Williams They Knew," 159.
93. Connell-Williams, interview by author, 31 May 2005.
94. Connell-Williams, "My Father," 6.
95. Ibid., 10.
96. James, *Convention Appraisal.*
97. Richardson, *Revolution or Evolution,* 56.
98. G. Lewis, *Growth of the Modern West Indies,* 213.
99. Simmel, *Sociology of Georg Simmel,* 185.
100. Freire, *Pedagogy of Freedom,* 30.
101. Ransby, *Ella Baker and the Black Freedom Movement,* 362.

Afterword

1. Fanon, *Wretched of the Earth,* 23.

2. "Trinidad: A Mutiny in the Armed Forces," intelligence note, Bureau of Intelligence and Research, Department of State, 22 April 1970, NARA, RG 2629, Pol 23-9, Trin Tob, box 269.

3. For more on the range of issues involved, see Craig, "Background to 1970 Confrontation."

4. Mitchell, "Making of Makandal Daaga," 99.

5. Daaga, "Making of 'Seventy,'" 181.

6. Mitchell, "Making of Makandal Daaga," 101.

7. Hennessy, "Intellectuals," 3.

8. *Trinidad Express,* 27 February 1970, quoted in Meeks, "1970 Revolution," 140. For more on the chronicle of events that were part of the disturbances, see Oxaal, *Black Intellectuals and the Dilemmas of Race.*

9. La Guerre, "Indian Response to Black Power," 287.

10. "Black Power Demonstrations," Amembassy, Port-of-Spain, to Department of State, A 58, 9 April 1970, NARA, RG 2629, Pol 13-10, Trin Tob, box 269.

11. Meeks, "1970 Revolution," 168; and Shah, "Takeover of Teteron." www.trinicenter.com/Blackpower5.htm.

12. Daaga, "Making of 'Seventy,'" 185.

13. Shah, "Black Power 1970 30 years later."

14. Hennessy, "Demise of the Intellectual?," 193.

Selected Bibliography

Archival Sources

Milton S. Eisenhower Library, John Hopkins University, Baltimore, Maryland.

National Archives and Records Administration (NARA), College Park, Maryland. RG 59. RG 2629.

National Archives, London. Colonial Office (CO).

National Archives, Trinidad and Tobago.

University of the West Indies Library, Mona, Jamaica.

University of the West Indies Library, St. Augustine, Trinidad. West India Section. Eric Williams Memorial Collection (EWMC).

Newspapers

Baltimore Evening Sun
Crisis
Nation
PNM Weekly
Sunday Chronicle
Tapia
Trinidad and Tobago Review
Trinidad Chronicle
Trinidad Express
Trinidad Guardian

Other Sources

Abrahams, Roger D. *The Man-of-Words in the West Indies: Performance and the Emergence of Creole Culture*. Baltimore: Johns Hopkins University Press, 1983.

Aldrich, Howard. *Organizations Evolving*. Thousand Oaks, CA: Sage, 1999.

Alexander, Wilfrid. "Birth of the PNM and Its Descent into the Political Arena." *Nation*, 21 January 1966.

Alleyne, Garth O'G., ed. *QRC 2004*. Glencoe, Trinidad and Tobago: QRC 2004 Committee, 2004.

Allsopp, Richard, ed. *Dictionary of Caribbean English Usage*. Oxford: Oxford University Press, 1996.

Arnold, A. James. *Modernism and Negritude: The Poetry and Poetics of Aimé Césaire*. Cambridge, MA: Harvard University Press, 1981.

Bachrach, Peter, and Morton Baratz. *Power and Poverty: Theory and Practice*. New York: Oxford University Press, 1973.

"Balisier, The." *Nation*, 21 January 1966.

Baptiste, Fitzroy André. "The Emergence of Eric Williams and the People's National Movement [PNM] in Trinidad and Tobago Politics as Gleaned from US State Department Records, 1952–1956." Paper presented at the annual meeting of the Association of Caribbean Historians, Cartagena, Colombia, May 2005.

Beckles, Hilary McD. "'The Williams Effect': Eric Williams's Capitalism and Slavery and the Growth of West Indian Political Economy." In Solow and Engerman, *British Capitalism and Caribbean Slavery*, 303–16.

Beckles, Lynne. "PNM Weekly Newspaper." *Nation*, 21 January 1966.

Bell, Daniel. *The End of Ideology: On the Exhaustion of Political Ideas in the Fifties*. New ed. New York: Free Press, 1966.

Benhabib, Seyla. "Models of Public Sphere: Hannah Arendt, the Liberal Tradition, and Jürgen Habermas." In Calhoun, *Habermas and the Public Sphere*, 73–98.

Benn, Denis. *The Caribbean: An Intellectual History, 1774–2003*. Kingston, Jamaica: Ian Randle, 2004.

———. *The Growth and Development of Political Ideas in the Caribbean, 1774–1983*. Kingston, Jamaica: Institute of Social and Economic Research, 1987.

Berger, Peter L., and Thomas Luckmann. *The Social Construction of Reality: A Treatise in the Sociology of Knowledge*. New York: Doubleday, 1966.

Berry, Mary Frances, and John Blassingame. *Long Memory: The Black Experience in America*. New York: Oxford University Press, 1982.

Birbalsingh, Frank. *The Rise of Westindian Cricket: From Colony to Nation*. St. John's, Antigua: Hansib, 1996.

Blau, Judith R., ed. *The Blackwell Companion to Sociology*. Malden, MA: Blackwell, 2001.

Bogues, Anthony. *Caliban's Freedom: The Early Political Thought of C. L. R. James*. London: Pluto, 1997.

Bolland, O. Nigel. *The Politics of Labour in the British Caribbean: The Social Origins of Authoritarianism and Democracy in the Labour Movement*. Kingston, Jamaica: Ian Randle, 2001.

Boodhoo, Ken. *The Elusive Eric Williams*. Port-of-Spain: Prospect; Kingston, Jamaica: Ian Randle, 2001.

———, ed. *Eric Williams: The Man and the Leader.* Lanham, MD: University Press of America, 1986.

———. "Eric Williams: The Myth and the Man." *Caribbean Issues* 8, no. 2 (March 1999): 1–16.

Bosch, Juan. *The Unfinished Experiment: Democracy in the Dominican Republic.* New York: Praeger, 1965.

Bottomore, T. B. *Critics of Society: Radical Thought in North America.* New York: Pantheon, 1968.

Bourdieu, Pierre. *Distinction: A Social Critique of Judgement of Taste.* Translated by Richard Nice. Cambridge, MA: Harvard University Press, 2002.

———. *Language and Symbolic Power.* Translated by Gino Raymond and Matthew Adamson. Cambridge, MA: Harvard University Press, 1991.

———. "Social Space and Symbolic Power." *Sociological Theory* 7, no. 1 (Spring 1989): 14–25.

Brereton, Bridget. *A Modern History of Trinidad, 1783–1962.* Portsmouth, NH: Heinemann, 1989.

———. *Race Relations in Colonial Trinidad, 1870–1900.* Cambridge: Cambridge University Press, 2002.

Breton, André. "A Great Black Poet." In Césaire, *Notebook of a Return to the Native Land,* ix–xix.

Burton, Richard. "Between the Particular and the Universal: Dilemmas of the Martinican Intellectual." In Hennessy, *Intellectuals in the Twentieth-Century Caribbean,* 2:186–210.

Calhoun, Craig, ed. *Habermas and the Public Sphere.* Cambridge, MA: MIT Press, 1992.

———. "Introduction: Habermas and the Public Sphere." In Calhoun, *Habermas and the Public Sphere,* 1–48.

Camp, Roderic A. "Mexican Intellectuals and Collective Biography in the Twentieth Century." In Hennessy, *Intellectuals in the Twentieth-Century Caribbean,* 2:211–24.

Campbell, Carl C. "Education and Black Consciousness: The Amazing Captain J. O. Cutteridge in Trinidad and Tobago, 1921–42." *Journal of Caribbean History* 18, no. 1 (1984): 35–66.

———. *The Young Colonials: A Social History of Education in Trinidad and Tobago, 1834–1939.* Kingston, Jamaica: Press University of the West Indies, 1996.

Cateau, Heather, and S. H. H. Carrington, eds. *Capitalism and Slavery Fifty Years Later: Eric Eustace Williams—A Reassessment of the Man and His Work.* New York: Peter Lang, 2000.

Césaire, Aimé. *Aimé Césaire: The Collected Poetry.* Translated with introduction and notes by Clayton Eshleman and Annette Smith. Berkeley and Los Angeles: University of California Press, 1983.

———. *Discourse on Colonialism.* Translated by Joan Pinkham. New York: Monthly Review Press, 2000.

———. *Notebook of a Return to the Native Land.* Translated and edited by Clayton Eshleman and Annette Smith. Middletown CT: Wesleyan University Press, 2001.

———. *A Tempest.* Translated by Richard Miller. New York: TCG Translations, 2002.

Clark, Heléne. "Sites of Resistance: Place, 'Race' and Gender as Sources of Empowerment." In Jackson and Penrose, *Constructions of Race, Place and Nation,* 121–42.

Cohen, Jean. "Strategy or Identity: New Theoretical Paradigms and Contemporary Social Movements." *Social Research* 52, no. 4 (Winter 1985): 663–716.

Collins, Patricia Hill. *Black Feminist Thought: Knowledge, Consciousness and Empowerment.* New ed. Boston: Unwin & Hyman, 2000.

———. *Fighting Words: Black Women and the Search for Justice.* Minneapolis: University of Minnesota Press, 1998.

Constantine, Learie. *Cricket in the Sun.* London: Stanley Paul, [early 1940s].

Corkran, Herbert, Jr. *Patterns of International Cooperation in the Caribbean, 1932–1969.* Dallas: Southern Methodist University Press, 1970.

Coser, Lewis. *Men of Ideas: A Sociologist's View.* New York: Free Press, 1997.

Craig, Susan. "Background to the 1970 Confrontation in Trinidad and Tobago." In *Contemporary Caribbean: A Sociological Reader,* edited by Craig, 2:385–423. 2 vols. Maracas: College Press, Trinidad and Tobago, 1981–82.

Cudjoe, Selwyn. "Eric Williams and the Politics of Language." In "Eric Williams and the Postcolonial Caribbean," edited by Sandra Pouchet Paquet, special issue, *Callaloo* 21, no. 4 (Fall 1997): 753–63.

Daaga, Makandal. "The Making of 'Seventy.'" In Ryan and Stewart, *Black Power Revolution,* 171–99.

De Barros, Juanita. *Order and Place in a Colonial City: Patterns of Struggle and Resistance in Georgetown, British Guiana, 1889–1924.* Montreal: McGill-Queen's University Press, 2002.

Deosaran, Ramesh. *Eric Williams: The Man, His Ideas, and His Politics (A Study of Political Power).* Port-of-Spain: Signum, 1981.

Du Bois, W. E. B. *Darkwater: Voices from Within the Veil.* New ed. Mineola, NY: Dover, 1999.

———. *The Souls of Black Folk.* New ed. New York: Dover, 1994.

Durkheim, Emile. *The Elementary Forms of the Religious Life.* New York: Free Press, 1965.

———. *The Rules of Sociological Method.* New ed. New York: Free Press, 1964.

Eisenstadt, S. N. "Intellectuals and Tradition." *Daedalus* 101 (Spring 1972): 1–19.

———, ed. *Max Weber on Charisma and Institution Building.* Chicago: University of Chicago Press, 1968.

Escoffier, Jeffrey. "Community and Academic Intellectuals: The Contest for Cultural Authority in Identity Politics." In *Cultural Politics and Social Movements,* edited by Marcy Darnovsky, Barbara Epstein, and Richard Flacks, 20–34. Philadelphia: Temple University Press, 1995.

Eyerman, Ron. *Between Culture and Politics: Intellectuals in Modern Society.* Cambridge: Polity, 1994.

Eyerman, Ron, and Andrew Jamison. *Social Movements: A Cognitive Approach.* University Park: Pennsylvania State University Press, 1991.

Fanon, Frantz. *The Wretched of the Earth.* Translated by Richard Philcox. New York: Grove, 2004.

Feagin, Joe R. *Systemic Racism: A Theory of Oppression.* New York: Routledge, 2006.

Fergus, Claudius. "Centring the City in the Amelioration of Slavery in Trinidad, 1824–1834." *Journal of Caribbean History* 40, no. 1 (2006): 117–40.

Ferree, Myra Marx. "The Political Context of Rationality: Rational Choice Theory and Resource Mobilization." In Morris and Mueller, *Frontiers in Social Movement Theory,* 29–52.

Feuer, Lewis. "What Is an Intellectual?" In Gella, *Intelligentsia and the Intellectuals,* 47–58.

Flacks, Dick. "Making History and Making Theory: Notes on How Intellectuals Seek Relevance." In *Intellectuals and Politics: A Social Theory in a Changing World,* edited by Charles Lemert, 3–19. Newbury Park, CA: Sage, 1991.

Foster, Michael B. *Masters of Political Thought.* Vol. 1, *From Plato to Machiavelli.* London: George G. Harrap, 1956.

Foucault, Michel. *Power/Knowledge: Selected Interviews and Other Writings, 1971–1977.* Edited by Colin Gordon. New York: Pantheon, 1980.

Franklin, John Hope. "Eric Williams and Howard University." In Cateau and Carrington, *Capitalism and Slavery Fifty Years Later,* 23–28.

Fraser, Nancy. "Rethinking the Public Sphere: A Contribution to the Critique of Actually Existing Democracy." In Calhoun, *Habermas and the Public Sphere,* 109–42.

Frazier, E. Franklin, and Eric Williams, eds. *The Economic Future of the Caribbean.* Dover, MA: Majority, 2004.

Freire, Paulo. *Pedagogy of Freedom: Ethics, Democracy and Civil Courage.* Lanham, MD: Rowman & Littlefield, 1998.

Frisby, David. *Georg Simmel.* London: Tavistock, 1984.

Gamson, William A. "Political Discourse and Collective Action." *International Social Movement Research* 1 (1988): 219–44.

———. *Talking Politics.* Cambridge: Cambridge University Press, 1993.

Gamson, William A., and David S. Meyer. "Framing Political Opportunity." In McAdam, McCarthy, and Zald, *Comparative Perspectives on Social Movements,* 275–90.

Ganz, Marshall. "Why David Sometimes Wins: Strategic Capacity in Social Movements." In *Rethinking Social Movements: Structure, Meaning and Emotion,* edited by Jeff Goodwin and James M. Jasper, 177–98. Lanham, MD: Rowman & Littlefield, 2004.

Garnsey, Peter. *Ideas of Slavery from Aristotle to Augustine.* Cambridge: Cambridge University Press, 1999.fff

Gella, Aleksander, ed. *The Intelligentsia and the Intellectuals.* London: Sage, 1976.

———. "An Introduction to the Sociology of the Intelligentsia." In Gella, *Intelligentsia and the Intellectuals,* 9–34.

Gendzier, Irene L. *Frantz Fanon: A Critical Study.* Rev. ed. New York: Grove Press, 1985.

Gilroy, Paul. *Black Atlantic: Modernity and Double Consciousness.* New York: Oxford University Press, 1994.

———. *There Ain't No Black in the Union Jack: The Cultural Politics of Race and Nation.* Chicago: University of Chicago Press, 1987.

Goffman, Erving. *Frame Analysis: An Essay on the Organization of Experience.* New York: Harper, 1974.

———. *The Presentation of Self in Everyday Life.* New York: Doubleday Anchor, 1959.

———. *Stigma: Notes on the Management of Spoiled Identity.* New York: Simon & Schuster/Touchstone, 1986.

Goldfarb, Jeffrey C. *Civility and Subversion: The Intellectual in Democratic Society.* New York: Cambridge University Press, 1998.

Gomes, Albert. *Through a Maze of Colour.* Port-of-Spain: Key Caribbean, 1974.

Gordon, Marilyn. "Oral Reminiscences: The Emergence of Women Activists as a Major Force in Party Politics; The Role of Eric Williams." *Caribbean Issues* 8, no. 2 (1999): 151–55.

Goulbourne, Harry. "The Institutional Contribution of the University of the West Indies to the Intellectual Life of the Anglophone Caribbean." In Hennessy, *Intellectuals in the Twentieth-Century Caribbean,* 1:21–49.

Gouldner, Alvin W. *The Dialectic of Ideology and Technology: The Origins, Grammar, and the Future of Ideology.* New York: Seabury, 1970.

———. *The Future of Intellectuals and the Rise of the New Class.* New York: Oxford University Press, 1979.

Gramsci, Antonio. *Selections from the Prison Notebooks.* Translated and edited by Quintin Hoare. New York: International, 1999.

Green, William A. "Race and Slavery: Considerations on the Williams Thesis." In Solow and Engerman, *British Capitalism and Caribbean Slavery,* 25–49.

Guidry, John. "Trial by Space: The Spatial Politics of Citizenship and Social Movements in Urban Brazil." *Mobilization* 8, no. 2 (June 2003): 189–204.

Habermas, Jürgen. *The Structural Transformation of the Public Sphere: An Inquiry into a Category of Bourgeois Society.* Translated by Thomas Burger with Frederick Lawrence. Cambridge, MA: MIT Press, 1991.

———. *The Theory of Communicative Action.* Vol. 2, *Lifeworld and System: A Critique of Functionalist Reason.* Translated by Thomas McCarthy. Boston: Beacon, 1989.

Hackett, Jeff. "Eric Williams, The Man, The Myth." *Trinidad Express,* 26 March 1998, 23.

Harvey, David. "The Political Economy of Public Space." In *The Politics of Public Space,* edited by Setha Low and Neil Smith, 17–34. New York: Routledge, 2006.

Hennessy, Alistair. "The Demise of the Intellectual?" In Hennessy, *Intellectuals in the Twentieth-Century Caribbean,* 1:191–97.

———. "Intellectuals: The General and the Particular." In Hennessy, *Intellectuals in the Twentieth-Century Caribbean,* 1:1–20.

———, ed. *Intellectuals in the Twentieth-Century Caribbean.* Vol. 1, *Spectre of the New Class: The Commonwealth Caribbean.* London: Macmillan, 1992.

———, ed. *Intellectuals in the Twentieth-Century Caribbean.* Vol. 2, *Unity in Variety: The Hispanic and Francophone Caribbean.* London: Macmillan, 1992.

Henry, Jeff. *Under The Mas': Resistance and Rebellion in the Trinidad Experience.* San Juan, Trinidad: Lexicon, 2008.

Henry, Paget. *Caliban's Reason: Introducing Afro-Caribbean Philosophy.* New York: Routledge, 2000.

Heywood, Linda M. "Eric Williams: The Howard Years, 1939–1948." *Caribbean Issues* 8, no. 1 (March 1998): 14–28.

Higman, B. W. *Writing West Indian Histories.* London: Macmillan, 1999.

Hoetink, Harmannus. "Ideology, Intellectuals and Identity: The Dominican Republic, 1880–1980." In Hennessy, *Intellectuals in the Twentieth-Century Caribbean,* 2:132–44.

Hoffer, Eric. *The True Believer: Thoughts on the Nature of Social Movements.* New York: HarperCollins, 1951.

Howat, Gerald. *Learie Constantine.* Devon: George Allen & Unwin, 1975.

Jackson, Peter, and Jan Penrose, eds. *Constructions of Race, Place and Nation.* Minneapolis: University of Minnesota Press, 1994.

———. Introduction to Jackson and Penrose, *Constructions of Race, Place and Nation,* 1–23.

James, C. L. R. *Beyond a Boundary.* London: Hutchinson, 1969.

———. *The Case for West Indian Self-Government.* Rev. ed. New York: University Place Bookshop; Detroit: Facing Reality, 1967.

———. *A Convention Appraisal.* Port-of-Spain: PNM, 1960.

———. *Party Politics in the West Indies.* Rev. ed. San Juan: Imprint Caribbean, 1984.

———. *Special Delivery: The Letters of C. L. R. James to Constance Webb, 1939–1948.* Edited with introduction by Anna Grimshaw. Cambridge, MA: Blackwell, 1996.

Jenkins, J. Craig. "Resource Mobilization Theory and the Study of Social Movements." *Annual Review of Sociology* 9 (1983): 527–53.

Jenson, Jane. "What's in a Name? Nationalist Movements and Public Discourse." In *Social Movements and Culture,* edited by Hank Johnston and Bert Klandermans, 107–43. Minneapolis: University of Minnesota Press, 1995.

John, Deborah. "Tribute to a Very Special Dad," *Trinidad Sunday Express,* 22 March 1998, sec. 2, p. 3.

Kelley, Robin D. G. "A Poetics of Anticolonialism." In *Discourse on Colonialism,* translated by Joan Pinkham, 7–28. New York: Monthly Review Press, 2000.

———. "Poetry and the Political Imagination: Aimé Césaire, Negritude and the Applications of Surrealism." In Césaire, *Tempest,* by Aimé Césaire, translated by Richard Miller, vii–xvi. New York: TCG Translations, 2002.

King, Martin Luther, Jr. "Non Violence." In *The Words of Martin Luther King, Jr.,* selected with introduction by Coretta Scott King, 65. New York: Newmarket Press, 1968.

Klandermans, Bert. "The Social Construction of Protest and Multiorganizational Fields." In Morris and Mueller, *Frontiers in Social Movement Theory,* 77–103.

———. *The Social Psychology of Protest.* Oxford: Blackwell, 1997.

———. "Why Social Movements Come into Being and Why People Join Them." In Blau, *Blackwell Companion to Sociology,* 268–81.

La Guerre, John. "The Indian Response to Black Power." In Ryan and Stewart, *Black Power Revolution,* 273–304.

Lamming, George. *In the Castle of My Skin.* New York: Longman, 1994.

———. "The Legacy of Eric Williams." In Cateau and Carrington, *Capitalism and Slavery Fifty Years Later,* 29–35.

———. *The Pleasures of Exile.* Ann Arbor: University of Michigan Press, 2012.

Lasch, Christopher. *The New Radicalism in America, 1889–1963: The Intellectual as a Social Type.* New York: Norton, 1965.

Lawrence, Dr. Stephen. "QRC 100: Being a Record of Queen's Royal College, 1870–1970." *Trinidad Chronicle,* 12 December 1918, 7.

Le Bon, Gustave. *The Crowd.* New ed. New York: Viking, 1985.

Lefebvre, Henri. *The Production of Space.* Translated by Donald Nicholson-Smith. Malden, MA: Blackwell, 2004.

Lewis, Gordon K. *The Growth of the Modern West Indies.* London: MacGibbon & Kee, 1968.

———. *Main Currents in Caribbean Thought: The Historical Evolution of Caribbean Society in Its Ideological Aspects, 1492–1900.* Baltimore: Johns Hopkins University Press, 1983.

Lewis, Rupert Charles. *Walter Rodney's Intellectual and Political Thought.* Kingston, Jamaica: University of the West Indies Press, 1998.

Lipset, Seymour Martin, and Asoke Basu. "The Roles of the Intellectual and Political Roles." In Gella, *Intelligentsia and the Intellectuals,* 111–50.

Lipset, Seymour Martin, and Richard Dobson. "The Intellectual as Critic and Rebel: With Special Reference to the US and the Soviet Union." In *Intellectuals and Tradition,* edited by S. M. Eisenstadt and S. R. Graubard, 137–98. New York: Humanities, 1973.

Lyons, Charles H. "The Colonial Mentality: Assessment of the Intelligence of Blacks and of Women in Nineteenth-Century America." In *Education and Colonialism,* edited by Phillip Altbach and Gail Kelley, 181–206. New York: Longman, 1978.

Mahabir, Errol. "The Eric Williams They Knew: Oral Reminiscences of Colleagues." *Caribbean Issues* 8, no. 2 (March 1999).

Mahabir, Winston. *In and Out of Politics.* Port-of-Spain: Imprint Caribbean, 1978.

Maingot, Anthony. "Politics and Populist Historiography in the Caribbean: Juan Bosch and Eric Williams." In Hennessy, *Intellectuals in the Twentieth-Century Caribbean,* 2:145–74.

Mannheim, Karl. *Essays on the Sociology of Knowledge.* New York: Oxford University Press, 1952.

———. *Ideology and Utopia.* New York: Harcourt, Brace & World, 1936.

Marston, Sallie A. "Locating Space in Social Movement Theory." *Mobilization* 8, no. 2 (June 2003): 227–32.

Martin, Deborah G., and Byron Miller. "Space and Contentious Politics." *Mobilization* 8, no. 2 (June 2003): 143–56.

Martin, Tony. "Eric Williams: His Radical Side in the Early 1940s." *Journal of Caribbean Studies* 17, nos. 1–2 (Summer 2002): 107–19.

———. "Eric Williams, ca. 1943—Early Stirrings of a Scholar Activist." Paper presented at the Conference "Eric Williams: His Scholarship, Work, and Impact," Schomburg Center for Research in Black Culture, New York, February 2002.

———. "Introduction—Eric Williams and the Anglo-American Caribbean Commission, 1942–1944." In Frazier and Williams, *Economic Future of the Caribbean,* ix–xxxvii.

Marx, Karl, and Frederick Engels. *The German Ideology,* edited with introduction by C. J. Arthur. New York: International, 2001.

Massey, Doreen. *Space, Place, and Gender.* Minneapolis: University of Minnesota Press, 1994.

McAdam, Doug. *Political Process and the Development of Black Insurgency, 1930–1970.* Chicago: University of Chicago Press, 1999.

McAdam, Doug, John D. McCarthy, and Mayer N. Zald, eds. *Comparative Perspectives on Social Movements: Political Opportunities, Mobilizing Structures, and Cultural Framings.* Cambridge: Cambridge University Press, 1997.

McCall, George J., and J. L. Simmons. *Identities and Interactions: An Examination of Human Associations in Everyday Life.* New York: Free Press, 1978.

McCarthy, John D., and Mayer N. Zald. "Resource Mobilization and Social Movements." *American Journal of Sociology* 82, no. 6 (May 1977): 1212–41.

Meeks, Brian. "The 1970 Revolution: Chronology and Documentation." In Ryan and Stewart, *Black Power Revolution,* 135–77.

Melucci, Alberto. *Nomads of the Present: Social Movements and Individual Needs in Contemporary Society.* Philadelphia: Temple University Press, 1989.

Merton, Robert K. *Social Theory and Social Structure.* New York: Free Press, 1968.

Mill, John Stuart. *On Liberty, and Other Writings,* edited by Stefan Collini. Cambridge: Cambridge University Press, 2005.

Miller, Byron. *Geography and Social Movements.* Minneapolis: University of Minnesota Press, 2000.

Mills, C. Wright. *The Sociological Imagination.* New ed. New York: Oxford University Press, 2000.

Mills, Gladstone. *Grist for the Mills: Reflections on a Life.* Kingston, Jamaica: Ian Randle, 1994.

Minkoff, Debra C., and John D. McCarthy. "Reinvigorating the Study of Organizational Processes in Social Movements." *Mobilization* 10, no. 2 (June 2005): 289–308.

Mitchell, Ray. "The Making of Makandal Daaga." In Ryan and Stewart, *Black Power Revolution,* 97–117.

Mohammed, Kamaluddin. "Dr. Williams' Political Education Campaign—1955." *Nation,* 21 January 1966.

———. "Oral Reminiscences." *Caribbean Issues* 8, no. 2 (March 1999): 156–58.

Mohammed, Patricia. "A Very Public Private Man: Trinidad's Eric Eustace Williams (1911–1981)." In *Caribbean Charisma: Reflections on Leadership, Legitimacy and Populist Politics,* edited by Anton Allahar, 155–91. Kingston Jamaica: Ian Randle; Boulder, CO: Lynne Rienner, 2001.

Moore, Brian L. *Cultural Power, Resistance and Pluralism: Colonial Guyana, 1838–1900.* Montreal: McGill-Queen's University Press, 1995.

Morris, Aldon D. *The Origins of the Civil Rights Movement: Black Communities Organizing for Change.* New York: Free Press, 1984.

———. "Political Consciousness and Collective Action." In Morris and Mueller, *Frontiers in Social Movement Theory,* 351–73.

———. "Reflections on Social Movement Theory: Criticisms and Proposals." *Contemporary Sociology* 29, no. 3 (May 2000): 29–52.

Morris, Aldon D., and Cedric Herring. "Theory and Research in Social Movements: A Critical Review." In *Annual Review of Political Science* 2 (1987): 137–98.

Morris, Aldon D., and Carol McClurg Mueller, eds. *Frontiers in Social Movement Theory.* New Haven: Yale University Press, 1992.

Mostern, Kenneth. *Autobiography and Black Identity Politics: Racialization in Twentieth-Century America.* Cambridge: Cambridge University Press, 1999.

Mueller, Carol McClurg. "Building Social Movement Theory." In Morris and Mueller, *Frontiers in Social Movement Theory,* 3–25.

Munro, Ian, and Reinhard Sander, eds. *KAS-KAS; Interviews with Three Caribbean Writers in Texas: George Lamming, C. L. R. James, and Wilson Harris.* Occasional Publications of the African and Afro-American Research Institute, 5. Austin: African and Afro-American Research Institute, University of Texas at Austin, 1972.

Nair, Supriya. *Caliban's Curse: George Lamming and the Revisioning of History.* Ann Arbor: University of Michigan Press, 1996.

"Nation, The: Ten Years of PNM and Good Government." University of the West Indies Library, St. Augustine, Trinidad.

Olson, Mancur. *The Logic of Collective Action: Public Goods and the Theory of Goods.* Cambridge, MA: Harvard University Press, 1971.

Ore, Tracy, ed. *The Social Construction of Difference and Inequality: Race, Class, Gender, and Sexuality.* Boston: McGraw-Hill, 2003.

Oxaal, Ivar. *Black Intellectuals and the Dilemmas of Race and Class in Trinidad.* Rochester, VT: Schenkman, 1982.

———. *Black Intellectuals Come to Power: The Rise of Creole Nationalism in Trinidad and Tobago.* Cambridge, MA: Schenkman, 1968.

Palmer, Annette. "The United States and the Commonwealth Caribbean, 1941–1945." PhD diss., Fordham University, 1979.

Palmer, Colin A. *Eric Williams and the Making of the Modern Caribbean, 1956–1970.* Chapel Hill: University of North Carolina Press, 2006.

———. Introduction to *Capitalism and Slavery,* by Eric Williams. Chapel Hill: University of North Carolina Press, 1994.

Paquet, Sandra Pouchet. Introduction to "Eric Williams and the Postcolonial Caribbean," edited by Sandra Pouchet Paquet, special issue, *Callaloo* 21, no. 4 (Fall 1997): v–viii.

Parmasad, Kenneth. "Among a Recalcitrant People." *Caribbean Issues* 8, no. 2 (1999): 76–91.

Pocock, Michael. *Out of the Shadows of the Past.* Port-of-Spain: Paria, 1993.

Posner, Richard A. *Public Intellectuals: A Study of Decline.* Cambridge, MA: Harvard University Press, 2003.

"Radiation: From a Correspondent in Britain." *Nation,* 13 November 1959.

"Radiation: What It Is and How It Affects You." *Nation,* 31 December 1959, 1.

Ramchand, Kenneth. Introduction to *Minty Alley,* by C. L. R. James, 5–15. London: New Beacon Books, 1971.

Ransby, Barbara. *Ella Baker and the Black Freedom Movement: A Radical Democratic Vision.* Chapel Hill: University of North Carolina Press, 2003.

Reddock, Rhoda E. *Women, Labour and Politics in Trinidad and Tobago: A History.* London: Zed, 1994.

———. "Women, the Creole Nationalist Movement and the Rise of Eric Williams and the PNM in Mid-20th Century Trinidad and Tobago." *Caribbean Issues* 8, no. 1 (March 1998): 41–65.

"Reflections on the Caribbean Economic Community." *Nation,* 8 October 1965.

Richardson, Elton. *Revolution or Evolution.* Port-of-Spain: Imprint, 1984.

Robnett, Belinda. *How Long? How Long? African-American Women in the Struggle for Civil Rights.* New York: Oxford University Press, 1997.

Rogers, De Wilton. "Out of This Womb Came PNM." *Nation,* 21 January 1966.

———. *The Rise of the People's National Movement.* Port-of-Spain, n.d.

Rohlehr, Gordon. "The Culture of Williams: Context, Performance and Legacy." *Callaloo* 20, no. 4 (Autumn 1997): 849–88.

Ryan, Selwyn D. *Eric Williams: The Myth and the Man.* Kingston, Jamaica: University of the West Indies Press, 2009.

———. "Passing of a Southern Gentleman." *Trinidad Express,* 28 September 2003.

———. *Race and Nationalism in Trinidad and Tobago: A Study of Decolonization in a Multiracial Society.* Kingston, Jamaica: Institute of Social and Economic Studies, University of the West Indies, 1974.

Ryan, Selwyn, and Taimoon Stewart, eds. *The Black Power Revolution: A Retrospective.* With the assistance of Roy McCree. St. Augustine, Trinidad: Institute of Social and Economic Research, 1995.

Samaroo, Brinsley. "The Race Factor in the Independence Discussions at Marlborough House, 1962." *Caribbean Issues* 8, no. 1 (March 1998): 119–35.

Sandiford, Keith. *Cricket Nurseries of Colonial Barbados: The Elite Schools, 1865–1966.* Kingston, Jamaica: Press University of the West Indies, 1998.

Schwartz, Barry. "Iconography and Collective Memory: Lincoln's Image in the American Mind." *Sociological Quarterly* 32, no. 3 (Autumn 1991): 301–19.

Scott, James C. *Domination and the Arts of Resistance: Hidden Transcripts.* New Haven, CT: Yale University Press, 1990.

Seecharan, Clem. *Muscular Learning: Cricket and Education in the Making of the British West Indies at the End of the 19th Century.* Kingston, Jamaica: Ian Randle, 2006.

Sewell, William A., Jr. "Space in Contentious Politics." In *Silence and Voice in the Study of Contentious Politics,* edited by Ronald R. Aminzade, Jack A. Goldstone, Doug McAdam, Elizabeth J. Perry, William H. Sewell Jr., Sidney Tarrow, and Charles Tilly, 51–89. Cambridge: Cambridge University Press, 2001.

Shah, Raffique. "Black Power 1970 30 years later." www.trinicenter.com/Blackpower4.htm.

———. "Takeover of Teteron." www.trinicenter.com/Blackpower5.htm.

Sherlock, Phillip. *Norman Manley.* London: Macmillan, 1980.

Shils, Edward. "The Intellectuals and the Powers: Some Perspectives for Comparative Analysis." In *On Intellectuals: Theoretical Studies/Case Studies,* edited by Philip Rieff, 27–53. New York: Anchor Books, 1970.

Simmel, Georg. *Georg Simmel on Individuality and Social Forms.* Edited by Donald Levine. Chicago: University of Chicago Press, 1971.

———. *The Sociology of Georg Simmel.* Translated and edited by Kurt Wolff. New York: Free Press, 1950.

Smelser, Neil. "Theoretical Issues of Scope and Problems." In *Readings in Collective Behavior,* edited by Robert Evans, 89–94. Chicago: Rand McNally, 1969.

———. *Theory of Collective Behavior.* New York: Free Press, 1965.

Smith, Faith. *Creole Recitations: John Jacob Thomas and Colonial Formation in the Late Nineteenth Caribbean.* Charlottesville: University of Virginia Press, 2002.

Snow, David A., and Robert D. Benford. "Master Frames and Cycles of Protest." In Morris and Mueller, *Frontiers in Social Movement Theory,* 133–55.

Snow, David A., E. Burke Rochford Jr., Steven E. Worden, and Robert D. Benford. "Frame Alignment Processes, Micromobilization, and Movement Participation." *American Sociological Review* 51, no. 4 (August 1986): 464–81.

Solomon, Patrick. *Solomon: An Autobiography.* Port-of-Spain: Imprint Caribbean, 1981.

Solow, Barbara L., and Stanley L. Engerman, eds. *British Capitalism and Caribbean Slavery: The Legacy of Eric Williams.* Cambridge: Cambridge University Press, 2004.

St. Pierre, Maurice. *Anatomy of Resistance: Anti-Colonialism in Guyana, 1823–1966.* London: Macmillan, 1999.

———. "The Chaguaramas Affair: An Intellectual Reassessment." *Journal of Caribbean History* 40, no. 1 (2006): 92–116.

———. "The 1823 Guyana Slave Rebellion: A Collective Action Reconsideration." *Journal of Caribbean History* 41, nos. 1–2 (2007): 142–69.

———. "The Old School Tie—The West Indian Public School Experience." In Alleyne, *QRC 2004,* 408–27.

———. "School Experience of the W.I. Elite." *Trinidad and Tobago Review* 25, no. 11 (November 2003): 13–15.

Sutton, Paul K. "The Historian as Politician: Eric Williams and Walter Rodney." In Hennessy, *Intellectuals in the Twentieth-Century Caribbean,* 1:98–114.

Szacki, Jerzy. "Intellectuals between Politics and Culture." In *The Political Responsibility of Intellectuals,* edited by Ian Maclean, Alan Montefiore, and Peter Winch, 229–46. New York: Cambridge University Press, 1990.

Tarrow, Sidney. *Power in Movement: Social Movements, Collective Action and Mass Politics in the Modern State.* Cambridge: Cambridge University Press, 1994.

———. "States and Opportunities: The Political Structuring of Social Movements." In McAdam, McCarthy, and Zald, *Comparative Perspectives on Social Movements,* 41–61.

Tarrow, Sidney, and Charles Tilly. *Dynamics of Contention.* Cambridge: Cambridge University Press, 2001.

Tilly, Charles. *From Mobilization to Revolution.* Reading, MA: Addison-Wesley, 1978.

Torres-Saillant, Silvio. *An Intellectual History of the Caribbean.* New York: Palgrave Macmillan, 2006.

Trotman, David V. "Public History, Landmarks and Decolonization in Trinidad." *Journal of Caribbean History* 40, no. 1 (2006): 39–63.

Tucker, Kenneth H. "Aesthetics, Play, and Cultural Memory: Giddens and Habermas on the Postmodern Challenge." *Sociological Theory* 11, no. 2 (July 1993): 194–211.

Urry, John. "The Sociology of Space and Place." In Blau, *Blackwell Companion to Sociology,* 3–15.

Walsh, Edward J., and Rex H. Warland. "Social Movement Involvement in the Wake of a Nuclear Accident: Activists and Free Riders in the TMI Area." *American Sociological Review* 48, no. 6 (December 1983): 764–80.

Warner, Michael. "The Mass Public and the Mass Subject." In Calhoun, *Habermas and the Public Sphere,* 377–401.

Weber, Max. *Economy and Society.* Rev. ed. 3 vols. Totowa, NJ: Bedminster, 1968.

———. *The Protestant and the Spirit of Capitalism.* London: Allen & Unwin, 1930.

———. *The Sociology of Religion.* Boston: Beacon, 1993.

———. *Theory of Social and Economic Organization.* Translated by A. M. Henderson and Talcott Parsons. New York: Oxford University Press, 1947.

Williams, Eric. *British Historians and the West Indies.* London: André Deutsch, 1966.

———. *Capitalism and Slavery.* Rev. ed. Chapel Hill: University of North Carolina Press, 1994.

———. *The Case for Party Politics in Trinidad and Tobago. A Public Lecture at Woodford Square, Port-of-Spain, Trinidad, September 13, Teachers' Economic and Cultural Association, People's Education Movement.* Public Affairs Pamphlet No. 4. Port-of-Spain: College Press, 1955.

———. *Constitution Reform in Trinidad and Tobago.* Public Affairs Pamphlet No. 2. Port-of-Spain: People's Education Movement, Teachers' Economic and Cultural Association, 1955).

———. *Education in the British West Indies.* Rev. ed. New York: A & B, 1994.

———. *Eric E. Williams Speaks: Essays on Colonialism and Independence.* Edited by Selwyn Cudjoe. Wellesley, MA: Calaloux, 1993.

———. "Establishment of a University of the West Indies." *Journal of Negro Education* 13, no. 4 (Autumn 1944): 565–68.

———. *Forged from the Love of Liberty: Selected Speeches of Dr. Eric Williams.* Edited by Paul K. Sutton. Trinidad: Longman Caribbean, 1981.

———. "The Idea of a British West Indian University." *Phylon* 7, no. 2 (1946): 147–56. First published in *Harvard Educational Review* 15, no. 3 (1945): 182–91.

———. *Inward Hunger: The Education of a Prime Minister.* London: André Deutsch, 1969.

———. *Massa Day Done by Dr. Eric Williams Political Leader P.N.M., delivered Wednesday, March 22, 1961.* Port-of-Spain: PNM, 1961.

———. *The Negro in the Caribbean.* Rev. ed. New York: A & B, 1964.

———. "The Origin of Negro Slavery." In *Black Society in the New World,* edited by Richard Frucht, 1–25. New York: Random House, 1971.

———. *Perspectives for Our Party. Address delivered to the Third Annual Convention of the People's National Movement, 17 October 1958.* Port-of-Spain: College Press, 1958.

———. *Perspectives for the West Indies.* Premier's speech delivered at San Fernando on Monday, 30 May 1960. Port-of-Spain: PNM, 1960.

Williams-Connell, Erica. "My Father: Interview with Erica Williams-Connell." In Boodhoo, *Eric Williams,* 3–12.

Wolford, Wendy. "Families, Fields, and Fighting for Land: The Spatial Dynamics of Contention in Rural Brazil." *Mobilization* 8, no. 2 (June 2003): 157–72.

Worcester, Kent. *C. L. R. James: A Political Biography.* New York: State University of New York Press, 1996.

Index

Recent Books in the New World Studies Series

Jeff Karem, *The Purloined Islands: Caribbean-U.S. Crosscurrents in Literature and Culture, 1880–1959*

Faith Smith, editor, *Sex and the Citizen: Interrogating the Caribbean*

Mark D. Anderson, *Disaster Writing: The Cultural Politics of Catastrophe in Latin America*

Raphael Dalleo, *Caribbean Literature and the Public Sphere: From the Plantation to the Postcolonial*

Maite Conde, *Consuming Visions: Cinema, Writing, and Modernity in Rio de Janeiro*

Monika Kaup, *Neobaroque in the Americas: Alternative Modernities in Literature, Visual Art, and Film*

Marisel C. Moreno, *Family Matters: Puerto Rican Women Authors on the Island and the Mainland*

Supriya M. Nair, *Pathologies of Paradise: Caribbean Detours*

Colleen C. O'Brien, *Race, Romance, and Rebellion: Literatures of the Americas in the Nineteenth Century*

Kelly Baker Josephs, *Disturbers of the Peace: Representations of Madness in Anglophone Caribbean Literature*

Christina Kullberg, *The Poetics of Ethnography in Martinican Narratives: Exploring the Self and the Environment*

Maria Cristina Fumagalli, Bénédicte Ledent, and Roberto del Valle Alcalá, editors, *The Cross-Dressed Caribbean: Writing, Politics, Sexualities*

Philip Kaisary, *The Haitian Revolution in the Literary Imagination: Radical Horizons, Conservative Constraints*

Jason Frydman, *Sounding the Break: African American and Caribbean Routes of World Literature*

Tanya L. Shields, *Bodies and Bones: Feminist Rehearsal and Imagining Caribbean Belonging*

Stanka Radović, *Locating the Destitute: Space and Identity in Caribbean Fiction*

Nicole N. Aljoe and Ian Finseth, editors, *Journeys of the Slave Narrative in the Early Americas*

Stephen M. Park, *The Pan American Imagination: Contested Visions of the Hemisphere in Twentieth-Century Literature*

Maurice St. Pierre, *Eric Williams and the Anticolonial Tradition: The Making of a Diasporan Intellectual*